MICHAEL JACKSON'S POCKET BEER BOOK

Revised, updated and expanded

1995

MITCHELL BEAZLEY

DEDICATION

To my late father, Jack Jackson
born Isaac Jakowitz, Yorkshire, 1909–84

Acknowledgments

Countless brewers and beer-importers worldwide, and their trade organizations, have gone to trouble and expense far beyond their self-interest to help me in my beery researches these past three decades. For their help in my most recent researches, my special thanks to Conrad Seidl, Erich Dederichs, Pierre-André Dubois, René Descheirder, Bernard Rotman, Stephen D'Arcy, Derek Walsh, Graham Lees, Lars Lundsten, Erik Hartmann, Eric Källgren, Unto Tikkanen, Gary and Libby Gillman, Drew Ferguson, Stephen Beaumont, Alan Dikty, Vince Cottone, Graham Howard, Willie Simpson and his many beer-loving friends, and the Japanese external trade organization Jetro ... and everyone else who helped me, or shared a beer, on the road.

Editor Stephanie Horner
Researcher Andree Hoffman
Executive Editor Anne Ryland
Production Michelle Thomas
Maps John Hutchinson

Michael Jackson's Pocket Beer Book
This edition edited and designed by
Mitchell Beazley
an imprint of Reed Consumer Books Limited
Michelin House, 81 Fulham Road, London SW3 6RB
and Auckland, Melbourne, Singapore and Toronto

A CIP catalogue record for this book is available from the British Library

ISBN 0 85732 333 5

The author and publishers will be grateful for any information that will assist them in keeping future editions up to date. Although all reasonable care has been taken in the preparation of this book, neither the publishers nor the author can accept any liability for any consequences arising from the use thereof or from the information contained therein.

Produced by Mandarin Offset
Printed and bound in Malaysia
Reproductions by M & E Reproductions Ltd, North Fambridge, Essex

CONTENTS

MAPS

INTRODUCTION

THE NEW APPRECIATION OF BEER

Go for a meal in San Francisco or Seattle, and the "wine" list may feature a choice of a golden lager or a dark one; Anchor Steam or Anchor Wheat; an ESB or an IPA; a Pottsville Porter or an Irish Stout ... This is beginning to happen in New York and London, and something similar has long prevailed in the brasseries of Brussels and Paris, where the offerings are more likely to be cherry Krieks, Trappist ales or *bières de garde*.

The respect accorded to wine is beginning to be enjoyed by beer. The grape is sharing the table with the grain, and not only to wash down the sausages and hams of Germany and the Czech lands.

As in the universe of wine, so in that of beer, many of the most exciting new products are being made in the New World. Some North Americans, most of them "micro" brewers, are making hoppier English-style ales, spicier "Belgian" wheat beers and maltier "German" lagers than can be readily found in Europe.

The bland, mass-market, beers of America are no longer the whole story, any more than the hamburger represents the height of culinary achievement in a land bubbling with inspired chefs.

Microbreweries

Once, all breweries were "micro". Germany, especially Bavaria, never lost those village taverns that brew their own beer, make their own bread, butcher their own meat. Britain was down to a handful of "homebrew houses" when they were rediscovered by the consumerist Campaign for Real Ale in the early 1970s. By the middle of that decade, a new generation of small breweries was springing up in Britain, and the movement quickly spread to the United States. After military service in Britain, Jack McAuliffe returned to his homeland and started the New Albion Brewery, in Sonoma, California. This later gave rise to the Mendocino County Brewing Company, which is still thriving. At that time, there were about 40 brewing companies in the USA. Two decades later, there are closer to 400. Today, parties of German brewers visit the USA to study microbreweries.

Within the new generation, the terms have become blurred, but a restaurant that makes its own beer is usually now known as a *brewpub*. This distinguishes it from a *microbrewery*, which exists primarily to serve other people's pubs. Next up the size scale is the old-established local or regional brewery, and finally the national, or global, giant.

Some beers are created by entrepreneurs who have no brewery of their own. These people hire time at established breweries to have their own products made, usually under the supervision of a technical consultant. These entrepreneurs are known as *contract brewers*. Often, their technical consultants are retired brewers, many of whom spent their working lives being obliged by their employers to make ever-blander beers. Now, they have emerged from retirement to make beers that they really like.

IS SMALL BEAUTIFUL?

There will always be a bigger market for bland beers, but they should not be allowed to wash away the more interesting choices for the discerning drinker. The world's second-largest brewer, Miller, failed with its absurd "Clear Beer" in 1993, continues to mass-market its "Lite" – but is now also enjoying some success with a tasty Amber Ale and a Stout. Large brewers have the skills to make distinctive beers, but sometimes their brew-kettles, and their marketing ambitions, are too big for specialities. Faced with the mass-market might of the giants, the smaller brewer should exist to specialize.

Food and drink are central to the quality of life. A good beer is a sensuous pleasure. The ever-present enemies of that pleasure are cost accountants who seek to cheapen its ingredients or make it faster; Head Brewers who want to collude in the interests of "science"; and marketing men who would render beer more "accessible" at the risk of persuading consumers that they should be drinking pop.

Once again, with no economies of scale, the smaller brewer does better to make traditional beers and hope that the consumer will pay a fair price for them. The evidence is that he, or she, will.

WHAT MAKES A GREAT BEER

Wine is more vulnerable to the mercies of soil and weather, but beer is the more complicated drink to make. The barley must first be malted and made into an infusion or decoction, the enigmatic (and none too hardy) hop added as a seasoning, and the whole brewed before it can be fermented, matured and conditioned.

In carrying out these procedures, the brewer is seeking to impart (in aroma, palate and finish) his own balance between the sweetness of the barley malt, the herby dryness of the hop, and the background fruitiness of the yeast used in fermentation. These characteristics are immediately evident in a fresh beer, especially one that has not been pasteurized (this process, unless it is carried out with the greatest of care, may merely deaden the beer to the ravages of travel and time).

The balance will be weighted differently according to the style of the beer, but it must always be achieved. A chef may intend one dish to be delicate, another to be robust, but each must have its own balance. After balance comes complexity. A wine-maker knows that each style is expected to have certain features, but beyond those there should be the individuality of its own character. Each time the drinker raises a glass of fine wine, new dimensions of aroma and palate should become apparent. So it is with a fine beer.

Any fine food or drink is enjoyed with the eyes and nose as well as the palate. The more individualistic beers, especially of the darker styles, can have a great subtlety of colour; most styles will present a dense, uneven "rocky" head if they have been naturally carbonated in fermentation, rather than having been injected with carbon dioxide; a properly carbonated beer will leave "Brussels lace" down the sides of the glass after each swallow. A good beer should be poured gently down the side of a tilted glass. A final, upright, flourish may contribute to its appearance, but the formation of a good head should not rest on the beer's being dumped violently into the glass.

Conventional beers are intended to be clear though excessive refrigeration can cause a "chill haze" in a good-quality, all-malt brew. The haze should subside once the beer reaches about 45°F (7°C). Conventional beers are also at risk of general deterioration (though they will not necessarily succumb to it) from the moment they leave the brewery. They are intended for immediate drinking, and not for keeping.

Brews indicated to be conditioned in the cask or bottle will contain living yeast. Unless the beer is poured carefully, the palate will have a "yeast bite", but the sediment is not harmful (in fact, its health benefits are quickly apparent). Very strong bottle-conditioned brews will improve with age.

Bottle-conditioned ales naturally have a very fruity aroma. In any beer, an unpleasant aroma reminiscent of damp paper or cardboard indicates oxidation (quite simply, the beer has gone stale). A cabbagey or skunky aroma means that the beer has been damaged by supermarket lighting or by being left in the sun. Beer is a natural product, and does not enjoy rough treatment.

Strength

This is not a measure of quality. The ideal strength for a beer depends upon the purpose for which it is intended. A beer that is meant to be quenching, and to be consumed in quantity, should not be high in alcohol. The classic example, the *Berliner Weisse* style, has around 3 percent alcohol by volume. A typical premium beer, whether in Germany, Britain or the United States, might have between 4 and 5 percent by volume. A strong "winter warmer" may typically have between 6 and 8 percent. Although there are specialities exceeding 13 percent, beers of this strength are hard to brew, and to drink in any quantity. At these levels, alcohol stuns beer yeasts to a point where they can no longer work, and the residual sugars make for heavy, cloying brews. There are, of course, wines of this strength, but they are not drunk by the half-pint.

Alcohol by volume is the system most commonly used to describe the strength of wine, and it is the simplest rating to understand. The European Community now uses this system, so does Canada, but American brewers usually quote alcohol by weight. Since water is heavier than alcohol, this produces lower figures. In several brewing nations, the authorities were traditionally more concerned to tax what goes into the beer: the malt, wheat or other fermentable sugars. This is variously described as density or original gravity. Each of the older brewing nations developed its own scale for measuring this, the German Plato and similar Czech Balling systems being the most commonly used. In those countries, drinkers are inclined to be less familiar with alcohol content than with gravity.

The two do not have a direct relationship, since alcohol content is also a function of the degree of fermentation. The more thorough the fermentation, the higher the level of alcohol produced from a given gravity. The less thorough the fermentation, the fuller the body. Alcohol content and body are quite different, and in this respect opposed, elements of a beer.

The Malts

As grapes are to wine, so barley malt is to beer the classic source of fermentable sugars. The barley is malted (steeped in water until it partially germinates, then dried in a kiln) to release the starches that are then turned into fermentable sugars by infusion or decoction in water in a mashing vessel. This process is parallel to that carried out in the first stages of production of malt whiskies. In addition to deciding the proportion of malts to be used to achieve the desired density, the brewer is also concerned with their origin.

Certain varieties of barley are grown especially to be malted for the brewing industry. Among them, those that are grown in summer are held to produce cleaner-tasting, sweeter malts, though there is some debate on this. Some brewers also feel that inland, "continental" barleys produce better results than those grown in maritime climates. With varying harvests, there are differences in the quality and availability of barley, and the brewer has to account for this in the fine detail of his mashing procedure, its durations and temperatures. He will also adjust these according to the precise character he is seeking in his beer. They are among the hundreds of variables, and thousands of permutations, that contribute to the final character of every beer.

The traditional malting barleys are of varieties that have two rows of grain in each ear. Six-rowed barley is also used, though it produces a huskier, sharper character in the beer. Traditionalists stick to two-row barley but some brewers claim to seek the character they find in six-row varieties.

To the consumer, the more immediately obvious influence is the way in which the barley has been malted. There are many different standard malting specifications, each intended to produce a different result in terms of both colour and palate. As to colour, the more intense the kilning of the malt, the darker the beer. In palate, the character of the barley and the way in which it is malted can impart tones that are reminiscent, for example, of nuts, caramel, chocolate, espresso or licorice. These variations in malting differ in the moisture of the grains at the time of the kilning, as well as in the cycles of temperature and duration.

Depending upon the style of beer being produced, the brewer may use only one or two different types of malt, or as many as seven or eight. He may also use a proportion of unmalted barley, sometimes highly roasted, as in the case of dry stouts like Guinness. German and Belgian "white" beers are made with a proportion of malted wheat. So, naturally enough, are *Weizen* beers (it means wheat, after all). Belgian *lambic* beers use a proportion of unmalted wheat. One or two highly specialized beers use other grains. Less traditional grains include proportions of rice and corn, both used to lighten beers, and the latter especially for its low cost. Also for reasons of cost, and to boost alcohol in expensive strong beers like American malt liquors, cane sugar may be used. In Belgium, candy sugar is used in strong Trappist monastery beers. In Britain, milk sugars are used in sweet stouts.

In a cheap beer, barley malt may represent 60 percent of the mash, and corn or other adjuncts the rest. In Bavaria, barley malt and wheat are the only fermentable materials allowed. Elsewhere in West Germany, the same goes for domestic beers but not for exports. One or two other countries have similar laws, the closest being those of Norway and Greece. Within the EC, a country may insist that its own breweries work within a "Pure Beer" law, but it cannot block imports for failing to conform.

The Hops

Early wine-makers lacked the knowledge to produce by fermentation alone products of the quality they sought, so they employed seasonings of herbs and spices, creating the forerunners of today's vermouths and of patent apéritifs like Campari. Distillers, faced with similar difficulties, used a spicing of juniper and coriander to dry the palate of their product, thus creating gin. Liqueurs like Chartreuse have a similar history of development. In the same tradition, early brewers used tree-barks, herbs and berries.

Juniper and coriander are still used in a handful of highly specialized beers, but the hop eventually became the standard choice. The hop is a climbing plant, a vine, that is a member of the same family as cannabis. In ancient times, its shoots were eaten as a salad, and in Belgium they still are. Its cone-like blossoms can have a sedative effect, and are used in hop pillows. The cones also produce tannins that help clarify and preserve beer, and resins and essential oils that are the principal sources of aroma and dryness.

This dryness, or bitterness, is a part of the flavour balance of beer. An especially hoppy beer is a marvellous apéritif because its bitterness arouses the gastric juices. Brewers have their own scale of Units of Bitterness. Some very bland beers have as few as 12 Units of Bitterness; one or two tasty classics have over 50. A very hoppy beer will be full of earthy, aromatic, herbal, flavour notes.

Since all hops contain elements of both bitterness and aroma, the same variety may be used for both purposes, but this is not generally done. Each variety of hop is usually identified as being ideal either for bitterness or aroma. A brewer may, indeed, use just one variety, but he is more likely to use two or three, occasionally even seven or eight. He may put hops into the kettle once, twice or three times. The early additions are to provide bitterness, the later ones to confer aroma. To heighten aroma, he may even add blossoms to the hop strainer, or to the conditioning vessel. This last technique is known as "dry hopping". At each addition, he may use only one variety, or a different blend of several. He may use hop oils or extracts, or the whole blossom, in its natural form or compacted into pellets.

There are many varieties of bittering hop, but few that enjoy special renown. Aroma hops are the aristocrats.

In continental Europe, the classic is the Saaz hop, grown in the area around the small town of Žatec, Bohemia, in the Czech Republic. In Germany, considerable reputations are enjoyed by the Hallertau Mittelfrüh and Tettnang aroma hops, named after areas near Munich and Lake Constance respectively.

In Britain, the delightfully named Fuggles are often used for their gentle, rounded, bitterness, though they are also regarded as aroma hops. The counties of Hereford and Kent are known for their hops, and the latter especially for a slightly more bitter and hugely aromatic variety called Goldings. These are at their finest in east Kent, near Faversham, allegedly in a strip of countryside a mile wide.

In North America the Cascade is the classic aroma hop, grown especially in the Yakima Valley of Washington State. There are hop-growing areas in British Columbia, Canada, too, and in similar latitudes of the southern hemisphere – in Tasmania.

The Yeast

Among wines, it might be argued – perhaps simplistically – that there is a central division along lines of colour, between the reds and the whites. Among beers such a division concerns not colour but the type of yeast used. For centuries, all brewing employed what we now know as top-fermenting, or "ale", yeasts. In those days yeast was barely understood, except as the foam which, when scooped from the top of one brew, acted as a "starter" for the fermentation of the next. In this primitive method of brewing, the yeasts naturally rose to the top of the vessel, and were able to cross-breed with wild micro-organisms in the atmosphere. In the summer, they did so to a degree where beer spoilage made brewing impossible.

Brewers in the Bavarian Alps discovered, empirically, that beer stabilized if it was stored (in German, *lagered*) in icy, mountain caves during the summer. Not only was it less vulnerable to cross-breeding; the yeast sank to the bottom of the vessel, out of harm's way. As scientists began to understand the behaviour of yeast in the 19th century, "bottom-fermenting" strains were methodically bred.

Today, all of the older brewing styles – ales, porters, stouts, German Altbier and Kölsch and all wheat beers – are (or should be) made with top-fermenting yeasts. All of the lager styles – Pilseners, Muncheners, Dortmunders, Märzen, Bock and double Bock and American malt liquors – are made with bottom-fermenting yeasts.

"Top" yeasts ferment at warm temperatures (classically 59–77°F/15–25°C), after which the beer may be matured for only a few days, or a couple of weeks, at warm temperatures. With modern means of temperature control, brewing in summer no longer poses a problem. A beer that has been "warm conditioned" will most fully express its palate if it is served at a natural cellar temperature, ideally not less than 55°F (12°C). This is why a well-run British pub will serve ales at such a temperature. British ale can be rendered worthless by refrigeration.

"Bottom" yeasts ferment at cooler temperatures (classically 41–48°F/5–9°C), and the beer is then matured by being stored (*lagered*) at around 32°F (0°C). Many mass-market beers are lagered for barely three weeks. Even in Germany,

many brewers are content with four weeks, but traditionalists argue for three months. Bottom-fermenting beers taste best if they are chilled to between 45°F (7°C) and 50°F (10°C), the lighter their body, the lower the temperature and vice-versa.

In both techniques, very strong ales and lagers are matured for longer periods, sometimes for nine, or even 12 months. For whatever duration, this is a period in which the remaining yeast settles, harsh flavour compounds mellow out, and the beer gains its natural texture and carbonation (its "condition").

In top-fermenting ales that have a short period of maturation, the yeast may be settled with the aid of finings, usually isinglass. In Britain the classic ales are delivered to the pub with some working yeast still in the cask, so that they may reach the prime of condition in the cellar. This is known as *cask-conditioning*. Some speciality ales are bottled without filtration, or with an added dosage of yeast, as in the *méthode champenoise*. This is known as *bottle-conditioning*.

Because they pre-date the true understanding of yeasts, some top-fermenting strains are hybrids. Others have picked up some "house character" from the micro-organisms resident in the brewery. Some brewers of top-fermenting specialities intentionally use a blend of yeast, or employ different strains at different stages. Many, of course, use single-cell pure cultures, as do almost all brewers of bottom-fermenting beers. Bottom-fermenting has its origins in a more methodical, scientific, approach to brewing.

Beers made with top-fermenting yeasts are inclined to have more individualistic and expressive palates, often with elements of fruitiness and acidity. Bottom-fermenting beers tend to be cleaner and rounder but the trade-off is that they may be less individualistic.

The Water

Claims about the water used in brewing were probably the most common feature of beer advertizing in the Victorian and Edwardian periods, and they are still to be heard.

In the 18th and 19th centuries, sources of pure water were not always easy to find. That is why towns or cities with good sources – among them, Pilsen and Munich in continental Europe; Burton and Tadcaster in England – became centres of brewing.

Even today, a source of water that requires little or no treatment is an asset to a brewery. A great many breweries have their own springs or wells (this may not be the rule, but it is by no means the exception). In a good few instances, the town supply is adequate once the chlorine has been removed. Only in isolated cases is a water supply a problem. There is at least one island brewery that has to de-salinate sea water.

Even if the water does come from the brewery's own spring or well, natural salts may have to be added or removed for the production of different types of beer. As environmental concerns grow, sources of pure water may once again be a marketable asset, but that time has not yet come.

"It's the water!" boast some breweries. "It's the beer!" would be a more convincing claim.

THE LANGUAGE OF THE LABEL

Abbey, Abbaye, Abdij Bier Not necessarily made in an abbey, or by monks, but imitating the Trappist style. Sometimes licensed by an abbey. See Trappist.

Ale The English-language term for a brew made with a top-fermenting yeast, which should impart to it a distinctive fruitiness. Ales are produced to a wide variety of colours, palates and strengths (see also Bitter, Brown Ale, India Pale Ale, Light Ale, Mild, Old Ale, Scotch Ale, etc). Only in some American states is the term determined by law (wrongly) to indicate a brew of more than 4 percent weight (5 by volume).

All barley Made only from barley-malt, with no other grains or sugars.

All malt Brewed only from malted grains, with no corn, rice, or other sugars.

Alt German word for "old". See Altbier.

Altbier A German term for a top-fermenting brew. Classic examples, copper in colour, mashed only from barley malt, fermented from a single-cell yeast and cold-conditioned, with an alcohol content of 4.5–4.7 by volume, are made in Düsseldorf.

Barley Wine An English term for an extra-strong ale (implied to be as potent as wine). Usually more than 6 percent by volume and classically closer to 11. Most often bottled. Both pale and dark versions can be found.

Bayrische German word for Bavarian.

"Beer" Confusingly, the Americans use the term "beer" to mean only lager. The British employ it to mean only ale. Neither is correct. Both lager and ale – as well as porter, stout, and all the Belgian and German specialities – are embraced by the general term "beer". It is all beer, so long as it is a fermented drink made from grain and seasoned with hops.

Berliner Weisse Berlin's classic "white" (cloudy), sedimented, top-fermenting wheat beer, with the quenching sourness of a lactic fermentation, the sparkle of a high carbonation, and a low alcohol content of around 3 percent by volume.

Bière de Garde French term originally applied to strong, copper-coloured, top-fermenting brews, bottle-conditioned for laying down. Today's examples have an alcohol content in the range of 4.4–7.5 by volume, and may be bottom-fermented and filtered.

Bitter English term for a well-hopped ale, most often on draught. Although examples vary widely, the name implies a depth of hop bitterness. There is usually some acidity in the finish, and colour varies from bronze to deep copper. Basic bitters usually have an alcohol content of around 3.75–4 percent by volume, "Best" or "Special" bitters come in at 4–4.75; the odd "Extra Special" at about 5.5.

Bo(c)k The German term for a strong beer. If unqualified, it indicates a bottom-fermenting brew from barley malt. In Germany, bock usually has more than 6.25 percent alcohol by volume, and may be golden, tawny or dark brown. Outside Germany, strengths vary, and a bock is usually dark, Bock beers are served in autumn, late winter or spring, depending upon the country. See also Maibock, Doppelbock, Weizenbock.

Brown Ale In the south of England, a dark-brown ale, sweet in palate, low in alcohol (3–3.5 by volume). In the northeast, a reddish-brown ale, drier, of 4.4–5. The slightly sour, brown brews of Flanders are also ales, though they do not generally use the designation.

Cask-conditioned Draught beer that is neither filtered not pasteurized and has a secondary fermentation and natural clarification in the cellar of the pub. This cannot take place if the beer is chilled.

Cream Ale An American designation, implying a very pale (usually golden), mild, light-bodied ale that may actually have been blended with a lager. Around 4.75 by volume.

"Dark beer" There are many, quite unrelated, styles of dark brew. If this vague term is used without qualification, it usually means a dark lager of the Munich type.

Diät Pils This has nothing to do with slimming, but was originally intended for diabetics. A German style so popular in Britain that many drinkers think there is no other kind of "Pils". Carbohydrates are diminished by a very thorough fermentation, creating a relatively high content of alcohol (about 6 percent by volume) and therefore lots of calories. In German law, the alcohol now has to be reduced back to a normal Pilsner level (5 percent by volume).

Doppelbock "Double" bock. German extra-strong bottom-fermenting beer, tawny or dark brown. Around 7.5 by volume or stronger. Southern speciality, seasonal to March and April. Names usually end in -ator.

Dort Abbreviation used in Belgium and The Netherlands to indicate a beer in the Dortmunder Export style.

Dortmunder This indicates merely a beer brewed in Dortmund, but the city's classic style is Export (see Export).

Draft beer in a can Nitrogen has been added to imitate the creaminess of a beer drawn by pump.

Dry Beer Originally a milder adaptation of the German Diät Pils, renamed Dry Beer by the Japanese. After its great marketing success in Japan, the term Dry Beer was taken up in North America. There, the style was made milder still. American Dry Beer has a conventional alcohol and calorie content but is notable for having scarcely any taste, and no finish.

Dunkel/Dunkles German word for "dark".

Eisbock An extra-strong (Doppel) bock beer in which potency has been heightened by a process of freezing. Because water freezes before alcohol, the removal of ice (eis) concentrates the beer.

Export In Germany, a pale, Dortmund-style bottom-fermenting beer that is bigger in body than a Pilsner, and less dry, but not as sweet as a Munich pale beer, It is stronger than either, at 5.25–5.5 by volume. Elsewhere, Export usually indicates a premium beer.

Faro Once Brussels' local style, a version of a lambic sweetened by candy sugar. 4.5–5.5 by volume.

Festbier In Germany, any beer made for a festival. Styles vary, but such beers are usually above average strength, often around 5.5–6 volume.

Framboise/frambozen Raspberry beer, usually based on *lambic*. Alcohol content varies.

Genuine Draft (and similar terms) Bottled or canned beer that, like most draughts, is unpasteurized. Unlike them, it is sterile-filtered for shelf-life.

Gueuze A blend of old and young *lambic* beers. Around 4.4–5.5 by volume.

Haute fermentation French for top fermentation.

Hefe- The German word for yeast, indicating that a beer is bottle-conditioned and sedimented.

Hell German word for "pale", indicating an everyday beer that is golden in colour. Ordered as a Helles (hell-es).

Ice beer (and similar terms) Otherwise conventional beers that have been frozen at some stage during fermentation or maturation, and in some cases reconstituted later. This knocks out some flavour components and perhaps concentrates others. A marketing-led technique inspired by Eisbock (see entry).

Imperial Stout See Stout.

India Pale Ale (IPA) A reminder of the days when the Indian Empire was supplied with ales (high in gravity, and well hopped, to stand the voyage) by the British. Today, the term implies a super-premium pale ale.

Kellerbier German term indicating an unfiltered lager, in which there is usually a high hop content and a low carbonation. Strengths vary according to the original style.

Kloster Bier "Cloister beer". German term for a beer that is, or formerly was, produced in a monastery or convent.

Kölsch Cologne's distinctive style of golden, top-fermenting brew. 4.3–5 by volume.

Kräusen In German custom, a traditional technique of carbonation is to add a small dosage of unfermented malt sugars (in English, wort) to the conditioning tank. In a normally *kräusened* beer, the wort ferments out and the beer is conventionally filtered. An unfiltered beer based on this technique is called *Kräusenbier*.

Kriek Cherry beer, usually based on *lambic*. 5–6 by volume.

Kruidenbier Dutch-language term for spiced beer.

Lager Any beer made by bottom-fermentation. In Britain, lagers are usually golden in colour, but in continental Europe they can also be dark. In the German-speaking world and The Netherlands, the term may be used to indicate the most basic beer of the house, the *bière ordinaire*.

Lambic Spontaneously fermenting style of wheat beer unique to Belgium, notably the Senne Valley. About 4.4.

Light Ale English term describing the bottled counterpart of a basic bitter. In Scotland, "Light" indicates the lowest gravity draught beer (usually dark in colour), neither term implies a low-calorie beer.

Light Beer American term, indicating a watery Pilsener-style beer. 2.75–4 by volume. Low in calories, and in interest. In some other countries, "Light" means lower in alcohol than a conventional beer.

Maibock A bock beer of super-premium quality. Usually pale. Made for the end of April/beginning of May to celebrate spring.

Malt Liquor Not especially malty, though they are usually low in hop character. Certainly not liquors, though they are usually the strongest beers in an American brewer's range. Malt liquor is the American term for a strong, pale lager, at anything from 5–7.5 by volume, often cheaply made. Regrettably, laws in some states encourage the term to be used on imported strong lagers of far greater character.

Märzen From "March" in German. Originally a beer brewed in March and laid down in caves before the summer weather rendered brewing impossible. Stocks would be drawn upon during the summer, and finally exhausted in October. In Germany, this tradition has come to be associated with one specific style. *Märzenbier* has a malty aroma, and is a medium-strong version (classically, more than 5.5 percent alcohol by volume) of the amber-red Vienna style. It is seasonal to the *Oktoberfest*, where it is offered as a traditional speciality alongside paler beers of a similar strength. Confusingly, in Austria the term refers not to style but to gravity.

Mild English term indicating an ale that is only lightly hopped. Some milds are copper in colour, but most are dark brown. These beers were devised to be drunk in large quantities by manual workers, and have in recent years suffered from their blue-collar image. Around 3 by volume, but often relatively full in body.

Münchener/Münchner Means "Munich-style". In international brewing terminology, this indicates a dark-brown lager, a style that was developed in Munich (although another Bavarian town, Kulmbach, also has a long tradition of – very – dark lagers). In Munich, such a brew is clearly identified by the word *Dunkel* ("dark"), and classic examples have an alcohol content of around, or just over, 5 percent by volume. The brewers of Munich, and Bavaria in general, also impart their own distinctively malty accent to their everyday, lower-gravity (alcohol content around 3.7) pale beers. These are sometimes identified as *Münchner Hell*, to distinguish them from the same brewers' Pilsener-style product.

Obergärig German for top-fermenting.

Oktoberfest beers See Märzen.

Old (Ale) In Australia, "Old" simply means dark ale. In Britain, it is most commonly used to indicate a medium-strong dark ale like Old Peculier, which has just under 6 percent by volume. However, by no means all ales describing themselves as "old" are in this style.

Oscura "Obscure" (ie dark) beer. Spanish word used on some Mexican labels.

Pale Ale Pale in this instance means bronze or copper-coloured, as opposed to dark brown. Pale ale is a term used by some English brewers to identify their premium bitters, especially in bottled form.

Pilsener/Pilsner/Pils Loosely, any golden-coloured, dry, bottom-fermenting beer of conventional strength might be described as being of this style (in its various spellings and abbreviations), though this most famous designation properly belongs only to a product of "super-premium" quality. Too many brewers take it lightly, in more senses than one. In their all-round interpretation, it is the German brewers who take the style most seriously, inspired by the Urquell (original) brew from the town of Pilsen, in the province of Bohemia, in the Czech Republic. A classic Pilsner, has a gravity of around 12 Balling and is characterized by the hoppiness of its flowery aroma and dry finish.

Porter A London style that became extinct, though it has recently been revived. It was a lighter-bodied companion to stout, and the most accurate revivals are probably the porters made by American micro-brewers like Sierra Nevada. Around 5 percent by volume. In some countries, the porter tradition remains in roasty-tasting dark brews that are bottom-fermented, and often of a greater strength.

Rauchbier Smoked malts are used in the production of this dark, bottom-fermented speciality, principally made in and around Bamberg, Franconia. Produced at around 5 percent by volume and in Märzen and Bock versions. Serve with Bavarian smoked ham, or bagels and lox.

Saison Seasonal summer style in the French-speaking part of Belgium. A sharply refreshing, faintly sour, top-fermenting brew, sometimes dry-hopped, often bottle-conditioned, 5.5–8 by volume.

Scotch Ale The ales of Scotland generally have a malt accent. In their home country, a single brewery's products may be identified in ascending order of gravity and strength as Light, Heavy, Export and Strong. Or by a system based on the old currency of shillings, probably once a reference to tax ratings: 60/-, 70/-, 80/-, 90/-. Alcohol content by volume might rise through 3, 4, 4.5 and 7–10. The term "Scotch ale" is something used specifically to identify a very strong, and often extremely dark, malt-accented speciality from that country.

Schwarzbier "Black" or very dark beer. The most famous type is made in Köstritz, Germany (see page 67).

Steam Beer A name trademarked by the Anchor Steam Beer brewery of San Francisco. This brewery's principal product is made by a distinctive method of bottom-fermentation at high temperatures and in unusually wide, shallow vessels. This technique, producing a beer with elements of both lager and ale in its character (though also distinctive in its own right), is said to have been common in California when, in the absence of supplies of ice, early brewers tried to make bottom-fermenting beers. The very lively beer was said to "steam" when the casks were tapped.

Stout An extra-dark, almost black, top-fermenting brew, made with highly roasted malts. Sweet stout, an English style, is typified by Mackeson, which has only about 3.75 percent alcohol by volume in its domestic market but more than 5 in the Americas. Sweet stout usually contains milk sugars (lactose), and is a soothing restorative. Dry stout, the Irish style, is typified by Guinness, which comes in at around 4 percent in the British Isles, a little more in North America and as much as 8 in tropical countries. Dry stouts sometimes contain roasted unmalted barley. Imperial Stout, originally brewed as a winter warmer, for sale in the Tsarist Russian Empire, is medium dry and distinguished by its great strength: anything from 7 to more than 10.

Trappist This order of monks has five breweries in Belgium and one in The Netherlands. By law, only they are entitled to use the term Trappist in describing their products. Each of them produces strong (6–12 percent by volume), top-fermenting brews, characteristically employing candy sugar in the kettle, and always bottle-conditioned. Colour varies from full gold to deep brown.

Tripel (various spellings) Dutch-language term usually applied to the strongest beer of the house, customarily top-fermenting and often pale in colour, occasionally spiced with coriander. The most famous example is made in Westmalle, Belgium (see pages 83–4).

Trub German term for sediment.

Vienna Amber-red, or only medium-dark, lager. This was the style originally produced in Vienna. Brewers still talk of a "Vienna malt" to indicate a kilning to this amber-red colour, but the beer-style itself is no longer especially associated with the city.

Ur-/Urquell "Original"/"source of", in German. Justifiable when applied to, for example, Einbecker Ur-Bock or Pilsner Urquell, but often more loosely used.

Weisse/Weissbier, Weizenbier The German term for "white" beer, implying a pale brew made from wheat. In the north, a special renown is enjoyed by Berliner Weisse, a style in its own right (see separate entry). A different style of Weissbier is made in the south, with a more conventional alcohol content (usually a little over 5 percent by volume), a higher proportion of wheat (at least 50 percent) and a yeast (again top-fermenting) that produces a tart, fruity, spicy palate, sometimes with notes of cooking apples and cloves. Often, instead of Weissbier, the southerners prefer the term Weizen (a similar-sounding word but it means, quite simply "wheat"). If the beer is sedimented with yeast, it may be prefixed Hefe-. Southern wheat beers are also produced in dark versions (these Dunkel Weizen brews have a delicious complex of fruitiness and maltiness), and in Export and Bock strengths. Weizenbock is sometimes served as a Christmas beer.

White A term once used in several parts of Europe to describe wheat beers. Apart from those of German-speaking countries, Belgium's white beers (Witbier, Bière Blanche) are of considerable interest.

Wiesen/Wies'n Among several words that are confusingly similar to the non-German speaker, this one means "meadow". It implies a beer brewed for a carnival or festival (an Oktoberfest beer may be described as a Wies'n Märzen) or a rustic speciality (such as Küppers' unfiltered Wiess).

Witbier A Dutch/Flemish term used in Belgium and, increasingly, the United States. See White.

Zwickelbier German term for an unfiltered beer without the distinguishing features of either a Kellerbier or a Kräusenbier.

THE WORLD'S BEERS REVIEWED

The appreciation of beer having been contemplated, its qualities studied, the language of the label decoded, and the time for a sampling determined, where is the brew to be found? What follows is the most comprehensive review ever compiled of the world's beers. It deals separately with each of the countries in which beer-brewing is an important tradition. Among them, it divides the most complex brewing nations into regions. These divisions are intended to be convenient for the traveller, but they also reflect style differences in the local beers. An overview of the local beer types is included in concise introductions to each major brewing nation or region. Each of these is followed by a "Where to drink" section introducing some of the most interesting establishments in which beer is available, including a number of specialist shops.

In the later sections, the less traditional brewing nations are grouped together under regional or continental headings. Throughout, this review attempts to highlight the most interesting and distinctive beers, often from very small breweries, as well as the better-known names. The figures mentioned in the text and appearing after a beer indicate its strength (see page 6). However, they are not a measure of its quality. For example, *Briljant* (12; 1048; 5.2; 6.3) has a density of 12; an original gravity of 1048; a percent alcohol by weight of 5.2; and a percent alcohol by volume of 6.3. The figures always appear in that order To avoid an endless recital of statistics, these details are given only where they might be helpful in distinguishing between two similar products, or where a beer of special interest is being discussed.

In the latter instance, there may also be a reference to Units of Bitterness (the significance of this scale is explained under Hops, page 8). Units of Bitterness are only a guideline, and cannot express the complex flavours imparted by the hops, but these figures are offered for the benefit of those beer-lovers who find them helpful. Many home-brewers, and some commercial beer-makers planning new products, like to have precise readings of bitterness in well-regarded examples.

The same is true with Units of Colour. Likewise, these cannot measure the subtlety and attractiveness of colour in some beers. The system used is that agreed by the European Brewing Convention. A figure of 6–8 units, for example, might indicate a golden beer; 20–40 suggests bronze to copper; a reading in the hundreds may reflect anything from mahogany to ebony.

In the traditional homes of the craft, every other brewery has interesting products, and the properly briefed traveller will be well rewarded. In more exotic parts of the world, the overwhelming majority of beers are in the "international" derivation of the Pilsener style, and there is not a great deal to distinguish one from another.

In this review, the description of each beer deals with what is salient and distinctive about its palate, and attempts to relate it to a classic style. Star-ratings are offered, but merely as a guide. They assess beers according to the standards of each region.

★ Typical of its country and style
★★ Above average
★★★ Worth seeking out
★★★★ World Classic

An Index at the back of the book acts as a quick reference guide to breweries and their beers.

THE CZECH REPUBLIC

The world's most widely known style of beer originates from the town of Pilsen, in Bohemia, the medieval kingdom of Wenceslas, and the province which, with Moravia, forms today's Czech Republic. The Republic's brewing traditions date back at least to the beginning of this millenium.

The international fixation with the term Pilsener can be dated, precisely, to 1842. Until then, all of the world's beers, whether ales or lagers, had been dark, or at least reddish, or murky. Dark malts can make for tasty beers but they were, in those days, also a way of covering up the haziness of yeasty instability.

In 1842, Pilsen's local brewery, which was then owned by the town, produced the world's first golden-coloured, clear, stable, beer by bottom-fermentation, thus "inventing" pale lager. This came at a time when opaque drinking vessels of stoneware or pewter were giving way to mass-produced glass.

At this time, the German-speaking Austrian Empire ruled Bohemia. "Pilsener-style" beer soon became chic throughout the German-speaking world and beyond. By the time steps were taken to protect the name, the drayhorse had bolted.

When the American brewer Adolphus Busch toured Europe in the late 19th century to study the lagering technique, he was particularly taken with the beers of a town called, in German, Budweis (in Czech, České Budějovice), once the home of the Bohemian royal court brewery. He decided upon this allusion when he set about launching his "King of Beers" in the USA in 1876, but he had the sense to protect the name Budweiser. Busch's "super-premium" trademark Michelob (from a town now known as Michalovce) is also protected.

The Republic has excellent malting barley — sweet and clean, grown in a protected, temperate continental climate. Bohemian hops have been famous since the earliest days, and still are. These are exclusively of the variety known as Bohemian Red, or as Saaz from the German-language name for Žatec, centre of the growing area. The hops' fresh fragrance is nurtured not only by the climate, but also by the soil, rich in clay and iron.

It is a paradox that Czech conservatism in brewing procedures, and especially the duration and traditionalism of lagering, was protected by the Communist regime's neglect of the industry. Now, Czech breweries are being tempted to sacrifice tradition in order to embrace the faster, more immediately profitable, methods of the capitalist world. In doing so, they may lose their selling point - the hop character, cleanness, softness and complexity of their beers - just as more of them become available in export markets.

The Czech brewing industry is undergoing a shake-out, and it will be a while before it settles. Must Czech brewers make all the mistakes already committed in the "Free World" before their Velvet Revolution is succeeded by their Micro-brewery Revolution? It is to be hoped not. On the credit side, some Czech breweries do now offer unfiltered beers (*Kvasnicová*) and wheat beers.

Where to drink

Almost every town in the Czech Republic offers its local beers. The capital, Prague, has 20-odd beer taverns. The most famous, U Fleků (11 Křemencova) in the "New Town" (the city centre), is the world's oldest brewpub, dating from 1499. It offers just one beer: a famous dark lager of 13 Balling, with a soft, spicy palate. U Fleků has a burlesque show. In the "Old Town", U Zlatého Tygra (17 Husova) is a famous literary tavern selling Pilsner Urquell. For the outstanding keeping of the beer, again Pilsner Urquell, some drinkers prefer U Kocoura, in the "Lesser Town" (2 Nerudova). Also in the "Lesser Town", U Svatého Tomáše (12 Letenska) serves beer from the small Braník brewery, of Prague; a lovely, firm, aromatic pale brew and a rather thin dark one. Prague's two larger breweries make the malty Staropramen and yeasty Prazanka beers.

Budweiser Budvar

Although it has a definite hop nose and finish, **Budweiser Budvar★★★→★★★★** is sweet by Czech standards, clean and rounded. The aromatic **Samson ★★→★★★** beer is marketed in Britain as Zamek. The Budvar brewery was not founded until 1895, so it must have been the similar beers from the older Samson brewery that inspired Busch.

Pilsner Urquell

The original Pilsner Urquell★★★★ has a slightly fuller colour than some of its latter-day derivatives. The local water imparts a softness and a faintly salty tang; the use exclusively of Zatec hops ensures a big, fresh bouquet and a bitterness balanced by softness of body (the yeast does not attenuate very far) A complex beer. Pilsen also has the Gambrinus brewery, producing hop-accented beers which evince the cleanness of Bohemian malt.

EASTERN EUROPE

There are few brewing treasures elsewhere in Eastern Europe. Beers similar in style to those of the Czech Republic are, not surprisingly, made in Slovakia, which also has a taste for bottom-fermenting porters like the coffeeish **Cassovar★★★**. Many other East European breweries have a range comprising a hoppy lager, perhaps also a dark one, and a bottom-fermenting strong porter. Perhaps the most unusual beer is Poland's **Grodzisk★★★→★★★★**, produced in the town of that name, near Poznan. This is made from malt smoked over oak, with some wheat content, and some wild yeast influence. It has an extraordinarily sourish, sappy, oak character.

In Poland and the Baltics beer has to compete with vodka; Russia also has *Kvass*, fermented from rye bread. In the Balkans beer dominates in Croatia and Slovenia, but gradually gives way to wine further south.

AUSTRIA

As an imperial capital, Vienna was a major brewing centre, famous for the amber-red, malty, style of lager first produced there by Anton Dreher in 1841. Its principal beers today are still accented towards malty sweetness, with a faint touch of bronze in the colour, but not nearly as assertive as some Vienna-style lagers produced elsewhere.

The city's local brewery, Ottakringer, makes the sweetish **Gold Fassl★★**, with some roundness. A lager in broadly the Vienna style is produced by the Wieden brewpub, in the district of the same name (5 Waag Gasse). More of a Munich type is made by the Fischer brewpub (17 Billroth Strasse), in the suburb of Döbling, on the edge of the Vienna Woods.

Baron Henrik Bachofen von Echt has a more colourful range, all top-fermenting, in a brewpub in the wine-cellars of his Schloss, where the tram stops at Nussdorf, also close to the woods. These include the chocolaty, fruity-dry **Sir Henry's Stout★★★** (4.8; 6); the copper, chewy, **St Tomas Brau★★→★★★**; the deep bronze, drier, complex, **Doppelhopfen Hell★★→★★★** (30 percent wheat); and a seasonal brew made with whisky malt.

Between Linz and Salzburg, the Eggenberg brewery produces a lightly smoky "whisky malt beer", **Nessie★★★**. It also makes a creamy but dryish **Urbock "23"★★★** (the figure indicates its gravity in degrees Plato). It has 7.9 percent alcohol by weight, 9.9 by volume. The monastery brewery of Schlägl, in Upper Austria, produces a rye beer, **Goldroggen** (not tasted). Austria also has one or two Alt and Weizen beers, and the occasional unfiltered brew.

Brau AG
This anonymous-sounding group owns the famous Schwechat brewery where Anton Dreher created the Vienna style of lager. That brewery has a premium **Hopfenperle★→★★**, relatively light in body and dry in finish, and a super-premium **Steffl★**, with a light-to-medium body and a hoppy finish. The group, which has its headquarters in Linz, also has a number of breweries producing the fruity **Kaiser★** beers, which are a national brand. Near Salzburg, Brau AG has a regional brewery known for its very pale **Zipfer Urtyp★→★★**, with a hoppy aroma and sherbety dryness.

Steirische (Styrian Breweries)
Second-biggest grouping, based in Graz, embracing the local Reininghaus-Puntigam brewery and a larger company that takes its name from its Styrian home-town of Leoben-Göss. The **Reininghaus-Puntigam★→★★** beers are generally malty and fruity. Gösser has a hearty **Spezial★★**, with a full, bronze colour, a smooth, malty palate and some hop bitterness in the finish. Its **Export★★** is slightly fuller-bodied, with a cleaner palate. Its new **Gösser Gold★** is lighter and relatively bland. **Gösser Stiftsbräu★→★★** is a dark, malty, sweet beer of 12.2 Plato but only 3.6 percent alcohol by volume.

SWITZERLAND

The world's strongest regularly produced bottom-fermenting beer, called **Samichlaus★★★★** ("Santa Claus"), is produced in Switzerland. This relatively new label has led lovers of individualistic brews to take a fresh look at Switzerland, which has more speciality beers than is suggested by a reputation for products that are well-made but not distinctive. Swiss beer-making tradition, at least in the German-speaking part of the country, is evidenced by monastic brewery ruins in St Gallen that date from the 9th century.

Samichlaus is brewed only once a year, on December 6, the day when the Swiss celebrate St Nicolas (Santa Claus). It is matured throughout the following year and released next December 6. Its starting gravity is 27.6 Plato (around 1110) and it emerges with 11.1–2 percent alcohol by weight; 13.7–14 by volume. Although it has a predictably malty nose and full body, its long maturation and high alcohol make for a surprising firmness and a brandyish finish.

This beer is produced by Hürlimann, of Zürich. Hürlimann's more conventional beers tend to be clean, light and dry, with a spritzy finish. South of Zurich, at Wadenswil, a new brewpub called Wadi Brau makes a Weizenbier of which there have been encouraging reports. To the east, Gasthof Frohsinn is a newish brewpub at Arbon, on Lake Constance.

Among the other major products, the beers of Cardinal are perhaps more flowery, those of Haldengut slightly smoky, and those of Feldschlösschen have a fruity bitterness; these are, however, only slight shades of difference.

A Swiss brewery's range might embrace a basic lager (at more than 11.5: 1046: around 3.8; 4.75); a deluxe beer (12; 1048; 4.1; 5.12); a "special" (12.5–6; 1050; 4.3; 5.37); a dark special (13.5; 1054; 4; 5); a "festival" brew of similar strength; a "strong" beer of 16; 1064; 5.4; 6.75; and perhaps a dark strong beer of 19; 1076; 5.9; 7.3.

Cardinal and Warteck both have Altbiers in their ranges. *Weizenbiers* are produced by Calanda, Frauenfeld (which now has the Back und Brau brewery tap) and the Ueli brewery at the Fischerstube (45 Rheingasse, Basel. ☎061–329495).

The strangest speciality from Switzerland's 30-odd breweries is a beer that is intended to taste of corn (maize) – and does. It is called **Maisgold**, contains 30 percent corn (which would hardly be unusual in the United States) and is produced by the Rosengarten brewery, of Einsiedeln.

GERMANY

As northern Europe is the home of brewing in the modern world, so Germany remains its hearth. Among its many claims to this central position, the strongest is that it has far more breweries than any other country. Their number is astonishing. Almost 40 percent of the world's breweries are in Germany; there are more than 1,200 covering the whole of the reunited country. The total in the past was far greater – there has been huge erosion in recent years – but there are also new breweries opening. Between one and two hundred new small breweries have opened since the late 1970s. Most of them are brewpubs, often specializing in unfiltered beers. Some, such as Johann Albrecht, are small chains.

Several of the new breweries use organically grown malting barley and hops, and some have attempted to create new speciality beers outside the classic styles.

Although now united, in history Germany has usually been a collection of separate states. The post-war division encouraged local loyalties. With Berlin in two, Germany's other great cities vied with one another, not least in their brewing traditions.

In general, the north has the driest beers; the southwest, especially the state of Baden-Württemberg, has softer brews, allegedly to suit palates weaned on wine; and the southeast (Bavaria) has sweeter, fuller-bodied products.

What is yet more interesting for the beer-lover is that each region has its own classic style. Berlin is known for its light, slightly sour, style of Weisse wheat beer, a summer quencher; Hamburg and the north in general are noted for extra-dry Pilsner-style beers; Dortmund, which makes more beer than any other city in Germany, has its confusingly named Export style, medium in both body and dryness; Düsseldorf drinks as its everyday brew a copper-coloured, top-fermenting Altbier. Cologne protects through *appellation contrôlée* its pale, top-fermenting Kölschbier. Einbeck and Munich share the strong *Bock* beer, especially in spring, though the latter city lays claim to winter's Dopplebock. Munich is the greatest of cities for stylistic variety. It also shares a tradition of dark or Dunkel beers with Kulmbach and other Bavarian towns (though Bamberg specializes in smoked-malt Rauchbier). Munich has a special interest in amber Märzenbier and various types of Weizen wheat beers.

Few of these varieties are wholly restricted to their own area or season, though they are always freshest at the appropriate time and taste best in their native place. Some brewers specialize in just one variety of beer, but more produce a range. Some brewers with regional roots have cross-bred with others to form semi-national groupings.

The biggest group includes, among others, DAB, of Dortmund; Binding, of Frankfurt; and Kindl, of Berlin. The second largest embraces Henninger, of Frankfurt; Eichbaum, of Mannheim; EKU, of Kulmbach, and others. A further group links Dortmund Union; Küppers, of Cologne; Einbecker; and Schultheiss, of Berlin. Famous exporters such as Holsten (of Hamburg) and Beck (of Bremen) also own other breweries. The biggest-selling beer in Germany, Warsteiner, is available throughout the country, but does not have a market-share comparable with those of national brands elsewhere in the world. Happily Germany is still a land of local beers – at least for now.

Within any style, German breweries – especially the larger ones – are apt to make similar products. This is in part because clear standards are laid down by law.

There is also the separate question of the *Reinheitsgebot*, the German Pure Beer Law of 1516. The industry maintains that it will continue to adhere to the Purity Law despite an EC ruling of 1987 insisting that it not be used to bar imports.

HAMBURG

Around the world, imported beer from Germany often means Holsten, Beck's or St Pauli Girl. The first comes from Hamburg, the others two from Bremen. These two cities remain the principal ports in Germany, a largely landlocked country, and they have been exporters of beer for more than 600 years. Their great importance in the brewing industry dates back to one of the early attempts at organized trade in Europe – the 15th-century Hanseatic League.

The extra-dry speciality Pilseners produced in this part of Germany owe their character to the same circumstance. In the days when transport by water was easier than travel across land, Hamburg was twice blessed. Not only did it, as a seaport, have Europe's greatest sales of beer, its requirement for hops was met by trade down the River Elbe from Bohemia, the classic area of cultivation. The dryness of these Pilseners echoes Hamburg's role as a great hop market. The hops were used not only for flavour but also as a natural preservative in beer that was destined for long sea journeys.

Holsten is the best-known of Hamburg's three breweries. Next is the confusingly named Bavaria St Pauli (nothing to do with St Pauli Girl of Bremen), then Elbschloss. All three produce generally dry beers, though with differences of emphasis. The Holsten products have an assertive dryness. Those from Bavaria St Pauli are perhaps a little fruitier. Elbschloss beers are very clean-tasting, reserving their dryness for a long, lingering finish.

Where to drink
Hamburg has three new-generation brew-pubs, all producing unfiltered beers. Dehn's Gröninger Braukeller (in the old warehouse district, at 47 Ost-West Strasse) offers a sweetish amber lager, confusingly presented as a "Pils", and a gentle amber, Weisse). The brewery has its own butchery and four adjoining restaurants. Zum Goldenen Engel (in a 1730 building at 7 Harburger Schloss Strasse) has a Vienna-style lager. Bierernest/Erlebnis Brauerie (30 Paulinen Allee, Eimsbüttel) has a cloudy Pils and a Dunkel. This pub, near the fish market, opens only in the evening (from 6 o'clock).

Bavaria St Pauli
Names like "Bavaria" were adopted in the late 19th century by brewers who were following the south's lead in lager-brewing. The Bavaria brewery of Hamburg and the more locally named St Pauli merged in 1922. As if its name were not confusing enough, the brewery markets its products under the Astra label. The company's basic lager, **Astra Urtyp★**, has a pleasant, light hop aroma and palate. The premium **Astra Pilsener★** has a very aromatic bouquet and palate. Astra also has a beer called **Exclusiv★**, in the style the Germans call **Export** (like the Dortmund variety) and a dark **Urbock★** (again a confusing name, since this is a Doppelbock).

In addition to that fairly standard range, there is a light-bodied but very dry Pilsener called **Grenzquell★** which was for some time heavily promoted in the USA. The company is best known for one outstanding product from its subsidiary Jever brewery, in the northern town of the same name in German Friesland.

Jever **Pilsener★★★★**, which is regarded as something of a

Frisian speciality, is the most bitter beer in Germany, despite a slight mellowing in recent years. Jever has a big bouquet (the aroma hops are of the Tettnang variety), a yeasty palate (the brewery has had its own strain since 1936) and an intense apéritif bitterness in the finish. A smooth **Jever Export★★** and a firm-bodied **Maibock★★** are hard to find outside Friesland.

A Frisian nation once straddled what are now the borders of The Netherlands, Germany and Denmark, and its traditional drinks suggest a liking for intense and bitter flavours. In its handsome resort town, Jever is a proud and prosperous brewery, with a very modern plant.

Elbschloss

This brewery takes its name from the River Elbe which flows parallel to the road on which the brewery stands. Masked by rowan, hawthorn and sycamore trees, the brewery is in its original, 1881, brick building. The *Schloss* is in the woods behind. Elbschloss is partly owned by the Dortmunder Union and Schultheiss group, Brau und Brunnen. It has a full range of products, including the very pleasant and splendidly dry **Ratsherrn Pils★★★**. there is also a good, malty Dopplebock called simply **Ratsherrn Bock★★**. None of the Elbschloss beers is pasteurized.

Holsten

In the days when the nobility controlled such matters as licenses to brew beer, the Duchy of Schleswig-Holstein held sway over Hamburg. The Duke of Holstein who granted the city the right to brew is remembered in the name of this company, and on its labels. The company's basic local beer is the firm-bodied **Holsten-Edel★**. It also has a German-style **Export★**, with a satisfying, wholesome texture and a soft, dry **Pilsener★**.

Holsten is the biggest German exporter to Britain, where one of its products has, to the uninformed drinker, become synonymous with the term "Pils". Ironically, the beer thus dubbed is not a regular Pilsener. It is the product that the company would prefer to be known by its full name of **Holsten Diät Pils★★→★★★**. This very dry low-carbohydrate beer was originally produced for diabetics. Since it has a relatively high alcohol content, at 5.8 percent by volume, its calorie count does not suit weight-watchers. Its real virtue is that it is a genuine import, with plenty of hop character. Holsten also has a **Maibock★★,** labelled in Britain as Urbock. This strong beer has a malty dryness, with a hint of apricot. Holsten's beers are *kräusened*.

Like its main local rival, Holsten also has a super-premium product from a subsidiary brewery. The brewery is in Lüneburg, a spa town of stepped-gable houses, their styles evolving from the 14th to the 18th centuries. A group of them forms the old brewery and guest-house, now converted into a beautifully arranged beer museum and a restaurant serving local dishes.

The new brewery is very modern, and its dry, hoppy beer is called **Moravia Pils★★★**. The name Moravia must have come down the Elbe at some time. The beer is notable for its big bouquet, and has a rather light body. In addition to Moravia, which enjoys some prestige, there are a number of minor products, some under the Bergedorf name, and associated breweries in other cities.

BREMEN

Churches and monasteries dedicated to St Paul have given their name to a good few breweries in Germany, including one in Bremen, long destroyed. This does not altogether explain how one of the city's famous export beers came to be known as St Pauli *Girl*, and the people who might know claim they can't remember. Another noted export is Beck's, while the local brewing company is called Haake-Beck.

Bremen had the first Brewer's Guild in Germany, in 1489, and such is its beery history that it still has a large number of brewery names. Most of these names are of brewing companies that were once independent and which are still separate but linked in a complicated corporate structure. Other labels to be taken into consideration are Hemelinger (nothing to do with the British brand of a similar name) and Remmer. Hemelinger produces a Spezial, a rather perfumy but sweetish beer. Remmer produces an interestingly malty Altbier.

All of the linked breweries in Bremen share a single complex of modern buildings, with two brewhouses, in the town centre, close to the River Weser. Outside of this group is Dressler, once famous for its porters, which no longer has a brewery but survives as a beer brand owned by Holsten.

Where to drink
The Old Town area of Bremen, known as the Snoor, is a delight, and has some lovely taverns. The quarter also has a brewpub at 12–13 Hinter dem Schütting and Bottcher Strasse. This Schüttinger Brauerei offers a full-coloured Pils, a malty Dunkel, a darkish Maibock, a dark winter brew (*Weihnachstbier*) and local dishes.

Beck's
The single product brewed by Beck's carries no description beyond a straightforward **Beck's Bier★→★★**. It is broadly within the Pilsener style, with a fresh aroma, a faintly fruity, firm, crisp palate and a clean, dry finish. It is light by German but heavy by international standards, and difficult to place in context. A very pale malt is used, and the hopping leans heavily towards the Hallertau aroma variety. Within the Beck's brand is a dark version, available in some markets. Beck's Bier is fermented with its own house yeast, at fairly low temperatures, and *kräusened*.

Haake-Beck
A traditional copper brewhouse is used to produce a full range of beers for Bremen and its hinterland, and also local

specialities. Both its regular **Edel-Hell★** and its **Pils★→★★** have a floral bouquet and a light, clean palate. While its cosmopolitan cousins do not make specific claims to the style, this Pils does, and properly has a little more bitterness than either in the finish. It is *kräusened*, and – unusually – is available locally (in the Old Town, for example) in unfiltered form. This version is identified as **Kräusen Pils★★★**, and has living yeast in suspension. As if to emphasize the resultant cloudiness, it is served in cracked-pattern glasses. Even by the standards of a German Pilsner, it has a mountainous head, followed by a soft palate, with just a suggestion of chewy, yeast bitterness.

Haake-Beck also produces, as a summer speciality, a Bremen interpretation of a northern wheat beer. **Bremer Weisse★★★** is served in a bowl-shaped glass similar to those used in Berlin, and is a wonderful summer refresher. In its natural state, it has a palate reminiscent of under-ripe plums, though it is usually served sweetened with a dash of raspberry juice. It has a gravity of 7.5 Plato, producing 2.2 percent alcohol by weight (2.75 by volume). In addition to a top yeast, there is a controlled, pure-culture lactic fermentation.

Yet a third speciality, **Seefahrt Malz**, cannot strictly be rated as a beer, since it is not fermented. It is a heavily hopped malt extract, of a daunting 55 Plato, with a syrupy viscosity but a surprisingly pleasant taste. Seefahrt Malz was for a time on sale, but is now available only to eminent citizens who are invited to the House of Seafarers' annual dinner in Bremen. It is ceremonially served in silver or pewter chalices. Despite its size, the company itself has a taste for traditions. From among its towering buildings each morning emerges a line of drays drawn by Oldenburg horses to deliver beer to the people of the inner-city area.

St Pauli Girl

This is produced in the older of Bremen's two brewhouses. Like Beck's, it has a lot of aroma hopping, though it emerges with a slightly lesser bouquet. **St Pauli Girl★→★★** has floral tones in its bouquet and palate, and is very clean. It has marginally less bitterness than Beck's, and is not *kräusened*. Although each of the two beers is made to its own specification, each with a different yeast background, the distinctions between them are less striking than the similarities. St Pauli Girl, too, is available in a dark version.

HANOVER AND LOWER SAXONY

Although this part of Germany is often associated with *Korn* schnapps and *Steinhäger* gin, it does also have its speciality beers. The very dry Jever and Moravia Pils (see pages 25–7) are actually brewed in the state of Lower Saxony. So is a newish speciality, called Duckstein, in character approaching something between a Belgian and an English ale. Duckstein is made in Braunschweig (Brunswick). That city also has an Altbier, as does Hanover.

More distinctively, this region is the original home of Bock beer. The Lower Saxony town of Einbeck was the biggest brewing centre in the medieval European federation of trading cities known as the Hanseatic League. The town brewed beers strong enough to survive being shipped far and wide, and its 'beck (later "bock") beers became famous. In the 1600s the Duke of Brunswick took Einbeck beer with him when he married a Bavarian noblewoman, and that is how Bock came to be so strongly associated with the southern state.

Where to drink
There are at least a dozen brewpubs in Lower Saxony. Brunswick has Schadt's (28 Höhe, at Am Marstall), producing a Pils with a slight wheat character. Hanover has two brewpubs. Ernst August (13 Schmieder Str; evenings only) makes a mild Pils. Roneburg (27 Königsworther Str) produces a hoppy Pils and a malty Dunkel. Statues on the facade depict emigrants to America. In Oldenburg, the brewpub Zum Heuglbräu (243 Ammerländer Heer Str) makes a very wide range of seasonal beers, including a hoppy Pilsener for Ascension Day, a dry "East Frisian" summer wheat beer in June, and malty, tasty, interpretations of a Märzen and a December Double Bock.

Einbecker Brauhaus
The town of Einbeck is worth a visit for its Late Gothic houses, their doors arched to provide access for a mobile brew-kettle, and their roofs vented to wind-dry the malt and hops. The Brodhaus tavern, on the town square, is the "tap" for the only surviving brewery, known simply as Einbecker. On the principle that the original Einbecker beers would have fermented-out on their journeys, and would have been well-hopped as a preservative measure, today's examples are made drier than those of Bavaria. The brewery produces three styles of Bock, all with a malty aroma, a clean palate and some hoppy dryness. The **Hell★★** starts malty and finishes long; the **Dunkel★★★** is more rounded; and the **Maibock★★★** faintly estery, spritzy and refreshing. The latter is available from March to the end of May.

Feldschlosschen
This sizeable brewery in Brunswick produces the top-fermenting beer **Duckstein★★→★★★**, a distant revival of a local style. It is an amber, malty-fruity brew, developing to a hoppiness and a distinct tartness in the finish. Duckstein is matured over beechwood chips. The archaic spelling Brunswiek is used on the brewery's **Alt★★**, which is made with a different yeast. This has a good malt character, and is very well balanced.

Lindener Gilde
The company takes its name from its origins as a civic brewery, operated by a guild. Today it produces a range of

very well-made beers. Its speciality **Broyan Alt★★★** is named after a great Hanover brewer of the 16th century. This is a top-fermenting Altbier in a similar style to those of Düsseldorf but a little stronger (12.4 Plato; 4.2 percent alcohol by weight; 5.25 by volume), slightly darker, relatively light-bodied, malt-accented, with a delicate hop character and a low bitterness. The brewery also has a regular **Gilde Pilsner★→★★** and a premium **Ratskeller Edel-Pils★★**, both with a complex hop character and some Saaz delicacy, as well as a German-style **Edel-Export★**.

MÜNSTER

The university city of Münster, rich in history as the capital of Westphalia, is regarded with affection by knowledgeable beer-lovers all over Germany for the specialities produced at its Pinkus Müller brewery and restaurant. Pinkus Müller is an institution, despite its being nothing larger than a *Hausbrauerei* producing fewer than 10,000hl a year. It makes some extra-ordinary beers and has the impudence to export to the USA.

Pinkus Müller's premises in the Old Town (what people in Münster call the "cow quarter" – *Kuhviertel*) were originally nine houses. Over the years they have been integrated, with considerable rebuilding in the 1920s and some more recently. There are four dining rooms; in the main one the centrepiece is a Westphalian oven, set among Dutch tiles illustrating Bible stories. The fireplace hangs with Westphalian hams, a good indication of the style of food.

Where to drink

Apart from Pinkus Müller, the Münster area has a tiny Heinrich Jürgens brewery (6 Huhl Str, Beckum), producing a pale Altbier. Southeast of Münster, at Oelde, the Pott-Feldmann's have a brewpub with rooms (☎02522–2209). A newer entrant in the Münster area is the Klute brewpub, at Havixbeck (28 Poppenbeck), serving a mild Helles and home-baked bread.

Pinkus Müller

The brewery produces no fewer than four beers and is best known for what it describes as **Pinkus Münster Alt★★★→★★★★**. In this instance, the term *alt* indicates simply an old style, without suggesting anything on the lines of the Düsseldorf classics. Pinkus Münster Alt is a very pale, top-fermenting beer made from an unusual specification of 40 percent wheat and 60 percent barley malt, to a gravity of 11.3 Plato. It has a long (six months) maturation, including a *kräusening*. The maturation takes place at natural cellar temperature, but in conventional lagering tanks in which there is a resident lactic culture. The result is a very crisp beer indeed, dry, with a faint, quenching acidity in the finish. In several respects, not least its higher gravity, relative clarity and restrained acidity, this is a different product from the Bremer or Berliner Weisse. It is wheatier than any Kölsch, yet it does not qualify as a Weizen; it is a unique speciality. In fact, the brewery does produce a **Pinkus Weizen★★→★★★**, which is worthy of special attention if only for its unusual lightness, though it is characteristically low on hop bitterness, and has a fruity finish. It is a rather northern-tasting Weizen, though it has a thoroughly southern ratio of 60:40 (wheat has the majority).

There are also two bottom-fermenting beers: **Pinkus Pils★→★★**, with a light but firm body and a hoppy dryness; and **Pinkus Spezial★★★**, a pale beer of 12.66 Plato, brewed with organically grown barley malt and hops. This clean, malty, dry beer, with a medium body, is sold in wholefood shops. Despite Pinkus Müller having all of these unusual brews, the house speciality is not a beer alone. The Müllers steep diced fresh fruit in sweetened water so that it forms its own syrup. They then add a tablespoon of the fruit and syrup to a glass of Pinkus Alt, so that its fresh flavours suffuse the beer and marry with the acidity of the wheat. The availability and contents of this confection depend upon which fruit is in season. Fruits with stones are not used, since they impart an incongruous, almondy bitterness. In summer, strawberries or peaches are favoured; in winter, oranges may be used. The fruit is steeped for a day in a pickling jar, with a kilo of sugar. When it is added to the beer, using a cylindrical glass, the result is known as an Altbier Bowl.

DORTMUND

The word "Dortmunder" features in the names of seven brewing companies, thus providing great confusion for beer-lovers who are not familiar with Germany. Some of these companies share facilities, but there are no fewer than half a dozen breweries in the city of Dortmund. Since each of the seven brewing companies has its own range of products in various styles, there are about 30 beers with Dortmunder names. In this respect, "Dortmunder" is an *appellation contrôlée*, since no beer brewed outside the city may, in Germany, bear the designation. In other countries, however, brewers have over the years produced beers that they have identified as being in the Dortmunder style. There was a vogue in The Netherlands and Belgium for a beer style described as "Dort".

There is, indeed, a Dortmunder style. In the days when the great brewing cities of Europe vied for ascendancy by promoting their own styles, that of Dortmund was a pale, medium-dry beer, very slightly bigger in body and higher in alcohol than its rivals from Munich or Pilsen. It was drier than a Munich pale beer, but less dry than a Pilsener.

As Dortmund's efforts were repaid with sales in other parts of Germany, and in adjoining countries, the local brewers began to refer to their characteristic beer as *Export*. That is how *Export* became a classic German style. Today a good Dort-munder Export beer has a gravity of 13 Plato, producing 4.4 percent alcohol by weight and 5.5 by volume, and with about 25 Units of Bitterness.

Unfortunately, the Dortmunder brewers' exposition of their classic style can be hard to find outside the city and hinterland. Although it made for a bigger local market, the industrial growth of Dortmund and the Ruhr was a mixed blessing for the city's image as a centre of fine brewing. In recent years especially, Dortmund brewers went through a phase of self-doubt: did a Dortmunder beer sound like a product for cloth-capped miners and steelworkers?

Although they have continued to make Dortmunder Export, the local brewers have in recent years neglected to promote it, preferring to concentrate on other products within their ranges, especially the Pilseners. This policy has not been a conspicuous success, nor does it deserve to be.

Dortmund is Germany's largest brewing city, and should be proud of its traditional style. Dortmund-inspired Export beers are, after all, included in the portfolios of brewers all over Germany.

Where to drink

For years, Dortmund was content to offer its beers to visitors at uninspiring bars (each representing a different brewery) set around the market square and church. Having been damaged in the war and quickly rebuilt during the recovery years of the 1950s, this area is a little lacking in colour.

In the mid-1980s, the two independents among the city's breweries separately decided to add a little romance. Both of them established brewpubs in the city-centre, each named after an early Dortmund brewer. Kronen opened Heinrich Wenker's Brauhaus on the Market Square. Wenker's is within the Zum Kronen restaurant complex.

Wenker's brewhouse stands among the drinkers in the bar area, and its speciality is an unfiltered, top-fermenting pale beer containing 15 percent wheat, called **Wenker's Urtrüb★★★** (12 Plato). It is a fresh, clean, lightly fruity beer with some yeast "bite". Other specialities are planned.

A few minutes' walk away, right outside the Thier brewery, is that company's offspring, Hövels Haus-Brauerei, at 5–7 Hoher Wall. There, the brewhouse is visible through a window of the restaurant.

All year round, Hövels serves a filtered brew, with a bronze colour and a malty aroma and palate, which is confusingly called **Bitterbier★★★** (13.5). This is a smooth, tasty, beer with a quite full body. Hövels has also produced some excellent specialities.

DAB (Dortmunder Actien Brauerei)

The middle name merely indicates a joint-stock company. Perhaps that is where the phrase "a piece of the action" originated. This very large brewing company is now part of a national grouping, with Binding, Berliner Kindl and others. In its modern brewery on the edge of Dortmund it produces beers that generally have a light, malty, dryness.

Its **Export★→★★** has a slight malt accent, while remaining dry, and is on the light side for the style. The brewery's **Meister Pils★** (marketed in the USA under the dismissive, lower-case name of dab beer), has a hint of malt in the nose but goes on to be dry, with some hop character in the palate and a fairly low bitterness.

There is more hop aroma, with a very clean and light palate, in the brewery's **Original Premium★**, marketed in the USA as Special Reserve. DAB also has an **Altbier★**, again with a dry maltiness and a light body. This is sold in the USA under the unflatteringly vague name of DAB Dark. In its local market, DAB has a pleasant **Maibock★→★★** and **Tremanator Doppelbock★→★★**. DAB is a very marketing-oriented company, distributing its products widely in the north of Germany.

Dortmunder Hansa

This is part of the same group as DAB, and the two share the one brewery. In Germany, Hansa has been very active in the supermarket trade. Its **Export★★** has a good malt aroma, a soft, full body, and a dry finish. Its **Pils★** is light and crisp, with some hoppy acidity.

Dortmunder Kronen

Among their home-town beers, the people of Dortmund favour those from the Kronen brewery, one of two privately owned breweries in the city. Its beers are, in general, big and malty, with a clean, delicate sweetness. These characteristics are evident especially in its **Export★★★**, and to a lesser degree in its super-premium **Classic★★→★★★**. **Pilskrone★★** has a flowery hoppiness. The brewery also has an **Alt★** with a relatively full body and a dense, rocky head. And there is a dark bock, called **Steinbock★★**, with an intense crystal-malt dryness. It is a shame that only the Classic, and not the whole range, is available in the bar at the adjoining museum (open Tuesday–Sunday, closed Monday; entrance free, through the main gates in Märkische Strasse).

Dortmunder Ritter

These robust, matter-of-fact Dortmunder brews are popular in the industrial Ruhr Valley. The fruitiness is perhaps most evident in the **Export★→★★**. The **Pils★** has a malty start and a dry finish. Ritter is an associate company of Dortmunder Union.

Dortmunder Thier

There is an attractive fullness, firmness and smoothness to the **Export★★★** from this brewery. It is to be hoped that the beer retains its character now that Thier is owned by Dortmunder Kronen. The Thier brewery continues to operate. Its other products include a dryish **Pils★★**.

DUB (Dortmunder Union Brauerei)

The "Union" refers to the merger of ten or a dozen breweries more than 100 years ago. That union sufficed until 1973, when

DUB linked with Schultheiss, of Berlin. The massive "U" of the Union logo, illuminated at night, is a Dortmund landmark atop the imposing brewery building which, looking rather like a 1920s power station, broods over the centre of the city. The DUB beers (all *kräusened*) have some malty sweetness and are generally mild in palate – perhaps on the bland side – and smooth. The **Export★★★** is malt-accented, and medium-bodied. The **Siegel Pils★** has an agreeably hoppy palate but not much finish. The super-premium **Brinckhoff's No 1★**, named after a founder-brewer, has a character somewhere between the two.

Dortmunder Stifts

Most production, and a majority shareholding, moved to Kronen after a series of changes of ownership. Stifts has a strong local following in the south of the city, and a minority shareholding in the community might ensure that the seasonal, top-fermenting *Hoeder Festbier* is in future produced in the old location. This beer, which contains a proportion of dark wheat malt, is made for a local festival at the beginning of each year.

DÜSSELDORF

Where a city is lucky, or sensible, enough to have retained a distinctive style of brewing, it often reserves a special beer for particular occasions or moods. Düsseldorf takes a different view and is one of those cities (like its neighbour and rival Cologne – or Dublin) that likes to serve its speciality as its daily beer.

Düsseldorf's prized beer is more instantly distinctive than that of its neighbour. It has a dark copper colour, is top-fermenting and is superficially similar to a British ale. The Düsseldorf beer has, though, a much cleaner palate, with a complex blend of malty body, sometimes a hint of roastiness, and hop bitterness. It has little of the yeasty fruitiness and acidity of the classic British ales. Since the Düsseldorf beer is a significant style in its own right, a German might resent its being compared to British ale. Internationally, however, the Düsseldorf style is little known, although it has been taken up by several brewers in the USA. In this context, its character can perhaps best be summed up by comparing it with ale.

The differences in the Düsseldorf product derive not only from the typically German barley malts and hops used, but also from the use of single cell, pure culture yeasts and – perhaps most significant – a period of cold conditioning in tanks, usually for several weeks. A German would no doubt argue that the Düsseldorf beer is cleaner and smoother than a British ale. The British would argue that their ales have more individuality. As always, this is to compare apples with oranges, neither is better; they are different.

A typical Düsseldorf beer has a gravity of 12 Plato, or a fraction more. It may be made with two or three malts. Some Düsseldorf brewers favour an infusion mash, but the decoction system is also widely used. Two or three hop varieties may be employed; Düsseldorf brewers have traditionally favoured Spalt. Open fermenters are sometimes used, especially in the smaller breweries. The warmer fermentation temperatures are reflected in slightly less intense cold conditioning, at between 32°F (0°C) and 47°F (8°C), for anything from three to eight weeks. Alcohol content is typically 3.6–3.8 by weight; 4–4.7 by volume. Units of Bitterness vary from the lower 30s to the 50s; colour around 35 EBC.

After its period of cold-conditioning, Düsseldorf beer is often dispensed in local taverns from a barrel, by gravity, with no carbon dioxide pressure, blanket or otherwise. Although this method is practised in several taverns and restaurants, notably in the Old Town, it is especially associated with the city's home-brew houses. Such is the joy of this city for the beer-lover: not only does it have its own style, of some character and complexity, it has no fewer than four home-brew taverns. In these establishments, the stubby, cylindrical glasses favoured in Düsseldorf are charged as quickly as they are exhausted.

The home-brew taverns are the shrines of the Düsseldorf brewing style, and as such their beers must be regarded as German classics. The beer-loving visitor to Düsseldorf will want to visit all of them – and also to sample the beers made in the local style by the city's four other breweries, and several others in neighbouring smaller towns.

Düsseldorf's brewers may well wish that a less imitable name had emerged for their style; they call their brews nothing more memorable than Düsseldorfer Altbier. No other city has such devotion either to the production or serving of beer in this style, but brewers in several other towns have in their portfolio something which they call Altbier. In most instances, though not all, it bears a great similarity to the Düsseldorf style. "*Alt*" simply means "old", and indicates a style that was produced before the widespread introduction of bottom-fermentation.

"Altbier" is the style of Düsseldorf and its brewers produce little else, except stronger brews variously called "*Latzenbier*" ("beer from the wood") or "*Sticke*" ("secret" beer) that appear very briefly in some places in winter, spring and autumn.

Of the Düsseldorf home-brew houses, three are in the Old Town (Altstadt seems especially appropriate in this instance). The fourth, Schumacher, is in the more modern part of the city centre. Among the bigger brewers' Altbiers, the popular Diebels is firm-bodied; Hannen is soft, rounded and well-balanced; Frankenheim is hoppy and light-bodied; Schlosser malty, but dry; Düssel the fruitiest; and Rhenania can be slightly thick-tasting.

Where to drink

None of the home-brew houses should be missed. A newer entrant, in the Oberkassel area, is a Johann Albrecht brewpub (102 Niederkasseler Str) which has a hoppy Pils, a top-fermenting, malty, mild, Dunkel, and local dishes.

Im Füchschen

"The Fox" is noted not only for its beer but also its food. This home-brew house, in Ratinger Strasse, produces a very good Altbier, simply called **Im Füchschen★★★→★★★★**. It is a complex and beautifully balanced beer, its firm, fairly full body at first evincing malty notes, then yielding to lots of hop flavour from Spalt and Saaz varieties. In the end, its hop bitterness is its predominant characteristic.

The tavern's big main dining room serves hearty *Eisbein* and *Schweinshaxe* (pork dishes). It can be very busy, but is a friendly place and diners are usually happy to share tables.

Zum Schlüssel

"The Key" is not to be confused with the larger Schlösser ("Locksmith") brewery, however easy that may be. Zum Schlüssel, in Bolker Strasse, is a home-brew house. The brewery is visible from its main room. **Zum Schlüssel Altbier★★→★★★** begins with an aromatic hoppiness of palate, but its predominant characteristic is a light maltiness, with a touch of "British" acidity in the finish. It has a fairly light body and a bright clarity. The restaurant is quite light and airy, too, with something of a coffee-shop atmosphere. It was founded in 1936 (a little late for Heinrich Heine (1797–1856), who was born in this street: the site of his home is now a roast-chicken restaurant). In 1963, the company opened a second, free-standing brewery, whose **Gatzweiler Altbier★★** is widely available in Düsseldorf.

Ferdinand Schumacher

Despite being in a modern part of the city this home-brew house in Ost Strasse, has the polite atmosphere of times past and is a quiet place at which to relax after shopping or a day at the office. Its **Schumacher Altbier★★★** is the lightest in palate and body, and the maltiest, very clean, with a lovely delicacy of aromatic, fruity hop character. The beer is also available at the Goldene Kessel, in Bolker Strasse.

Zum Uerige

This rambling tavern in Berger Strasse is named after a cranky proprietor. Cranky he may well have been, but it is a friendly enough place today – and produces the classic Düsseldorfer Altbier, an aromatic, tawny brew, deep in colour and flavour, with a slowly unrolling hop bitterness in its big and sustained finish. **Zum Uerige★★★★** beer is the most assertive, complex and characterful of the Alts. It is also the most bitter. Like all of the Düsseldorfer "house" beer, it is produced in traditional copper kettles, but this is the most beautiful brewery of them all. It also has a traditional copper cool-ship, and a Baudelot cooler, both still in use, and it is impeccably maintained and polished. The brewhouse can be seen from the most picaresque of the many bars. Every few minutes, barrels are rolled through Zum Uerige on their way to the various dispense points, while drinkers jink out of the way. Meals are not served, but Zum Uerige has its own sausage kitchen on the premises. Here, sausages of pork and liver, *Blutwurst* (blood sausage) and brawn, are produced, with spiced dripping left over to serve with malodorous Mainzer cheese that has been marinated in beer. If those flavours are not sufficiently intense, robust gastronomes are encouraged to look for the "secret" *Sticke* beer usually on the third Tuesday of its designated months: January and October. This is an Altbier of 14 Plato, with an extra dash of roasted malt – and it is dry-hopped in the maturation tanks. Very intense indeed. The brewery has recently added a wheat beer.

COLOGNE

German beer-lovers greatly admire the speciality brewing style of Cologne, even if most of the world has not so far noticed it. It would be widely imitated, too, if it were not protected by its appellation Kölschbier (the beer of Cologne). Except in cases of lengthy precedent, a beer may not label itself Kölsch unless it is made in the Cologne metropolitan area. Imitations are thus pointless: they cannot identify their aspirations.

Happily, there are a baker's dozen breweries in Cologne and as many again in its hinterland. All of them produce Kölschbier, and some do nothing else. At least one has dropped other, more conventional, styles from its portfolio. Kölschbier dominates Cologne: it is possible to go into an ordinary bar in the city and be unable to find a Pilsener – even though it may be advertized outside. In the city's "home-brew" houses, of course, Kölsch is the only beer available.

Cologne has more breweries than any other city in Germany (indeed, in the world). Being so blessed, it naturally has a great many bars and taverns, including its home-brew houses. For most of the year, it is an engrossing place in which to sample beers, except during its pre-Lenten carnival, when the drinking becomes less considered. Whether its wealth of drinking places results from, or serves to attract, the tourist is a matter for conjecture. Some people apparently go to Cologne to study its history, see its huge cathedral, or take trips down the Rhine. They should not be distracted from the city's distinctive beer by such diversions, though it is comfortably possible to enjoy both.

For all the envy it attracts, Kölschbier is not at first sight especially distinctive. It is a pale beer, much the same colour as a Pilsener, but – as its lightly fruity aroma and palate should reveal – it is made by top-fermentation.

A classic Kölsch has that fruitiness in the beginning, a notably soft palate (influenced by the local water) and a very delicate finish. Although Kölschbier brewers pay a lot of attention to hop character (two or three varieties are used, often with a Hallertau accent), their aim is to achieve a light dryness in the finish and nothing too assertive.

The very subtle character of this style is no doubt influenced also by the background palate imparted by the typical Cologne yeasts. These generally create a very vigorous fermentation, followed by two, three or four weeks of cold conditioning at 32°–41°F (0°–5°C). The gravity range of Kölsch beers is from just over 11 to just under 12 Plato. A typical example has 11.5 Plato and emerges at between 3.5 and 4 percent alcohol by weight. Most often, it is 4 (5 by volume). Bittering units are typically in the upper 20s.

Kölschbier is a lovely apéritif (not a bad digestif, either), often consumed as an accompaniment to snacks. On its home ground, this may mean "half a hen" (Rhineland whimsy for a wedge of cheese with a roll) or "Cologne caviare" (blood sausage). *Mettwurst* is the tartare type. "With music" means an onion garnish.

Among the home-brew beers, P.J. Früh's is especially clean-tasting, that of Päffgen the hoppiest and Malzmühle, appropriately, the maltiest. Each has its own support as a local classic, though none of the three has a clear claim to be the definitive Kölsch. Nor among the rest of the Kölschbiers does one stand out, though a good claim is staked by Garde. This is a pronouncedly fruity Kölschbier, produced by an old-established private company at Dormagen-bei-Köln. Garde is one of several companies in Germany with a woman brewer.

Differences between the more widely available Kölschbiers are so subtle as to be very open to the influence of freshness (of beer or the taster). Sion is flowery and hoppy; Gereons fruitier, with a dry finish; Sester fruity and dry; Gilden fruity, with a rather heavy texture; Zunft creamy; Reissdorf light, soft and delicious; Küppers soft and sweetish; Kurfürsten and Dom sweet at the front, with a drier finish.

Where to drink
Visitors who go to Cologne to see the Roman museum or the cathedral will find P.J. Früh's Kölner Hofbräu conveniently opposite, in Am Hof. Behind Früh is the Old Town, lined with bars and restaurants, especially on the Heumarkt (Haymarket). At the near end of the Heumarkt, the Päffgen Kölsch brewery family has a restaurant. At the far end is the Malzmühle home-brew café. Beside the Rhine, a pleasant ride on tram number 15 or 16 to stop at Schönhauser Strasse leads to the Küppers Kölsch brewery, where there is a restaurant serving local dishes and Wiess beer, and a very worthwhile museum of brewing (157 Altenburger Str. ☎0222–373242). The Cologne metropolitan area also embraces Bonn, where the new generation of brewpubs is represented by Brauhaus Bönnsch (4 Sternbrücke), in the city centre. This establishment has created its own specialities in a style that it describes as "Bönnsch". Its brews are cloudy-white, quenching and fruity, like a wheaty version of an unfiltered Kölsch. They are served in an arched elaboration of a Kölsch glass. This commercially minded enterprise is linked to Sieg-Rheinische Germania brewery, in nearby Hersel, Bornheim.

P. J. Früh's Cölner Hofbräu
Because it is the parent of its own beer, P.J. Früh's is still regarded as a home-brew house. In fact, the brewery behind

the restaurant became too small to cope with demand for the beer in the free trade. The Früh brewery is now away from the city centre. However, the bar and restaurant remain an institution in Cologne. **Früh Echt Kölsch★★★** is a soft beer, delicate in both its fruitiness of entrance and its hoppy dryness of finish. It is made with only barley malt – no wheat – and hopped with the Hallertau and Tettnang varieties.

Gaffel

This brewery traces its origins to 1302, and is in the heart of town, just behind the railway station. It was once a brewpub, but now has a handsome "tap" at 20–22 Alter Markt, in the Old Town. **Gaffel Kölsch★★★** is very dry, almost nutty.

Hellers

New-generation brewpub, in the premises that formerly housed a distillery making a liqueur bitters. Organically grown barley and hops are used. **Hellers Kölsch★★★** is creamy in texture, and robust in its maltiness, hoppiness and fruitiness. There is also an unfiltered beer, called **Ur-Wiess★★★**. Hellers Brauhaus is at Roon Strasse. There are two other new-generation brewpubs: Weiss-Bräu (24 AmWeidenbach), making a Kölsch, and a Dunkel; and hoppy Pils and Papa Joe's (14 Unter Käster, in the Old Town), producing an unfiltered, top-fermenting beer. The latter has an antique collection of mechanical novelties.

Küppers

By far the biggest producer and exporter of Kölschbier despite being a newcomer. Küppers was established 20-odd years ago in Cologne to meet the rules of appellation, so that a Kölschbier could be added to the portfolio of the large Wicküler Pils company, then brewing in Wuppertal. This move followed a court case over the appellation. Sales since, supported by hefty marketing efforts, have justified the determination behind Küppers' establishment, but tradition is harder to build. No doubt this was in mind when Küppers established its excellent restaurant and museum. The soft and sweetish **Küppers Kölsch★→★★** is unexceptional, but the brewery wins bonus points for another gesture to tradition, its confusingly named *Wiess* beer. Although *Wiess* is the Rhineland dialect pronunciation of *Weiss* ("white"), the designation perhaps has less to do with the cloudy tone of this beer than its rustic style; Bavarians talk in the same vein about a *Wies'n* beer when they mean something that is to be served at a country fair. **Küppers Wiess★★★** is an unfiltered version of the normal Kölsch. It still has yeast in suspension, imparting the cloudiness and an astringent, refreshing, bitter-fruit quality. The name is not intended to suggest a wheat beer. Although some wheat is used, it is present only in the small proportion typical of Kölschbier.

Malzmühle

This is a home-brew café and restaurant with a pleasantly insouciant, relaxing atmosphere. Being at the far end of the

Heumarkt, it is easily missed, but shouldn't be. Its **Mühlen Kölsch★★★→★★★★** is mild and rounded, with a warm, spicy aroma and palate, reminiscent almost of marshmallow. It is a distinctive and delicious beer, lightly hopped with Hallertau blossoms and fermented in open vessels.

Päffgen

A beautifully kept home-brew restaurant in Friesen Strasse which has a small beer garden. Its **Päffgen Kolsch★★★→★★★★** has a soft palate with a big, hoppy bouquet. By the standards of Kölschbier, it has a very hoppy finish, too.

Sion

Originally a home-brew, too. Its tavern, in Unter Taschen-macher, in the Old Town, offers brisk service and a very fresh glass of its pleasantly flowery beer. Since **Sion Kölsch★★→★★★** is now produced under contract by the brewers of Gereons Kölsch, knowing drinkers whisper that the two beers are one and the same. This is not true; each is produced to its own specifications. The flowery bouquet and dry finish of Sion Kölsch derives in part from Hersbrucker hops. **Gereons★★** is hopped exclusively with Hallertau.

RHINELAND'S PILSENERS

Apart from those cities that are islands of their own style, the whole of the Rhine and its hinterland is dotted with well-regarded breweries. Towns without a speciality style of their own have in several cases put their best efforts behind a Pilsener, developing, as Madison Avenue might term it, a super-premium product and in several instances producing nothing else.

Several of these products were among a selection dubbed "The Premium Beers" in an article some years ago in the influential newspaper *Die Welt*. The writer, Hans Baumann, is a journalist who frequently comments on both the business and social aspects of the brewing industry. His intention was not to say that these "premium" beers were the best, but that they were labels that seemed capable of commanding a high price. His "premium" tag was gratefully seized by the breweries and he now has mixed feelings about its continued use. There are, he points out, many other good beers, not all of them as intensively marketed.

The German consumer has, however, come to believe in recent years that a brewery concentrating on one style is likely to do a better job than those with a whole portfolio of products. This is a questionable proposition. If a chef prepares the same dish every lunchtime, he is unlikely to undercook or burn it, but are his skills necessarily those of an Escoffier?

While the Pilseners of the far north are generally the driest, the same leaning is evident in Rhineland, perhaps with a softness and lightness emerging as the brewers enter wine country. Several of the most popular breweries are in the hill-and-lake region called the Sauerland. Its clean air and fresh water do much to inspire the thirst of the consumer.

Where to drink

In Essen, home town of the Stauder brewery, one of the company's shareholders established a "house brewery" in 1984. The Borbecker Dampfbier brewery, bar and restaurant is in Heinrich Brauns Strasse. D*ampf* refers to the fact that the premises were a steam-powered brewery in the 1880s and not to the style of beer. The brew, called **Salonbier★★★**, is in the Vienna style and of Export strength. It has a clean, dry, malty palate and is available filtered or as a Zwickelbier. It's a long way from the Pilseners of the region – and a delightful contrast. Essen now has a second brewpub, Graf Beust, at 95 Kastanien Allee. This produces a golden, mild Zwickelbier and sweetish, dark Altbier.

At the opposite end of Premium Pilsener country, across the border and into Saarland, another Zwickelbier can be found, also in a "house brewery". This is the brewery guesthouse Zum Stiefel, run by the Bruch family, in the town of Saarbrücken. Another Saarland speciality, though not from a house brewery, is Bier Eiche (oak beer). This was originally produced for a festival concerning oak trees, but is now available all year round. It is a pale, top-fermenting beer of everyday gravity, with a delicate hop aroma and dryness. It is produced in Merzig, by Saarfurst, a local subsidiary of the region's Karlsberg brewery. Karlsberg, in the Saarland town of Homburg, has – of course – nothing to do with the Danish brewery of a similar name but different spelling.

Bitburger

Taking its name from its home town of Bitburg, this is a specialist "Premium" Pilsener brewery. It is a very modern place indeed, producing a Pilsener with a low original gravity by German standards: 11.3 Plato. This is thoroughly attenuated, to produce an alcohol content of 3.9 by weight, 4.8–9 by volume. **Bitburger Pils★★★** is very pale, extremely light, and dry. It has a soft maltiness, a pronounced hop flavour and a very subtle, elegant, bitterness. A much-admired beer.

Herforder

Principally a Pilsener brewery though it does also produce beers in other styles. **Herforder Pils★★→★★★**, is full-bodied, with a clean, mild palate. Its gravity is 12.1 and its alcohol content 3.9; 4.8–9. Herforder also produces a malty but dry **Export★→★★**; a pale **Mai-Bock★→★★** and a dark **Doppelbock★→★★**, both very malty. Herford is on the northern borders of Rhineland-Westphalia.

Irle

Another specialist Pilsener brewery. Its **Irle Edel-Pils★→★★** has the classic combination of a 12 Plato gravity and an alcohol content of 4; 5, and it has a lovely clean palate and is very mild.

König

Known as a "Premium" Pilsener brewery but also produces other styles. Its Pilsener is very full-bodied but clean and notably dry. König Pilsener★★★ has a rich aroma, a sustained, very smooth, bitterness and a perfumy finish. It has an original gravity of 12.1 but this is fermented down to an alcohol content of only 3.8; 4.6. The company also has a **König-Alt★** that is fractionally less full-bodied, and much milder in hop character.

König-Alt has a rival in its home town of Duisburg. A beer called **Rheingold-Alt★→★★** is the speciality of a smaller brewery in the town.

Königsbacher

Coblenz brewery which produces several styles. It has a number of subsidiaries, whose products include **Richmodis Kölsch** and **Düssel Alt**. The enjoyable **Königsbacher Pils★★→★★★** is complex and satisfying, medium-bodied with a fresh, hoppy bouquet and a well-sustained bitterness in the finish.

Krombacher

Taking its name from its location in Kreutzal-Krombach, this house is a specialist "Premium" Pilsener brewery, proud to announce that its water comes from a rocky spring. **Krombacher Pils★★** is medium-bodied, with a slight malt accent in the nose, a clean palate, and a pleasing hop bitterness in its late finish. In the American market, the beer has been promoted as having a crispness, a "hop taste", and "a noticeable lack of bitterness". It is hard to say whether the copywriter was being intentionally dishonest, or cloth-tongued.

Stauder

This is known as a "Premium" Pilsener brewery although Stauder does have other products. **Stauder Pils★★** is marketed especially to expensive hotels and restaurants. Its advertizing in Germany emphasizes cold maturation, making a play on the verb to rest. Brewers sometimes describe their beer as "resting" in maturation, and Stauder is promoted as a product to enjoy in tranquillity. Since a long maturation also "cleans" beer, there is an implication that Stauder-drinkers are strangers to the hangover. Stauder Pils does not, however, have an unusually clean nose or palate, and there is a hint of fruitiness in its character.

Veltins

This brewery led the movement to speciality Pilsener brewing in Germany and is owed a debt of fashionability by its fellow "Premium" producers, especially its neighbours in Sauerland. It is a relatively small brewery, and its **Veltins Pilsener★★** still has something of a cult following. It is a sweetish, robust beer, with an elegant hop bitterness in the finish.

Warsteiner

Although it does have other styles this concern is known as a "Premium" Pilsener producer. It is a very up-to-date brewery, aggressively marketing and exporting its premium-priced product. **Warsteiner Pilsener★→★★** has a light hop bouquet, a dry palate, and a moderately bitter finish. It is the biggest-selling beer in Germany, with a growing following in the USA.

FRANKFURT AND HESSE

In the Old Town of Frankfurt, the *Sachsenhausen*, the bars and restaurants serve Apfelwein, a cloudy, medium-dry alcoholic cider. If Frankfurt has a speciality for the drinker, then this is it. There is a theory that Europe once had a cider belt, separating the wine-growing and beer-brewing areas. It is a tenuous theory, but in this instance the argument could, indeed, be put that Frankfurt has wine to its south and west; beer to its north and east.

In this pivotal position, Frankfurt has no beery leaning of its own, no varietal style. Nor has Hesse, the surrounding state. In so far as Germany has a centre, Frankfurt is the city that stands there. If its beers are middle-of-the-road, that is only to be expected.

What Frankfurt lacks in style, it makes up in scale. With an output in the region of 2.5 million hl, the Frankfurt brewery company of Binding is the biggest in Germany. Binding belongs to the group that also includes Dortmund's DAB and Berlin's Kindl breweries. Frankfurt's other brewing company, Henninger, is better known internationally. It has an output in the region of 1.75 million hl.

Just as it is an important state in the matter of large breweries, so Hesse has some significance for small – or, at least, independent – ones. A nationwide organization of privately owned breweries, the Bräu Ring, has its headquarters in Hesse, at Wetzlar, which is also the home of one of its members, the Euler company. Several other member-breweries are in Hesse, including Alsfeld, the Andreas Kloster brewery, Busch, Marburger and the Unionbrauerei of Fulda.

Where to drink

Frankfurt has three brewpubs. Zwölf Apostel (1 Rosenberger Str) produces a hoppy Pils and a robust Dunkel. Wäldches Bräu (52 Woog Str) makes a wide range of seasonal beers, most of them dark. Zum Mainkur (568 Hanauer Land Str, Fechenheim) produces hoppy Pils and a very malty Dunkel, and serves local dishes

In the cellar of the town hall at Wiesbaden, the Rathsbräu brewpub makes a mild Hell and Dunkel, and offers food grown on its own farm. In a former ice-house, once used to store wine, in Mainz, the Eisgrub brewpub (1 Weisslilien Gasse) offers a Pils, a Märzen and a porter called Gambrinus.

Otto Binding, once owner of the big Frankfurt brewery, has established a somewhat smaller enterprise between Wiesbaden and Mainz, at Eltville, in wine country. He brings water by tanker from the Taunus Mountains, uses organically grown malting barley and hops, and produces an unfiltered Pilsener and a full-bodied, malty, dark beer of low alcohol content (3.2 by weight). His Kleines Eltviller Brauhaus (☎06123–2706) even serves free-range pigs' knuckles.

In the artists' and philosophers' town of Darmstadt is a shop stocking around 1,200 beers, from 250 countries. The shop is named B. Maruhn, "Der Groesste Biermarkt Der Welt", and is at 174 Pfumgstaete Strasse, in the district of Eberstadt, (☎06151–54876). The owner, Bruno Maruhn, is a jolly, enthusiastic chap, and his claim to have the world's biggest beer shop is probably safe, despite earnest competition from the USA. East of Darmstadt, Gross-Umstadt has a brewpub bearing the town's name, at 28 Zimmer Strasse. This serves an unfiltered Pilsener and a dark Export.

Binding

Germany's biggest brewing company producing a full range of beers and perhaps most noteworthy for its premium version of a German-style Export called **Export Privat★★**. It has a fresh, light hoppiness in the nose; a clean, malt-accented palate; and a faintly fruity dryness in the finish. A very similar beer, but fractionally less dry, marginally fuller bodied, and slightly paler, has been brewed for the American market under the name **Steinhauser Bier★★**. This has a little extra maturation, and is micro-filtered, to retain its freshness. Binding has been very successful with Clausthaler, one of the more acceptable low-alcohol beers.

Busch

A famous name in brewing. Southwest of Frankfurt is Mainz, whence Adolphus Busch emigrated to the USA to start the world's biggest brewing company. Northwest of Frankfurt is Limburg, where a family called Busch runs a rather smaller brewery. The American Busch make 90 million hl of beer in the time it takes its German counterparts to brew 15,000hl.

The two families are not related and neither, of course, has anything to do with a product called Bush Beer (no "c"), made in Belgium. There are, on the other hand, historical connections, though distant, between the German town of Limburg and the Belgian and Dutch provinces of the same name. As to Limburger cheese, it originated in Belgium and is still made there and in The Netherlands, but its principal centre of production is Germany. The three Limburgs also share an interest in beer. The German Limburg produces a pleasant, very mild **Golden Busch Pils★→★★** and a **Limburger Export★★**.

Euler

The cathedral in Wetzlar gives its name to Euler's **Dom Pilsener★★**, which is medium-dry. The brewery is also known for its slightly fuller-bodied **Euler Landpils★★**. Other products include a deep amber, malty **Alt Wetzlar★★** (*alt* in this instance refers to tradition, not style. This is not an Altbier but a bottom-fermenting "dark" beer). Its basic **Euler Hell★→★★**, a pale, malty beer, has an export counterpart called **Kloster Bier**. The Landpils is served unfiltered at the Wetzlarer Braustuben, adjoining the brewery.

Henninger

This may be the smaller of the two principal breweries in Frankfurt, but it is still a sizeable concern and the better known internationally. Its principal products, within a considerable range, include **Kaiser Pilsner★** and the drier **Christian Henninger Pilsener★→★★**. The latter has not only more hops but also a second "e". Exports widely.

STUTTGART AND BADEN-WÜRTTEMBERG

This is the place for the eclectic drinker. Here, wine and fruit brandies oblige beer to share the table, even though the state of Baden-Württemberg still contrives to have over 180 breweries.

In the Black Forest – or, at least, its greener valleys – village brewers produce tasty, sometimes slightly fruity, beers that reveal the softness of the local water. East of Stuttgart, towards the Swabian Mountains, one or two maltier beers emerge. (The term "Swabian" is widely used in Germany to indicate the culture and kitchen of an imprecise region that might be considered to stretch from Stuttgart to Augsburg.)

Where to drink

Stuttgart has a brewpub in its pedestrianized shopping area in the city centre. The Stuttgarter Lokalbrauerei (31 Calwer Str) serves an unfiltered, Pilsener-style beer: light, clean and soft, with a fruity start and a very dry finish.

Beer-lovers will want to have a nostalgic glass at the former Sanwald Brewery *Gasthof* in Silberburg Strasse. There is also a small beer garden round the corner in Rotebühl Strasse. The old Sanwald brewery's wheat beers are now made by Dinkelacker, in Tübinger Strasse. In front of the Dinkelacker brewery is a pleasant restaurant serving the company's beers and offering Swabian dishes like *Fladlesuppe* (clear soup with strips of pancake); *Maultaschen* (Swabia's salty retort to ravioli); and *Spätzle* (egg noodles). No one ever went to Germany to lose weight and the Swabians clearly subscribe to this view.

At the end of September and for the first two weeks in October this business-like city lets its hair down for its annual fair on the Cannstatt meadows. This *Cannstatter Volksfest* is Stuttgart's counterpart to Munich's *Oktoberfest*. Beer is supplied by all three of the local breweries (three more than some cities have, though it is only half the number mustered by Munich). Special *Volksfest* beers are produced, in the Märzen style, and similar *Weihnachts* brews at Christmas.

In Heidelberg, always more swashbuckling, the old-established Café Schöneck (9 Steingasse) now houses a brewpub. Vetter's Alt-Heidelberger Brauhaus, producing a beer called 33 (denoting degrees Plato) that is one of several unratified claimants to being the world's strongest. Not far away in Weinheim, the Woinemer Hausbrauerei (23 Friedrich Str) produces an unfiltered Pilsener, a very dark Dunkel and seasonal specialities. In nearby Hemsback, the Burgbrauerei brewpub (3 Hilda Str) has a similar range.

In Karlsruhe, the Vogel brewpub (Kapellen Str) produces a very hoppy unfiltered Pils. This brewery, in a modern apartment block, works in the evenings, so that drinkers can see their beer being produced.

About half way between Heidelberg and Stuttgart, at the salt-water spa of Bad Rappenau, the Haffner brewery has its own resort hotel (33 rooms, ☎07264–8050). Its house beer is called *Kur* ("Cure") Pils.

South of Stuttgart, on the way to Lake Constance, is a brewery called Löwen (there are about 30 such, unrelated, "Lion" breweries in Germany). This Löwen brewery, at Tuttlingen, serves a Kellerpils in its restaurant. Drinkers who enjoy this excessively should be warned that there are no bedrooms. Between Tuttlingen and Ulm, at Bingen, the Lamm brewery serves a *dunkles Hefeweizenbier* and, yet more exotic, *Bierhefebrannt*, a clear spirit distilled from beer. Closer to Ulm, at Trochtelfingen, the Albquell brewery (five rooms, ☎07124–733) serves a Kellerbier.

Where to drink in Swabian Bavaria

South of Ulm, there are four breweries with restaurants, three with bedrooms. At Roggenburg-Biberach the Schmid brewery restaurant specializes in Dunkel and Märzen beers, but has no bedrooms. Hotel Löwenbrau (20 rooms, ☎08247–5056), at Bad Wörishofen, has a Kurpils, and is proud of its Doppelbock. The Hirsch brewery, at Ottobeuren, has several interesting specialities including a house liqueur made by Benedictine brothers in the local monastery. The brewery's kettles are visible to guests who soak away their hangover in the indoor pool at the adjoining hotel (80 rooms, ☎08332–799/115). Nearby at Irsee, a secularized monastery brewery produces some beers of outstanding interest – as well as having a very good kitchen. The Irseer Klosterbrauerei (26 rooms, ☎08341–432200) specializes in unfiltered beers, some matured for more than six months. A speciality called Abt's Trunk, conditioned and sold in hand-made clay flasks, has been reported to have reached a record-shattering 15 percent alcohol by weight. This sounds unlikely and the owner reckons that 12 percent by volume is more realistic. This brewery also has a *Bierbrannt*. There is also a colourful range of home-produced beers and schnapps at the Post Brewery Hotel (22 rooms, ☎08361–30960) in the mountain resort of Nesselwang. The hotel has a small museum of beer.

Dinkelacker

The biggest brewery in the southwest; it might just achieve this ascendancy on the basis of local sales, but exports are the decider. The brewery is best known for its **CD-Pils★★**. Although this is marketed as a prestige beer, the name stands not for *corps diplomatique* but for Carl Dinkelacker, who founded the brewery in Stuttgart in 1888. The Dinkelacker family, brewers since the mid-1700s, still control the company. The brewery, not far from the city centre, is a blend of the traditional and the modern. Copper kettles are used, and the CD-Pils is hopped four times with half a dozen varieties (the final addition being Brewers' Gold, as the brew kettle is emptied). The CD-Pils is also fermented in the classic square type of vessel and *kräusened* during lagering; other products go into an ugly forest of unitanks.

Dinkelacker produces a range of bottom-fermenting beers that adopt a middle stance between those of its local rivals Stuttgarter Hofbräu and Schwaben Bräu. In general, Hofbräu's are the sweetest, Dinkel's medium, Schwaben's the driest, but these are fine distinctions since all three breweries produce typically soft southwestern beers. In addition to its pale beers, Dinkelacker has a dark single bock, **Cluss Bock Dunkel★★**, from its affiliate Cluss brewery in nearby Heilbronn – very malty in aroma and palate, but rather weak in finish. At its Stuttgart headquarters Dinkelacker also produces a number of specialities inherited when the local Sanwald brewery was absorbed. These include a rather thin **Stamm Alt★** and two wheat beers, each made to the same specifications: the sparkling **Weizen Krone★★** and the **Sanwald Hefe Weiss★★**.

Fürstenberg

The "Premium" ratings were perhaps something of a northern notion and Fürstenberg is the only southern brewery to have been dubbed in this way. It is also a house of some nobility, controlled by the aristocratic Fürstenbergs, who have been brewing for more than 500 years. The family are patrons of the arts and there is an impressive collection of German masters in the Fürstenberg Museum, at the palace of Donaueschingen, in the Black Forest. In the palace grounds, the Danube emerges from its underground source. Donaueschingen is also the home of what is now a very modern brewery. A full range of styles is produced, but the brewery is especially well known for its **Fürstenberg Pilsener★★→★★★**. This has quite a full body, a sustained, lasting bead, and a nicely hoppy taste in its dry finish.

Schwaben Bräu

The smallest of Stuttgart's three breweries, in the pleasant suburban township of Vaihingen. It has a large, traditional copper brewhouse and splendidly cavernous lagering cellars. The relative dryness of its beers is best exemplified by its **Meister Pils★★→★★★**. The parent company, Rob Leicht, also owns the Kloster brewery at Pfullingen-Reutlingen. Its **Kloster Pilsner★→★★**, is available not only in the local market but travels as far as the USA. It has a lightly hoppy aroma and finish, a quite full, soft, texture, and a hint of sharpness in the finish. Another subsidiary, Bräuchle, in Metzingen, produces a pale **Bock★★** for the whole group. The company plans a small museum of brewing, perhaps as a gesture to beer as a parent product – in the local market, it is almost as well known for its soft drinks.

Stuttgarter Hofbräu

The Hofbräu rivals, and may surpass, Dinkelacker in local sales. Its brewery is not far beyond that of Dinkelacker, on the edge of Stuttgart. It's a curiously rural fold of the city, and Hofbräu's turn-of-the-century buildings have flourishes that could be Scottish baronial. Inside, however, the brewery is uncompromisingly modern. The name Hofbräu derives from a former royal brewery, but the present company is publicly held, with most of the stock in the hands of one person. The notion that drinkers of German wines have a soft, sweetish palate is emphatically accepted by Hofbräu, and the brewery also takes pride in its beers' not being pasteurized. Its premium product is called **Herren Pils★→★★**.

BAVARIA: MUNICH AND THE SOUTH

Beer-lovers in other countries may be jealous of Germany in general but the focus of envy must be the state of Bavaria. No entire nation, nor even Germany's other states put together, can rival Bavaria's tally of breweries, which still exceeds 800. Between them, they produce about 5,000 beers. Only nine or ten of Bavaria's breweries are, by any standard, large (each producing more than half a million hl a year). More than 500 are very small – 10,000hl or less and of those, about half are tiny, producing less than 2,000hl.

Almost every village has a brewery and some have two or three. The very small breweries almost have their own inn, and often their beer is available nowhere else. There are breweries in monasteries – and convents – and in castles. The castles and baroque-rococo churches are a reminder that Bavaria was a nation of extrovert pride in the 17th and 18th centuries and when in 1919 it joined the German Republic, one of the conditions was that its Pure Beer Law be retained. Bavaria is the home of more beer styles than any other part of Germany. Its everyday beers are not especially potent, but its specialities include the strongest beer in Germany. It grows good malting barley and virtually all of Germany's hops (and exports them all over the world), it has water in the Alps and the icy caves where the usefulness of cold maturation – lagering – first came to be understood.

The mountain and forest isolation of village Bavaria has helped its culture to survive, not only in costume, everyday dress, worship, music and dance, but also in its sense of being a beer land. Isolation was favoured by the founders of monasteries, too, in the days when they were the sanctuaries of all knowledge, including the art of brewing. If there was communication in these matters, it was across the mountains and within the forests. From the Dark Ages, the cradle of modern brewing has been slung from St Gallen in Switzerland to Munich, to Vienna, to Pilsen in Bohemia. That cradle is filled to bursting point with hearty, thirsty, Bavarians, crying *ein prosit!* at every opportunity.

While Germany as a whole drinks 140-odd litres of beer per head each year, this figure is greatly exceeded in Bavaria where the figure is closer to 220. No other state has such a defined calendar of drinking dates and styles. It may not matter much which beer you drink in the madness of the pre-Lenten *Fasching* (an answer in southern cities like Munich and northern ones like Cologne to the *Mardi Gras* of Nice and New Orleans, or the *Carnival* of Rio). However, in March and April, the appropriate beer is Doppelbock; in May, single Bock; in June, July and August Export-type beers at village festivals and Weissbier or Weizenbier in the beer gardens; at the end of September, and for the weeks that follow, Märzen-bier for the Oktoberfest; by November, it is time to think of Weihnachts (Christmas) beer, which may be a variation on the festival speciality, or could be a Weizenbock.

Even the beer's accompaniments have a timetable. With the mid-morning beer, the appropriate snack is *Weisswurst*, a pair of succulent veal sausage coddled in a tureen of warm water. The veal is tempered with small proportions of beef and coarse bacon, and there is a seasoning of parsley (occasionally chives) and sometimes onion or lemon. *Weisswurst* is so important that purists argue over its proper contents. For lunch, the beer might be accompanied by *Leberkäse*, which is neither liver nor cheese but a beef and pork loaf, served hot. For an early evening snack, the ubiquitous large radish of the region, which has a black skin and white flesh. The flesh is sculpted into a spiral and assaulted with salt. If the salt on the radish doesn't make you thirsty, the granules on the big, fresh, soft pretzels will do the trick.

To the foreigner, not least the beer-lover, the state of Bavaria may be synonymous with its capital city, Munich. Within Bavaria, while its claims are universally recognized, Munich and its hinterland have competition from other cities and regions where yet more breweries are to be found.

Munich boasts that it has some of the biggest and most famous breweries, and that it has nurtured more styles of beer than any other city. Within its hinterland, stretching through the regions known as Upper and Lower Bavaria, into the Alps and to the Austrian frontier, are hundreds of breweries. The city itself is ringed by small breweries making excellent beers. The Maisach and Schloss Mariabrunn breweries are just two examples. To the southwest, it is only 20 miles to the lakes and the beginning of the mountains, with more local breweries to serve the terraces and beer gardens.

South of Herrsching, on the lake called Ammersee, is the monastic brewery of Andechs, whose immensely malty beers were the extremely distant inspiration for the American Andeker brand. The brothers also have their own bitter liqueurs and fruit brandies, and there is a well-patronized *Stube* and terrace. Further into the Alps, near the ski resort of Garmisch-Partenkirchen, is another famous monastery brewery, Ettal, producing well-made and typically Bavarian beers but better known for its fruit brandy. Northeast of Munich near Landshut is the Klosterbrauerei Fürth and also the celebrated convent brewery of Mallersdorf, just off the road to Regensburg.

Another convent brewery, St Josef's, is at Ursberg, west of Augsburg, near Krumbach, on the road to Ulm.

A monastery brewery founded in 1040 at Weihenstephan, near Freising, less than 20 miles northeast of Munich, was to have great historical significance. Although the evidence for continuous production is hazy, the brewery survived long enough to be secularized by Napoleon and continues today under the ownership of the State of Bavaria. The Bayerische Staatsbrauerei Weihenstephan thus claims to be the oldest brewery in the world. Although there are vestiges of the monastery from the 12th century, and today's buildings are set in a restored cloister from the 17th century, the brewery is modern. It also offers some training facilities to the adjoining brewing institute.

There is only a handful of Faculties of Brewing in the world, and Weihenstephan — part of the Technical University of Munich — is the most famous. In recent years it has had difficulties, arising originally from its efforts to deal with brewers who do not work in *Reinheitsgebot* countries, but its name remains a by-word in the industry. The Weihenstephan brewery produces a full range of beers but is perhaps best known for its Kristal Export Weizenbier (very fruity, with hints of blackcurrant, and extremely dry in the finish) and its Hefeweissbier (light for the style and refreshing).

Wheat-beer brewing is especially associated with the area to the east of Munich. About 20 miles out of the city is the Erding wheat-beer brewery, perhaps the best-known of the specialist and certainly the fastest-growing. Further east, in Mühldorf, the Jägerhof house brewery of Wolfgang Unerti produces a wonderfully turbid wheat beer.

To the south of Munich another tiny brewery specializes in wheat beers: Gmeineder, at Deisenhofen near Oberhaching. Much further south, at Murnau, off the road to Garmisch, another notable example of the turbid style of wheat beer is made by the Karg brewery.

Where to drink
Each of the principal Munich breweries has several of its own special outlets in the form of gardens, beer halls and restaurants. Kaltenberg has an offshoot called Das Kleine Brauhaus, which specializes in wheat beer, in the Luitpoldpark (2 Brenner Str). Among several other newish brewpubs in the area, Schmied von Kochel-Bräu (at 14 Ramung Str, behind the Bavarian Parliament building) is notable for its hoppy Hell and very dark Unimator Doppelbock. There is also a wheat-beer brewpub, Flieger-Bräu, at the old Munich airport (2 Sonnen Str, Riem). To the west of Munich, closer to Augsburg, the *Schloss* brewery at Odelzhausen specializes in a double bock called Operator (nothing sinister about the name — it is dedicated to the Munich opera). As is often the case, the *Schloss* (nine bedrooms, ☎08134–6021) is more like a country house, but it has a restaurant. To the north of Munich, the brewery guest-house Goldener Hahn (☎08461–419) is at

Beilngries, about half way to Nürnberg. Further north, at Lengenfeld-Velburg, the Winkler brewery guesthouse (☎09182–170) is widely known for its Kupfer Spezial beer. This much-loved brew is a dark copper colour, with gravity of 14 Plato, bottom-fermented in open vessels and matured for between 10 and 16 weeks. A remarkable feature of this family concern is that it grows and malts its own barley. Its beer is hopped with both Bavarian and Bohemian varieties. There are also brewery guest-houses to the northeast of Munich at Adlersberg (Prösslbrau, ☎09404–1822); Böbrach (Brauereigasthof Eck, ☎09923–685); Zwiesel (Deutscher Rhein, ☎09922–1651); and Zenting (Kamm, ☎09907–315).

Augustiner

The favourite brews among serious beer-drinkers in Munich are those from Augustiner. The beers are generally the maltiest among those produced by the city's major brewers and in that sense are closest to the palate traditionally associated with Munich. This is especially true of Augustiner's pale beers. The everyday **Augustiner Hell★★★** qualifies as the classic pale beer of Munich, with its malty aroma and palate, soft entrance and firm, smooth finish. The brewery's interpretation of the German Export type has the brand name **Edelstoff★★★** in Germany and, confusingly, is described as Augustiner Munich Light in the American market. "Light" refers, of course, to its colour and not to its body. This is hardly the lightest of German beers and even the slenderest of those is big by American standards. In recent years Augustiner has been emphasizing its pale beers, perhaps to the detriment of its dark styles. The basic dark beer is called **Dunkel Vollbier★★★**. There is also a **Dunkel Export★★→★★★**, which has occasionally appeared in Germanic areas of the USA. The company has a number of other styles; its **Maximator Doppelbock★★★** is marketed in the USA under the unexciting description "Munich Dark".

The maltiness of Augustiner's beers has sources close to home. No fewer than three of Munich's brewers have their own maltings and Augustiner is one. Its malt is produced in cellars that stretch like the tunnels of a mine underneath the brewery, which itself belongs to industrial archaeology. Constructed in 1885 and a magnificent example of the proud brewery edifices of the time, it is now a protected building. In the brewhouse only one in three vessels is made from copper; the other two are of stainless steel. The dark beers have the benefit of a triple decoction; the pale a double. Only aroma hops are used, in five varieties, from both Bavaria and Bohemia. Fermentation is in unusual vessels, open but with a lid that can be brought down, without pressure, to collect carbon dioxide. Fermentation is at very cold temperatures and lagering is in traditional vessels, with *kräusening*. The brewery uses wooden casks to supply beer gardens and some inns in the Munich area. The casks are pitched at the brewery, adding another traditional aroma to that of the malty air.

Augustiner has as its near neighbours Hacker-Pschorr, Spaten and Löwenbräu; all four are in the traditional "brewery quarter" behind Munich's central railway station. Paulaner and Hofbräuhaus are elsewhere in the city. In the heart of the brewery quarter, on Arnulf Strasse, is the Augustiner Keller, relatively small and much loved by the people of Munich. In the centre of the city on Neuhauser Strasse, Augustiner has its elegant, somewhat eccentric, 1890s restaurant and brewery tap, with a small Italianate garden. This building was originally constructed in 1829 to house the brewery after secularization. As its name suggests, Augustiner was originally a monastic brewery, and its first site was close to Munich's landmark cathedral, the Frauenkirche. The brewery dates at least from the 15th century, though there is some uncertainty about the claimed foundation date of 1328. It is without doubt an institution in Munich, favoured by yet a third famous outlet, the beer garden at the Hirschgarten, a public park near Nymphenburg Castle. This popular picnic spot is said to accommodate as many as 8,000 drinkers, while Löwenbräu's beer garden in Munich's huge central park holds a mere 6,000. How carefully this has been counted is open to dispute.

Ayinger

In Munich, the best-known country brewer is Ayinger. The position it enjoys in the city is evident: its beers are served in the restaurant and cabaret called the Platzl, on the square of the same name, directly opposite the Hofbräuhaus. The restaurant is owned by Ayinger and a special Platzl brew is produced – a miniature barrel of the beer is customarily set in the centre of the table, to accompany the evening's burlesque. After dinner, there might also be a clear fruit brandy, made from apples and pears and served in pot vessels shaped like tobacco pipes.

The Platzl beer is pleasant enough but a half-hour journey out of Munich to the village of Aying will provide just that freshness to make it taste delicious. In Aying (and in the USA) this brew is known as Jahrhundert. The name dates from the brewery's centenary in 1978. **Jahrhundert★★** is a German Export-type beer. It has some herbal hoppiness in the nose and a big, malty palate that dries in a crisp finish.

Ayinger has a full range of styles, among which several are noteworthy. **Altbairisch Dunkel★★→★★★** is a splendid example of the Bavarian dark style, with a warm, sweetly fruity aroma and coffeeish finish. **Fest-Märzen★→★★** is a little pale for the style but has a lovely malt bouquet, carrying through in the soft palate. **Maibock★→★★**, too, is a classically malty Bavarian beer, with spicy, apricot notes. Most characterful of all is the double bock, labelled in Germany as Fortunator and in the USA as Celebrator. By whichever name, **Fortunator/Celebrator★★★** is an outstanding example of double-bock style and a beautifully balanced beer, its richness mellowing out in a long, dryish finish. When strong brews are served at the end of winter, Germans talk about taking the "springtime beer cure". Ayinger goes further: it dubs its home village a "beer spa".

Where the Munich basin, with its crops of malting barley, gives way to the foothills of the Alps the village of Aying provides for gentle exploration. Ayinger, with its own elderly maltings and modern brewhouse, stands on one side of the road, facing its guest-house on the other. A small beer garden, little more than a terrace, and an early baroque church complete the village square. In the square, the typical Bavarian maypole is set into a wooden tun that was once a maturation vessel in the brewery.

Ayinger also owns Höll wheat-beer brewery in Traunstein, further up the road. This imposing brewery was built in the late 19th century and has not changed markedly since. It leans sleepily into a hillside in the valley of the River Traun. Four wheat beers are produced at Traunstein. **Export Weissbier**★→★★ is filtered and has a full, relatively sweet, fruitiness (ripe plums, perhaps?). The unfiltered **Hefe-Weissbier**★→★★ is much more tart. **Ur-Weizen**★★→★★★ has a fuller, amber-red colour and bursts with fruitiness. It is also unfiltered and has the classic apples-and-cloves spiciness of a traditional wheat beer. A **Weizenbock**★★★, 17 Plato, pale and filtered, is available in the local market at Christmas.

Erdinger

The biggest-selling wheat beers in Germany. The very pretty town of Erding is near the new Munich airport. A building dating from 1513, at 1 Lange Zeile, is the "tap", and was once the brewery. Production switched in 1983 to a showpiece brewery on the edge of town. Local farmers are supplied with seed and contracted to produce much of the barley and all the wheat. Among the wheat beers of Bavaria, those from Erdinger are among the cleaner, lighter and more delicate in aroma and palate. They are aimed at the popular audience rather than the traditionalist. Products include a **Kristall**★→★★, with a touch of vanilla and dessert apple in its aroma and palate; a version described as **Mit feiner Hefe**★→★★, with more fruitiness; a lightly chocolatey **Dunkel**★★; and a very smooth Weizenbock, called **Pikantus**★★→★★★. A marginally fuller version of the **Mit feiner Hefe** is served at Erding's autumn festival, which starts on the last Friday of August and continues for ten days.

Forschungs

A secret well kept by the beer-lovers of Munich is the existence of a house-brewery in the market-gardening suburb of Perlach. The place does have the qualities of a mirage. For one thing, it operates only in summer (and even then closes on Mondays). For another, it looks like a cross between a seaside ice-cream parlour and the control tower at a small and dubious airport. It also happens to make the highest-gravity brew in Munich. Its speciality is a 19 Plato beer called **St Jacobus Blonder Bock**★★★. This potent product is soft and sweet but very clean with a big, malty finish. The supporting potion is curiously called **Pilsissimus**★★→★★★. It has both hops and malt in its big aroma and contrives to be both dry and soft in palate. The Forschungs brewery and its small, pebbled beer garden are at 76 Unterhachinger Strasse, Perlach (☎089–6701169).

Hacker-Pschorr

There is a resonance about the names of Munich's principal breweries. Not so long ago, Hacker and Pschorr were two of them. They merged, and much more recently have been taken over by Paulaner. Despite that, the brewery continues to operate, with its own range of beers. They are on the dry side and perhaps not as smooth as some Munich brews. However, by the standards of some other regions and countries, they still have a fair degree of character. Hacker-Pschorr has never been identified with any single speciality, though it has recently been concentrating on its **Pils**★. Its *Oktoberfest* **Märzen**★→★★ and **Animator**★★ double bock are both pleasant. The company's beers can be tested at Zum Pschorr-Bräu, in Neuhauser Strasse, and in summer on a terrace in the Marienplatz.

Hofbräuhaus

Perhaps in Germany the label "HB" speaks for itself, but elsewhere the allusion is not instantly clear. It stands for "Hofbräu" ("court brew"), and is the label of brews produced for the world's most famous beer hall. Munich's Hofbräuhaus was originally the beer hall and garden of the Bavarian Royal Court Brewery. Lesser Hofbräus remain elsewhere in Germany, having passed from minor royalty into commercial hands, but the most important one still belongs to Bavaria, albeit to the state government. The garden is pleasant, though the rambling beer hall smells of stale cigarettes and the detritus of tourism. The beers are excellent, the conventional brews being malt-accented with a spritzy finish. Although the everyday beer is a fresh-tasting, malty **Export**★★→★★★, the Hofbräuhaus (founded in 1589) is credited with having, in its early days, introduced Bock beer to Munich. Its immensely tasty, malty **Maibock**★★★★ (18 Plato) has a very deep amber-red colour. Its winter double bock, **Delicator**★★★→★★★★ has the same gravity but a yet darker colour. When the first cask of the springtime beer is tapped at the Hofbräuhaus on May Day, the Prime Minister of Bavaria usually takes part in the ceremony. Maibock tastes especially good accompanied by a couple of *Weisswurst*. Since its earliest days the Hofbräuhaus has also had a tradition of wheat beers. Its **Edel Weizen**★★→★★★ has long been enjoyed, but **Dunkel-Weizen**★★→★★★ is not to be ignored: a complex beer with dense head, lavish lacework, a sweet start, toasty maltiness, and a lemony tartness in the finish.

Hofbräuhaus Freising

Dating from at least the 1100s, and originally the Bishop's household brewery. It is now owned by the Count of Moy.

The brewery is in a visually dramatic *Jugendstil* building. Its very fruity wheat beers include the distinctive **Huber Weisses★★★**, quite heavily sedimented, and intentionally lower in carbonation than some of its contemporaries.

Kaltenberg

Although by no means the only brewery owned by an aristocrat, Kaltenberg is perhaps the best known, not least because it is in a classic Bavarian castle. The castle dates from the 13th century, but the present structure was built in the 17th century based on designs by the architect who created Neuschwanstein for "mad" King Ludwig II of Bavaria. The third King Ludwig was the last and his great-grandson, Prince Luitpold, runs the Kaltenberg brewery. In export markets Kaltenberg is known for a well-made **Diät-Pils★★**, but in its local market it is noted for a malty, dark beer, with a coffeeish finish, **König Ludwig Dunkel★★→★★★**, which has a gravity of 13.3 Plato.

Kaltenberg Castle is near Geltendorf, less than 30 miles west of Munich. It has a beer garden and restaurant, and in June holds a beer festival and costumed jousting between "medieval" knights (for information, ☎08193–209). A **Dunkel Ritter Bock★★★** 23 Plato is made during Lent ("Ritter" means "rider" or "knight"). Kaltenberg has a second brewery in a nearby town, and additionally makes a range of sherbety-tasting wheat beers.

Löwenbräu

Internationally, the best-known name among the Munich breweries is Löwenbräu. About a quarter of its output is exported and it licenses its name to be used on products in other countries. Löwenbräu's Munich-brewed beers are somewhere in the middle of the league table. In general, the beers are malt-accented but well-balanced, with a late hint of hoppiness in the finish. Löwenbräu is not especially associated with any one style, but promotes its **Pils★★**, which is quite hoppy by Munich standards. The brewery owns the biggest beer hall, the 5,000-seat Mathäser, in Bayern Strasse, near the central railway station. The Mathäser has the look of a railway station itself, with its cafeteria entrance, but its 15 or so inner halls are worth exploring. There is an ornate beer-restaurant and terrace opposite the Löwenbräu brewery, and the company has one of the city's biggest beer gardens, at the landmark "Chinese Tower". This pagoda is, confusingly, in a park called the English Garden.

Paulaner

The biggest brewery in Munich is especially associated with its classic **Salvator★★★★** double bock. This extra-strong, very dark beer, with deep amber highlights, has a gravity of 18.5 Plato and is made with three malts. Only Hallertau hops are used, though of both bittering and aroma varieties. The beer has a very rich start, drying out in a long finish. Its alcohol content is around 6 percent by weight, 7.5 by volume. The brewery has its origins in the early 17th century with a community of monks of St Paul, who became well known throughout the city for the strong beer they brewed, called Salvator (Saviour) to sustain themselves during Lent. Being a very strong beer, it came to be known as a "double" bock and gave rise to that style. Most other double-bock beers echo the Saviour's brew by bearing names ending in -*ator*. Double-bock beers are drunk to warm the soul as winter gives way to spring and the beer gardens think about reopening. The first new barrel of Salvator is ceremonially tapped by the Mayor of Munich or Prime Minister of Bavaria at the brewery's 3,500-seat beer hall and garden on Nockherberg three to four weeks before Easter.

The brewery was secularized in the early 19th century and has since had several owners, but it still stands on the same site, though it has grown to straddle the hill. From the modern office block, a tunnel through the hillside leads to the maltings and the brewhouse, which is still in traditional copper. The brewery uses classic fermenters and traditional lagering cellars, maturing its everyday beers (which are *kräusened*) for five or six weeks and its stronger specialities for three to eight months. Paulaner has one of Germany's first refrigeration machines, made for the brewery by Carl von Linde, and an early water turbine powered by a stream that runs down the hill. Paulaner's beers are firm-bodied and dry for Munich, often with an assertive finish. The dark **Alt-Münchner Dunkel**★★→★★★ has a fine colour, a smooth, full body and a maltiness in that dry finish. The export-style **Urtyp 1634**★★ has, again, a full, smooth body but a slightly tannic finish. The pale **Original Münchner Hell**★★→★★★ is similar but milder. The brewery produces a full range of styles – with about ten principal beers – including a dry, rounded **Altbayerische Weissbier**★★→★★★ that has helped popularize wheat beers in the USA. Paulaner also has a brewpub on Kapuziner Platz. The premises were once the Thomas brewery.

Rauchenfels Steinbier

A famous speciality produced by the addition of white-hot rocks to the brew-kettle. This technique was widely used in the days when brew-kettles were made from wood, and could not be placed over a fire. The style was revived by the inventive and entrepreneurial German brewer Gerd Borges in 1982. Originally, he brewed in Neustadt, close to the border with the former East Germany. The brewery there had lost much of its market with the division of Germany, and Rauchenfels Steinbier was seen as a speciality that might compensate in volume. Since reunification, the production of Steinbier has been moved to the Borges brewery at Altenmünster, near Augsburg. The company says it is still using the same technique, in which the kettle is brought almost to the boil by conventional methods, then finished with the hot rocks, which cause considerable caramelization of the malt sugars. The sugar-coated rocks are then allowed to cool, and placed in the maturation vessels. The brew already tinged with caramelization in the kettle begins to enjoy a secondary fermentation when it renews its contact with the rocks. The beers are made to conventional strengths, of 3.8; 4.7 **Rauchenfels Steinbier**★★★→★★★★ is brewed from equal proportions of barley and wheat malt, and has a smoky, treacle-toffee palate, less dry than smooth, with a long, rounded, finish. A version called **Rauchenfels Steinweizen**★★★, made with 60 percent wheat, is very lively, a little less hoppy, with slightly more sharpness. It is to be hoped that these beers retain their integrity and character in their new home. The brewery has also made an Export under the name Altenmünster, and a range with the Sailer label.

Schneider

The Schneider family, specialists in wheat beer, were once the brewers at the Hofbräuhaus in Munich, and more recently at premises in the street called Tal ("Dale"). The famous Schneider beer-hall in the Tal still serves the family's beers, but production is now in the Bavarian town of Kelheim, near Regensburg. The Schneiders own a brewery there that has been making wheat beer since the 1600s. There is also a "tap" at the brewery in Kelheim (closed in November). **Schneider-Weisse**★★★→★★★★ has a distinctively tan colour and a characteristic spiciness. This is named after Johannes Aventinus, the historian who first described Bavaria and its people. **Aventinus**★★★ (18.5; 1074; 6.1; 7.7) has a huge head, an insistent sparkle, malty notes in the nose; chocolate, fruit and spices in the palate; and a lightly clove-like finish.

Spaten

One of the world's most important brewing companies, because of its influence on the beers most nations drink today. All lager beers, whether dark, amber or pale, owe much to the work of the Spaten brewery in the 19th century. The influence of this company should be far more widely recognized internationally, but perhaps its reputation has been subsumed, with those of its neighbours, into that of Munich itself.

Although it still takes great pride in earlier styles such as wheat beers (notably the dry, spicy, full-bodied and fluffy **Franziskaner Hefe-Weissbier**★★→★★★ and its cleaner, sparkling **Club-Weisse**★★), Spaten's greatest contributions were in the development of bottom-fermenting beers; in the perfecting of the Bavarian dark style, as typified by its own **Dunkel Export**★★★→★★★★; in the popularization of the amber type, as represented by its world classic **Ur-Märzen**★★★; and in the perfecting of the Munich pale variety, as exemplified by its **Münchner Hell**★★★. From a historical viewpoint all these beers are classics, and they are still produced in a manner that blends tradition with modern technology. Spaten has its own maltings, uses traditional kettles and lauter tuns (copper in the old brewhouse, stainless steel in a new one), closed classic fermenters and horizontal lagering tanks.

An especially interesting feature of Spaten's methods is that three different yeasts are used in the production of bottom-fermenting beers. The pale beers of conventional gravities (including a very dry **Spaten Pils★★→★★★**) have one yeast; the **Franziskus Heller Bock★★** another; the darker brews a third. Most breweries would use only one strain for all those types, but Spaten feels that yeasts should be chosen according to their suitability to ferment the different worts and their contribution to background palate.

The company traces its origins to a brewery of 1397, and its name (meaning "spade") is a jocular corruption of Spaeth, an early owner. The royal court brewmaster Gabriel Sedlmayr took over the company in 1807 and his son, Gabriel the Younger, became the father of modern lager-brewing. Studies carried out by Gabriel in the 1830s introduced Bavaria to more scientific methods, notably the use of the saccharometer in the control of fermentation. Sedlmayr gathered disciples who spread the reputation of Bavarian bottom-fermenting techniques, and Sedlmayr's friend and rival Anton Dreher went on to introduce the amber style of lager in Vienna in 1840–1. A year later, the Pilsen brewery produced the first pale lager. In 1873, Sedlmayr worked with von Linde on his first refrigerator, at the instigation of Dreher (Paulaner's Linde machine came later) and in 1876 he introduced the world's first steam-heated brewhouse (companies that followed liked to call themselves "steam breweries"). The present company was constituted originally from Gabriel's business and his brother Joseph's Franziskaner brewery.

Spaten is still predominantly owned by the Sedlmayr family. It is proud of its family ownership and of its traditions, and still delivers beer in Munich by horse and dray. Regrettably, the building from which they emerge looks less like a brewery than a fair-sized airport.

NORTHERN BAVARIA: FRANCONIA

For the beer-drinker, Munich and southern Bavaria might seem like the pearly gates, but heaven is further north. Up there Bavaria has a region that is almost a state within a state: Franconia (Franken), with Nürnberg as its largest city and Bamberg and Amberg as its most heavily breweried towns, with nine or ten apiece, subject to planned new brewpubs.

There are more small breweries in Franconia than anywhere in the world. It remains a centre of production for dark Bavarian lagers. It has more unfiltered beers than anywhere else and a greater number of eccentric specialities.

From south to north, the region stretches from Regensburg to Bayreuth, Kulmbach and Coburg, on the former border with East Germany. Due east the Bohemian Forest forms the frontier with the Czech Republic, with České Budějovice (Budweis) and Pilsen nearby. To the west the small-brewery country of the Steigerwald reaches to Würzburg and wine territory.

Bamberg is the centre for a highly unusual speciality, namely the smoky Rauchbier. Kulmbach is the traditional centre for dark beers and produces some especially strong Doppelbock brews. Bayreuth has a proprietary speciality: the Maisel brewery's Dampfbier, and Schierling has its own Roggen (meaning rye) beer.

Even in towns not specifically associated with a single style, many breweries have their own minor specialities. Sometimes these are dark beers. Often they are unfiltered. While an unfiltered Kräusenbier is cause for comment elsewhere in the country, such brews are not uncommon in Franconia. As its name suggests, this type of beer is *kräusened*. Then, before the kräusen has worked out, the maturation vessel is tapped, revealing intentionally cloudy beer.

Another type of unfiltered beer is not *kräusened*. This is Kellerbier, which is allowed to settle in the maturation tanks before being tapped. As might be expected it has a notably low carbonation. Traditionally, this type of beer has been heavily hopped to guard against infection. An outstanding example is made by St Georgenbräu, of Buttenheim, just south of Bamberg. Another excellent Kellerbier comes from Maisel of Bamberg (there are four Maisel breweries in Bavaria, each quite separate but linked by family).

Bamberg is a town of only 70,000 people but it is a remarkable centre of brewing. On the hill that overlooks the town is the 17th-century Romanesque church of St Michael, part of a former monastery which had a brewery (the monks' brewhouse has now been converted into a Franconian Beer Museum ☎0951–53016). The town itself is a living museum, not only for its German Renaissance buildings but also for its selection of breweries. There is plenty of half-timbering and gilding about the breweries and their guest-houses, too, but their principal contribution is in terms not of architecture but of social and economic history. Two even have their own maltings so that they can do the kilning necessary to produce Rauchbier (which is made by kilning the malt over beech logs). There are also two free-standing maltings.

By no means do all of Bamberg's nine breweries regularly feature Rauchbier and, though the town is the centre for production, companies elsewhere have been known to produce a beer in this style. In Bamberg, the Heller brewery has Aecht Schlenkerla Rauchbier as its principal product; the family Merz's Hausbrauerei Spezial produces nothing else; Kaiserdom Rauchbier is produced in Eltmann for Bürgerbräu-Bamberg; Maisel's Rauchbier is made by another Eltmann brewery. An unfiltered, but bright, Rauchbier is made by Fischer Greuth, in Herscheid, south of Bamberg.

Among other Bamberg breweries, Fässla offers as its specialities a Kellerbier and a Märzen and splendid dark pre-Christmas Bock called Bambergator; Keesman emphasizes its malty but dry Herren Pils; the secular Klosterbräu has a dark beer; Löwenbräu has a range of products; Mahrs has a relatively well-carbonated Kellerbier and a delicious, rich dark brew called Wunderburger Liesl. The pale beers of Bamberg all have a dry maltiness.

To the west is the Steigerwald, with woodland walks and scores of small breweries, many with their own taverns. About 15 miles north of Bamberg, at Pferdsfeld, the Kunigunda Leicht brewery lists its production at 250hl a year, which probably makes it the smallest in Germany. To the east, in the country-side known as the Frankische Schweiz are more small breweries.

Some towns and villages have communal breweries where members of the public can brew their own beer. Falkenburg, Neuhaus-on-Pegnitz and Sesslach are examples. This facility is generally exercised by barley farms or tavern keepers. In the days before commercial production, a communal brewer who had a new batch ready would display a garland or a six-pointed star outside his house. The latter is a symbol of the brewer, deriving from alchemy rather than from any religious significance. In some places this practice is still followed, although it is also used by small commercial brewers. Ecclesiastical brewing was significant in the past in Franconia, but only one monastery brewery remains, the Klosterbrauerei Kreuzberg at Bischofsheim, north of Würzburg.

Where to drink

In Bamberg, the obvious places to stay are the guest-houses of Brauerei Spezial (10 Obere König Str. ☎0951–24304), which is in the shopping area; or Brauerei Greifenklau (20 Laurenziplatz. ☎0951–95310) which has a spectacular valley view. The mandatory stop for a drink is the Schlenkerla tavern, in Dominikaner Strasse, but other brewery taps are also worth a visit; the low-ceilinged tavern of the Mahrs brewery, in Wundeburg, is a delightful "local". The Steigerwald can be explored from the Klosterbräu Hotel in Ebelsbach (☎09522–6027), which specializes in a dark Märzen beer.

To the north, between Bamberg and Coburg, the Goldener Stern at Ebersdorf (24 bedrooms, ☎09562–106163) has a splendid Zwickelbier. Northwest of Coburg, at Gauerstadt, near Rodach, the Wacker brewery (20 bedrooms, ☎09564–225) has a pale draught beer. Northeast of Coburg, the Grosch brewery (17 bedrooms, ☎09563–4047) in Rödental, on the way to Neustadt, has an excellent dark beer. In the old brewing town of Lichtenfels, the Wichert *Gasthof* has a Kellerbier but no bedrooms. The Frankische Schweiz can be explored from the Drei Kronen brewery inn at Memmelsdorf (☎0951–43001), where an unfiltered lager and a dark Märzen are served.

Another Drei Kronen ("Three Crowns") in nearby Strassgeich produces a lovely, firm-bodied Kronenbräu Lager with a gravity of 12.7 Plato and a "1308" Pilsener of 12.4 (unusual, in that everyday lagers usually have lower gravities than their companion Pilseners). The "1308" is named for the foundation date of this tiny (3,000hl) brewery, which so captured the imagination of an executive from a large international company that its name was bought for use on somewhat lesser beers in Canada and South Africa. This Drei

Kronen has no rooms. Neither does the Schinner brewery restaurant in Richard Wagner Strasse, Bayreuth, but it serves an excellent Braunbier. In Nürnberg, the Altstadt brewery is an essential visit, with beer on sale by the bottle and available on tap nearby. Regensburg has a number of beer-restaurants. In Arnulfsplatz, the Kneitinger brewery produces beer mainly for its own restaurant. The Spitalgarten, in Katharinenplatz, dates from the 14th century and serves local beer.

Altstadthof

The name indicates "Old Town Courtyard", which is the corner of Nürnberg where this delightful *Hausbrauerei* is to be found. The brewery, a bakery and one or two wholefood shops share a restored courtyard off Berg Strasse. In the Old Town, in a building dating from the 16th century and with brewing rights from that time, the *Hausbrauerei* first charged its traditional copper kettle in 1984, taking care to use organically grown barley malt and hop blossoms. Fermentation is in open wooden tuns like those in drawings of medieval breweries and lagering is in wooden hogsheads of the type often kept as museum pieces in large breweries. The year-round product is an unfiltered dark beer with a gravity of 12–12.5 Plato. **Hausbrauerei Altstadthof★★★** beer has a deep, tawny colour, almost opaque; yeasty fruitiness and malty sweetness in the aroma; a yeasty dryness overlaying the rich, smooth, malty palate; dark malt tones in the finish, with some local, Hersbrucker hop coming through. A Helles, seasonal Bock and Märzen versions have also been produced. A tiny antique bottling machine fills the beer into swing-top litres, which are then sold at the brewery in crude wooden six-packs. The beer is also available on draught at two Altstadthof cafés (one, open at lunchtime, is called the Dampfnudel and specializes in sweet steamed puddings; the other, open in the evening, is the Schmelztiegl). The brewery has only two full-time employees.

The *Hausbrauerei* was established, initially out of enthusiasm for beery history, by the owners of the Lamms brewery in Neumarkt, south of Nürnberg. Lammsbräu provides not only the yeast but also the water for Altstadt. The *Hausbrauerei* does not have an adequate supply of its own water, nor space for treatment facilities.

EKU

The EKU brewery in Kulmbach boasts the highest ratified gravity of any bottom-fermenting beer in the world, with its **Kulminator 28★★★→★★★★**. As its name suggests, this beer has a guaranteed gravity of 28 degrees – though analysis has revealed levels as high as 30.54. The brewery claims to mature the beer for nine months with a short period of freezing to settle protein. Since this is not done specifically for the purpose of raising alcohol content, Kulminator 28 is not labelled as an Eisbock. As the name Kulminator implies, it is a Doppelbock by style, though it is labelled merely as Urtyp ("original") and Hell ("pale"). In fact it is not especially pale –

the great density of malt provides an amber cast – but it is not a dark beer. It has an intensely malty nose and palate, with some estery notes and a strongly alcoholic finish. It usually has an alcohol content of 9.2–9.6 by weight, 11.5–12 by volume, but this varies. Some samples have reached 11.1 by weight, 13.7 by volume.

The world heavyweight title is contested between Kulminator 28 and the Swiss Hürlimann brewery's Samichlaus (a Christmas beer). Samichlaus has a lower gravity (27.6), a longer period of maturation (a year) and a higher alcohol content (11.2 by weight; 13.7–14 by volume). While this contest is too hard to resist, such muscle has limited application. These are beers of excellent quality but they would best be dispensed from small barrels suspended from the necks of mountain-rescue dogs. Whether they revive or stun the recipient depends upon the constitution of the drinker. Certainly, in their fermentation, the yeast is stunned by the alcohol it produces. That explains why these beers take so long, and are so difficult to make. Nor do they contain any of the sugars (or, sometimes, enzymes) that are used in the relatively lightweight strong beers (or "malt liquors") of the USA.

EKU also has a dark double bock, simply called **Kulminator**★★→★★★ (19.2; 1077; 6; 7.6); a pale, single **Edelbock**★★; a conventional dark export-style beer called **Rubin**★★★; a rather full-bodied **Pils**★→★★; and a pleasant **Weizen**★.

The first two initials of EKU stand for Erste ("first") Kulmbach. The "U" derives from the union of two earlier breweries that created the company in 1872.

Hofmark

The traditionalist Hofmark brewery is interesting for a number of reasons: its location, east of Regensburg at Cham on the Bavarian side of the Bohemian Forest, means that its soft water emerges from the same quartz-granite bed as that of Pilsen; it was founded in 1590 and has been in one family for more than 200 years; and it still uses some traditional techniques, not least the method of fining with beechwood chips. It is also unusual in that its premium beer Das feine Hofmark is prepared in two variations: mild and bitter (designations that sound more English than German). Both are firm, smooth, beautifully balanced beers of some complexity. Das feine Hofmark **Würzig Mild**★★ has a malt accent; **Würzig Herb**★★→★★★ (meaning "dry" or "bitter") has a lovely hop character in both nose and finish. This brewery was a pioneer in the use of swing-top bottles.

Kaiserdom

A full range of beers is marketed under the Kaiserdom label by the Bürgerbräu brewery of Bamberg. Most tend towards the dry maltiness of the region but are unexceptional. However **Kaiserdom Rauchbier**★★★ has the distinction of being the only Bavarian smoked beer exported to the USA.

Kulmbacher Mönchshof

The dark-beer tradition of Kulmbach is best maintained by the "Monks'" brewery. Its **Kloster Schwarz-Bier★★★★** rates as a classic, with a gravity of 12.5, a full smooth body and a dark-malt palate unrivalled among major labels. The connoisseur of Bavarian dark beers might, of course, prefer the earthier character to be found in some of the many *Hausbrauerei* examples. Mönchshof goes back to the beginnings of monastic brewing in Kulmbach in 1349. It was secularized in 1791, becoming a family brewery, and is now part-owned by Kulmbacher Reichelbräu. Even at the peak of Kulmbach's international repute as a brewing centre, at the turn of the century, Mönchshof was one of the smaller houses. Its range includes a very full-bodied dark double bock called **Urstoff★★→★★★;** a very flavourful single **Klosterbock Dunkel★★★**; a malty **Märzen★★**; a malty export called **Maingold★★**; and what is for Bavaria an unusually dry **Mönchshof Pilsener★★**.

Kulmbacher Reichelbräu

If Germany can have Eiswein, then it can have icy beer, too. The tradition of Eisbock is especially kept alive by Kulmbacher Reichelbräu. Eisbock is a strong beer in which the alcohol content is enhanced by freezing and then removing the ice. Because alcohol has a lower freezing point than water this concentrates the brew. The resultant **Eisbock Bayrisch G'frorns★★★→★★★★** ("Bavarian Frozen") has a gravity of 24 and an alcohol content of around 8 percent by weight, 10 by volume. It is a most interesting beer, smooth, dense and potent with suggestions of whisky and coffee. Reichelbräu, which is named after its founder, has the biggest local sales and offers a full range of styles.

Maisel

Among the four Bavarian brewing companies called Maisel, this one in Bayreuth is by far the biggest. It has also become well known for its speciality brews, notably its highly individualistic **Maisel's Dampfbier★★★**. This is a top-fermenting beer, very fruity, with vanilla-like tones. It has a gravity of 12.2 Plato, is made with a triple decoction mash from four barley malts, hopped with Hallertaus and fermented with its own yeast in open vessels. It emerges slightly redder and paler than a Düsseldorfer Altbier, and about 4 percent alcohol by weight, 5 by volume. It is not pasteurized, even for export to the USA. "Dampfbier" is a registered name, not intended to indicate a recognized style and Maisel earnestly disavows any intention to sound like Anchor Steam (which is different both in production process and palate). In the late 1970s, the brewery decided that "all beers were beginning to taste the same. We wanted something distinctive. We experimented, and this was the brew we liked." The decision may also have had something to do with the move out of a magnificently castellated and steam-powered brewery of 1887 into a remorselessly modern plant next door. There is an element of nostalgia to a "steam beer" (which is how *Dampfbier* would, inescapably, translate). For the two Maisel brothers who own the brewery, nostalgia is not cheap. The entire old brewery has been mothballed, in working order, and is now open for tours, at 10 o'clock each morning, or by appointment.

Meanwhile, Maisel continues in its spotless new brewery to produce an interesting range of products, including three wheat beers. **Weizen Kristall-Klar★★★** is, as its name suggests, a crystal-clear beer, very pale, with a champagne-like sparkle and a tannic, apple fruitiness. **Hefe-Weiss★★** is fermented out with a mixture of yeasts, *kräusened* and given a dosage at bottling. It has a deep bronze colour, an apple-like palate and a big, fluffy body. **Weizenbock★★→★★★**, at 17.5 Plato, has a deep tawny colour, a big body, and a sharpness that recedes into smooth vanilla and licorice tones at the finish.

Schäffbräu

This brewery is notable for its "Fire Festival" double bock. **Schäff-Feuerfest★★★** has a gravity of 25 Plato, and the brewery claims that it is matured for 12 to 18 months before emerging with an alcohol content of more than 8 percent by weight; 10 by volume. It is a dark, fruity beer, with a low carbonation. Although the brewery recommends Feuerfest as an apéritif, both its name and prune-brandy palate seem more suited to accompany *crêpes Suzette*. So does its bottle, with wax seal and limited-edition number. The brewery is south of Nürnberg, in the Altmühltal Natural Park at Treuchtlingen.

Schierlinger Roggen

"The first rye beer for 500 years", says the advertizing, discounting the Finnish speciality *Sahti*. The local brewery in Schierling is a subsidiary of the aristocratic Thurn und Taxis, of Regensburg. *Roggen* simply means rye. **Schierlinger Roggen★★★** is a newish, top-fermenting, speciality. It has a tawny, dark, colour; the dense head and fruity aroma of a wheat beer; a dry, grainy palate; and a dash of spicy, slightly bitter, rye character in the finish. A welcome innovation.

Schlenkerla Rauchbier

The most famous Bamberg Rauchbier is Schlenkerla, made for the tavern of that name by the Heller brewery. Like Scotch, Rauchbier gains its smoky palate at the malting stage. The method stems from the available means of kilning the malt. What the Scots had at hand was peat; the Franconians had beech-wood. As more modern methods of kilning evolved, a degree of tradition survived in both Scotland and Franconia, especially in the wooded countryside that surrounds the town of Bamberg.

Ricks of beech logs still wait to burn in the tiny maltings (though it has both Saladin and drum systems) of the Heller brewery, which dates from 1678. The traditional brewhouse, in copper trimmed with brass, sparkles. In another room, a whirlpool makes a strange contrast before the open fermenters.

Ninety-five percent of the brewery's production is Rauch-bier, usually at a Märzen gravity of just over 13.5 percent. It is made entirely from smoked malt, mashed by double decoction, hopped only once (the magic cone can hardly fight the smoke), bottom-fermented, matured for six or seven weeks without *kräusening* and not pasteurized. The resultant beer has a smoky aroma and a dryness the moment it hits the tongue, and a full, smoky flavour that lingers in a long finish. Some people have to drink as many as five litre glasses before they begin to enjoy Rauchbier. It is, not only among beers but also among all alcoholic drinks, a classic. **Aecht Schlenkerla Rauchbier Märzen★★★★** is the definitive example, and in October, November and December there is a 19 Plato version called **Ur-Bock★★★**.

The brewery also has a Helles, but even that has a hint of smokiness.

Spezial

The oldest Rauchbier producer is believed to be Bamberg's Brauerei Spezial, which dates from 1536. It is an unassuming *Hausbrauerei* in a main shopping street. The Christian Merz family have their own tiny maltings and produce only smoked beers. Their everyday product, if it can be called that, is a Rauchbier simply named **Lager★★★,** at 12 Plato. It has a gently insistent smokiness and a treacle-toffee finish. A **Märzen★★★→★★★★** version of around 13.5 is even smokier in texture, bursting with flavour in the finish. There is also a November **Bock★★★**.

Tucher

One of the two large breweries that dominate the Nürnberg market is Tucher, the other being Patrizier. On their home ground, both have upset beer-lovers by swallowing smaller breweries, but Tucher's exports have brought a welcome taste of Germany to parts of the New World.

The Tucher brewery has a full range, which includes a dryish **Pilsener★→★★**, a tasty malty dark beer called **Alt Franken Export Dunkel★★**; a smooth double bock called **Bajuvator★★**; and also a couple of wheat beers, **Weizen★** and **Hefe-Weizen★**. Sad to say, the splendidly bitter **Doppel-hopfen** has not been available in recent years.

Würzburger Hofbräu

Würzburg is in wine country and tried, in 1434, to banish its brewers forever. A couple of hundred years later it had acquired a Hofbräuhaus, which still produces pleasant beers, malt-accented but well-balanced. Its **Pils★→★★** has a malty nose, a firm body and a hoppy finish. **Burkardus★** (in some export markets "Bavarian Dark") is tawny and translucent with a dry, malty palate. **Oktoberfest★** is on the dark side and quite dry. There is also a **Maibock★**, a **Sympator★** double bock and the fresh, plummy **Julius Echter Hefe-Weissbier★★**.

"The champagne of beers" is a sobriquet too generously disposed. It is appropriate only to wheat brews, notably Berliner Weisse. Napoleon's troops during their Prussian campaign coined the description "the champagne of the north". Long after Napoleon was vanquished, the same "champagne" was a fitting toast in Imperial Berlin.

"Berlin white beer" has a very pale colour, an insistent sparkle, a fragrant fruitiness in the nose, a sharp, dry palate and a *frisson* of quenching, sour acidity in the finish. It is served in large bowl-shaped glasses, like beer-sized champagne saucers. To soften its acidity, it is often laced with a dash (a *Schuss*) of raspberry syrup, as though it were a *kir royal*. The green essence of the herb woodruff is also sometimes used for this purpose.

The term "white" has been used over the centuries throughout northern Europe to describe pale, sometimes cloudy, wheat beers. In the north of Germany it became the practice for such beers to contain a relatively low proportion of wheat and be characterized by a lactic fermentation. No doubt the lactic fermentation was originally accidental, but it is now a feature of the style. There are vestiges of this type of brewing elsewhere in the north, notably in Bremen, but it is mainly associated with Berlin. Because it is intended as a light, refreshing drink, Berliner Weisse is produced to a low alcohol content and with a very gentle hop rate. A typical gravity is around 7.5–8 Plato, with an alcohol content of just under 2.5 percent by weight; around 3 by volume. The beer may well have only four or five Units of Bitterness.

Between a quarter and a half of the mash comprises wheat, which is malted. The rest is barley malt. A top-fermenting yeast is used, in a symbiosis with a lactic culture. In the production of the Schultheiss brewery's Berliner Weisse, there is also a blending with a wort that is three to six months old. The brew then has between three and six months' maturation at warm temperatures, is re-inoculated, and has three to four weeks' bottle-conditioning at the brewery. Devotees of the style will keep the beer for a further one to two years in a cool, dark place (but not a refrigerator) to bring out the delicacy and complexity of its fruitiness and fragrance.

Schultheiss Berliner Weisse★★★★ is a beautifully complex example. **Berliner Kindl Weisse★★★**, made by the biggest producer, scores points for assertiveness, but is lacking in complexity and length.

Where to drink

Berliner Weisse is widely available, and is especially popular at the city's various lakes in summer. The Berlin Museum (14 Linden Str) has a Weissbierstube, with an interesting collection of glasses, the Kindl version of the beer, and traditional snacks. (It is currently closed for long-term renovations.) "Haus der 100 Biere", at 45 Mommsen Strasse, Charlottenburg, is worth a visit. Opposite the Charlottenburg

Palace, the Luisen-Bräu brewpub produces a soft, sweetish, unfiltered amber beer. On Berlin's bustling Kurfürstendamm (at no. 26), the Aschinger brewpub produces a range of lagers, including the odd seasonal Bock. In the Neuköln district, a branch of Johann Albrecht makes a malt beer called Kupfer ("Copper"). In the Nikolai quarter of the old East, Georgsbraeu (4 Spreeufer) produces a Hell and Dunkel, and also features Korn schnapps.

THE EASTERN LANDS

There were few speciality beers in the former East Germany, though the firm-bodied **Radeberger★★★** and the dry **Wernersgrüner★★★** are both good Pilseners. The smooth **Köstritzer Schwarzbier★★★→★★★★**, with a flavour reminiscent of bitter chocolate, is a distinctive, very dark, lager, of conventional strength. It is made in the old spa town of Bad Köstritz, near Gera, in Thuringia.

While most of the old-established breweries in the former East are now owned by West German companies, and several others have closed, there is a new generation of brewpubs. In the North, there is a brewpub in a cellar dating from the 1200s, on the marketplace at Lübeck. The Berger brewpub (13 Markt) offers a sweetish Hell, a drier Dunkel and a Bock.

Between Brunswick and Magdeburg, at Quedlinburg (14 Blasii Str), the Lüdde brewpub offers a Pils and a sweet, dark top-fermenting house speciality. In Thuringia, the city of Weimar has the Felsenkeller, offering a Hell, a Dunkel and seasonal specialities. In the same state, the town of Mühlhausen has the brewpub Zum Löwen (3 Korn Markt), offering a full range of styles. The town is between Kassel and Erfurt.

SCANDINAVIA

The northernmost nations of Europe evoke images of icy *fjords* bristling with longboats full of Norsemen inflaming themselves with mead or some early form of beer. Nordic legend certainly lays great stress on brewed beverages, but the modern reputation of Scandinavia in this respect derives from elegant, civilized Copenhagen.

Outside Germany, the Danes did more than anyone to popularize lager brewing, and they did so with great resourcefulness. In 1845, pots of bottom-fermenting yeast were brought from Munich to Copenhagen by the founder of the Carlsberg brewery. During a journey by stagecoach of at least 600 miles, he is said to have kept the yeast cool under his stovepipe hat, dousing it with cold water at every stop. In 1883, the Carlsberg laboratory crossed another frontier by isolating for the first time a single-cell yeast culture. Pure bottom-fermenting yeasts were subsequently identified as *carlsbergensis*.

Denmark continues to remember its earlier, top-fermenting wheat beers by producing a barley malt derivative, of low alcohol content, called *hvidtøl*. But it is, of course, best known for pale lagers, brewed in an unusually wide variety of strengths, and typically with a malty mildness of palate.

Not only in tradition but also in consumption of beer per head, Denmark is an important brewing nation. It has, though, fewer than 20 breweries. Among these, the Carlsberg group owns Tuborg and Wiibroe. It also has stakes in two smaller groups: one formed by Faxe, Ceres and Thor; the other by Albani and Slotsmøllen. There are about half a dozen independents, and a couple of related brewpubs: St Clemens (10–12 Kannikegade, Aarhus) and Apollo (3 Vesterbrogade, near the Tivoli Gardens). The brewpubs make light, tart, yeasty, unfiltered lagers.

Several of the Nordic countries impose rigid classifications of permitted strengths, and these are used as the bases for high taxes, which are intended to discourage drinking. This can make it hard, and expensive, to venture beyond the standard golden lagers and to find the more interesting Vienna types (often made for Easter, Whitsun or Christmas), darker Munich (or "Bavarian" interpretations, and strong porters or stouts. They are worth seeking.

Norway has perhaps the most standardized range of styles, though its beers gain a cleanness from a Purity Law similar to that of Germany. Other laws are being softened as some of the Nordic countries approach membership of the European Community.

Norway's dominant brewery is Ringnes, which also has the brands of the defunct Frydenlunds and Schous companies. In recent years, it has also acquired Nordlands, Dahl, Arendal and Tou. There are a further half-dozen old-established breweries, a new micro, Akershus, and a couple of brewpubs: Oslo Mikro Brygerri (6 Bogstadveien), producing British and

"New American" styles; and, also in the capital, Studenten (45 Karl Johansgt), making unfiltered pale and dark lagers.

Sweden's dominant companies are Pripps, Spendrup and Falken, with a couple of breweries each. There are also three medium-sized breweries and three newcomers, all making conventional brews. For the moment, brewpubs are not permitted under Swedish law.

Finland's biggest company is Hartwall, which also owns the Lapin Kulta ("Lapp Gold"), Mallasjuoma and Aura breweries. The second company, Sinebrychoff, also owns the Karhu brewery, and an excellent brewpub in Helsinki. The third, in Lisalmi, is Olvi, which also has a micro-brewery in the town. A new lager brewery has opened near Tampere.

Hartwall, having closed its brewery at Lappeenranta ("Shore of the Lapps"), in South Karelia, has now made a minority investment in its rebirth. The brewery is making a very clean, malty lager, with a good Saaz bouquet. Another partner is the owner of the Lammi *Sahti* brewery. Finland has five small companies commercially making *Sahti*, an indigenous style traditionally made in farms and homes. It is sometimes brewed with rye, and heavily aromatized with juniper, and often has a strong character of wild yeast. It is a living embodiment of Norse tradition.

Aass

Embarrassingly named (at least to English-speakers) brewery in Drammen, near Oslo. The name means "summit"; perhaps the owning family came from the mountains. Products, all lagers, include a firm, smooth **Export★★**; an aromatic, malty **Amber★★** (the English word is used); a malty but firm **Bayer Øl★★** ("Bavarian"-style); a tawny, deliciously nutty, **Jule Øl★★★**, (Christmas beer); and a splendidly creamy **Bokk★★→★★★**.

Akershus

New Norwegian micro, producing a crisp, orangey-tasting, filtered **Krystall Weissbier★★→★★★**; a **Pale Ale★★★**; with a superbly hoppy, cleansing, finish; and a complex **Irish Stout★★→★★★** with a dryness and complexity of flavours worthy of its designations.

Albani

Medium-sized independent producing a typical range of Danish beers, with some good strong seasonal specialities as well as the popular **Giraf★★** pale lager (15.4 Plato; 1063; 5.4 percent alcohol by weight; 6.8 by volume) and an all-malt **Porter★★→★★★** (20; 1083; 6.2; 7.8).

Carlsberg

International name, producing or licensing its beers in at least a dozen countries, some of which have as many as four or five different strengths and styles of Carlsberg. The company also makes at least half a dozen special export beers, and within its own country has yet more. The basic **Lager Beer★→★★** (known in some markets as Hof, after the Danish Royal Court), has the soft, smooth, malty dryness that is typical of Carlsberg and its home country.

The same character can be found in the much stronger **Elephant★★** (in some markets, Carlsberg '68), which has 16 Plato; 1064; 5.7; 7.1. There is, predictably, a chewier character to the yet stronger **Carlsberg Special Strong Lager★★★** (6.8; 8.5), representing something of a style in itself.

At Easter, Danes have the pleasure of **Carlsberg Påske Bryg 1847★★★** (17.4; 1069; 6.2; 7.8), which has a lovely, deep-amber colour, a restrained sweetness in the nose and a malty dryness in the finish. A beautifully balanced and delicious beer. A similar brew, of slightly lower gravity, is produced for Christmas. **Gamle Carlsberg Special Dark Lager★★** is a true Munich-style beer, of conventional gravity. **Gammel Porter** (or **Imperial Stout**)**★★★** has a gravity of 18.8; 1075, producing 6.1; 7.5. It is bottom-fermenting, but has a splendidly stouty "burnt toffee" palate.

Carlsberg's premises include the world's most beautiful brewhouse, like a cathedral of beer. The original owners turned the company into a foundation to support the arts and sciences, and it remains such.

Ceres

Specialist brewery, in Aarhus. Its principal product is a strong (6.2; 7.7) interpretation of a **Dortmunder★→★★**, somewhat fruity for the style. From the group's Thor brewery, **Buur★★** (an old Danish word for "beer") is similar, perhaps sweeter. **Bering Bryg★★→★★★** is another strong lager, blended with lemon, rum and the brewery's spicy tasting (peppery?) **Stowt★★→★★★** (rendered in a less phonetic spelling in export markets).

Faxe

This brewery's beers are less interesting than they were. **Faxe Premium★→★★** is malty and dryish. Other products include a slightly syrupy **Bock★★**.

Hansa

Bergen company making the hoppy **Ludwig Pils★★**, and operating for visitors a traditional farmhouse brewery that makes a strong (7.2; 9.0) juniper beer in rustic tradition.

Koff

The abbreviated brand-name of Sinebrychoff. Its products include a clean, malty, Vienna-style lager for Christmas, called **Jouluolut★★→★★★**; the lightly fruity, chocolatey, **Brewmaster's Brown Ale★★→★★★**; and the famously satisfying **Koff Porter★★★→★★★★**. The company's brewpub, on the esplanade in Helsinki, is in a building known as "the Chapel" (in Finnish *Kappeli*). Early products have included a (for Finland) notably hoppy golden lager and commensurately malty dark example.

Mack

Seagulls' eggs are consumed in May with the grassy-malty **Mack Øl★★**, from the world's most northerly brewery, in Tromsø, Norway. The English-speaker might think the stronger (5.2; 6.3) **Gull★★** more appropriate, but that name means "Gold". Other products include a chocolatey **Bayer★★→★★★**; and a toasty **Bok★★→★★★**.

Polar Beer

Iceland (with only 200,000 people) has just one brewery, and severe laws mean that its local products, a "Pilsner" and (surprisingly) a "Märzen-type", have only 6.2; 1025; 1.78; 2.25. However, the brewery does export a well-made **Polar Beer★→★★** of 13; 1052; 4.2; 5.3.

Pripps

The Pilsener-style **Royal★★**, with a lot of German hop aroma, is the pride of the brewery. Its **Julöl★★→★★★** has a memorably sweet maltiness. **Carnegie Porter★★→★★★★**, has a big, dry, burnt-tasting palate. Its vintage-dated editions, are a particular treat.

Spendrup's

Spendrup's Premium★★ is firm-bodied, with a malty start and a refreshingly hoppy finish. **Old Gold★★→★★★** is hoppier and very appetizing.

Tuborg

International name, producing a full range of Danish styles. Tuborg's beers are perhaps a little lighter in body and hoppier than those of its partner Carlsberg.

THE NETHERLANDS

The Netherlands is the homeland of international names like Heineken, Amstel, Oranjeboom and Grolsch, all known for relatively light interpretations of the Pilsener style – but in recent years the country has begun to develop a selection of more colourful beers. All of the national brewers have launched speciality products in their home market, but they have done so in response to the interest created by beers from the smaller independents, micros and brewpubs. In all, the country has 30-odd breweries.

While the Protestant north traditionally leavened abstinence with jenever gin, and trading cities like Amsterdam and Rotterdam have a history of brewing in volume for export, the Catholic provinces of North Brabant and Limburg culturally have much in common with neighbouring Belgium to the south – including its tradition of small breweries. This is especially true around the Limburg city of Maastricht. (For the visitor, geographical names can be confusing. There are also adjoining provinces called Brabant and Limburg in Belgium, and there is a city of Limburg in Germany.)

For many years, Dutch breweries were inclined to offer only an Oud Bruin (a sweetened dark lager, with low alcohol content, at about 9.0 Plato; 1036; 2–3 percent by weight; 2.5–3.5 by volume); a Pilsener (in The Netherlands, this term indicates the classic gravity of 11–12; 1044–48; around 4.0; 5.0); perhaps a "Dortmunder" (usually stronger than its German inspiration); and a seasonal Bock (15.6–17.0; 1062–68; 5.0–5.5; 6.25–7.0), sometimes spelled without the "c".

An annual festival of Bo(c)k beers, usually held in Amsterdam in October or November, is organized by the consumerist organization PINT (PO Box 3757, Amsterdam 1001 AN; fax 010–2122162).

Many of the newer beers are more Belgian in inspiration. Several score bonus stars for assertiveness and individuality, but only a handful rate highly for consistency or keeping-quality.

Where to drink

(*Cities listed from north to south*)

Alkmaar In the centre of this tourist town, famous for its cheese market, is a beer museum, with a bar, called De Boom (1 Houttil), which attempts to serve every beer in The Netherlands. Opens Tuesday–Saturday, and Sunday afternoons in summer.

Amsterdam The Dutch pioneered speciality beer bars, and run them very well. One of the best, not to be missed by any visitor, even though it is tricky to find, is In De Wildeman, 5 Nieuwe Zijds Kolk and Kolksteeg, off the shopping street Nieuwendijk, in the city centre. Interesting guest beers, and a good selection, in a former gin tasting-room. Opens at noon, and closes on Sundays.

As a member of the Alliance of Beer Tappers, this establishment makes available a pocket-sized brochure listing about 30 others elsewhere in The Netherlands.

There is also a café specializing in Belgian beers, De Zotte, at 29 Raam Straat, near Leidseplein, one of the main squares. Noisy and smoky. Opens at 11.00 am daily; 4.00 pm on Sundays.

Amsterdam has several speciality beer shops. The most convenient, and highly recommended, is De Bierkoning, 125 Paleis Straat, near the royal palace. See also entries for brewpubs 't IJ and Maximiliaan.

Utrecht Jan Primus, 27 Jan van Scorel Straat, is a pioneering speciality beer bar. Opens 3.00 pm, closed Sundays. Café Bwelgie, 196 Oude Gracht, has 20 taps, the most in any café in The Netherlands, and offers *cuisine à la bière*.

The Hague Den Paas, 16a Dunne Bierkade, is a beer café in the old town. Opens 3.30 pm. De Wijn en Bier Boetiek, 803 Leyweg, just to the southwest of the centre, is a shop highlighting small Dutch brewers, and also offering malt whiskies.

Rotterdam Cambrinus, 4 Blaak (near metro station of same name) does some cooking with beer. Opens noon weekdays, and 2.00 pm weekends. Locus Publicus, 364 Oostzeedijk (Oostplein metro), is a well-established beer café. Opens 5.00 pm daily, 9.00 pm Sundays.

Breda De Beyerd, 26 Bosch Straat, is a pioneering beer café in this Brabant town.

The breweries

A note on brewery names: Where breweries are named after towns, grammar may require a final "e", or a longer ending, on the company's name, but perhaps not on the beer itself. Grolsche, for example, is the brewery name, but the beer is called Grolsch.

Alfa

Small, old-established (1870), Limburg brewery making exclusively all-malt beers, smooth and well-balanced, with German and Czech hops. Pre-dated the speciality beer boom with its sweetish, malty, **Super-Dortmunder★★★**, the strongest example of the style (16–16.5; 1064-66; 5.5; 7.0). The brewery is at Schinnen, north of Maastricht.

Arcense Stoom ("Steam")

After a lively period as a revived independent, and very much a pioneer of speciality beers in The Netherlands, Arcen is now owned by Oranjeboom, and is thus back in the hands of Allied Breweries.

There has been an Arcener Steam, reminiscent of a Kölsch, but the current emphasis seems to be on a dry, faintly salty, **Pils★→★★**, with a touch of wheat; the dry, thinnish, **Altforster Altbier★★→★★★**; and various forms of Bock. In a varying portfolio, the most interesting beer has been **Arcener Grand Prestige★★★**, arguably an Old Ale, but described as a barley wine. It would be sad if this strong (8.0, 10.0), rich, dark brown, smoothly fruity, brew fell by the wayside. The brewery is at Arcen, north of Venlo, Limburg.

Bavaria

Family-owned, but sizable, brewery that caters primarily to the supermarket and own-label trade. The brewery is in Lieshout, North Brabant. The name probably dates from the days when the term "Bavarian" suggested lager beer. Has been known for light, sweetish, mainstream, beers but recently launched a wheat Bock (not tasted).

Brand's

Oldest brewery in The Netherlands, perhaps dating from the 1300s, known as Brand's since 1871, and still protective of its individuality, despite a takeover by Heineken in 1989. Its all-malt regular **Pils★★** has a touch of very fresh bread on the nose, a hint of grassiness in the palate, then perfumy and dry hop notes. The super-premium **Brand UP** ("Urtyp Pilsener") ★★→★★★ (12.5; 1050; a little over 4.0; 5.0) has become slightly more malty and less hoppy in recent years, but is still beautifully balanced and elegant, with a long finish. It has 36 Units of Bitterness. **Imperator★★★** is a soft, clean, amber-coloured, year-round Bock (16.4; 1066; 5.2; 6.5), notable for its complexity of aromatic maltiness. **Dubbelbock★★★** is a stronger (18.4; 1074; 6.0w; 7.5v), ruby-coloured, early winter Bock, with a great depth of aromatic, oily, buttery, fruity, maltiness. **Sylvester★★★**, intended for midwinter, is top-fermenting strong ale (18-18.5; 1072-4; 6.4; 8.0), with a deep bronze colour and a sophisticated palate, fruity, sometimes oaky; an *eau-de-vie* among beers. In spring of 1994, Brand's launched a golden-to-bronze, top-fermenting, **Meibock★★★** (17; 1068; around 5.6; 7.0), with a creamy, spicy nose; a touch of Seville orange in the palate; and a suggestion of clovey yeastiness in the finish. The brewery is in Wijlre, just to the east of Maastricht.

Breda

The old Three Horseshoes brewery (founded in 1538), in the historic north Brabant town of Breda, and the Oranjeboom ("Orange Tree") brewery, of Rotterdam, were for years both owned by Allied Breweries, of Britain. Today, only Breda operates, but the company calls itself Oranjeboom. It has in recent years produced a wide range of brands, from the light **Royal Dutch Posthorn★** to the firmer-bodied **Oranjeboom Pilsener★**. Among its newer products is **Het Elfde Gebod★★→★★★** ("The Eleventh Commandment"), a strong (5.6; 7.0) top-fermenting ale, with a full gold colour, and a creamy, malty, aroma and palate, drying towards a fruity, perfumy, banana-like, finish.

Budelse

Very small, old-established (1870), brewery in North Brabant, at Budel, near the Belgian border. The Kölsch-like **Parel★★→★★★** (14; 1056; 4.8; 6.0) and **Budels Alt★★→★★★** (13.5; 1054; 4.4; 5.5) are both slightly stronger than their styles would suggest. The abbey-style

Capucijn★★→★★★ (16; 1064; 5.2; 6.5) is malty, fruity, spicy and smoky, with hints of applewood. All are notably smooth.

St Christoffel

Noted for a world-class, assertively dry, Pilsener-style beer, originally called simply **Christoffel**★★★→★★★★, now additionally described as Blond (with the sub-title Dubbel Hop). A newer beer, designated "Double Malt" (4.8; 6.0), is called **Robertus**★★→★★★. This name is a personification of Robijn, the Dutch description for the reddish-brown colour of the beer. It has an aromatic malt character, a creamy palate, and a dryish finish. Both beers are all-malt, unfiltered and unpasteurized. St Christoffel is a micro, established in the 1980s by Leon Brand, a member of the Limburg brewing family. The brewery is located in Roermond, a former coal-mining town, whose patron saint is Christoffel.

Dommelsche

Owned by the Belgian group Interbrew (Artois/Jupiler). Dommelsche's products include **Dominator**★→★★, a strongish (4.8; 6.0) pale lager, dry and lightly fruity; a surprisingly dry (by Dutch standards) **Bok**★★; and **Jubilator** (too early to rate), brewed to celebrate the brewery's 250th anniversary in 1994. The brewery is in North Brabant, at Dommelen, not far from the Belgian border.

Drie Horne

Commercial home-brewery, founded in 1991, in Kaatsheuvel, north of Breda. Products include bronze **Trippelaer**★★ (6.8; 8.5), bronze in colour, with a sweet, spicy, aromatic, faintly medicinal, palate.

Drie Kruizen

"Three crosses". Micro established in 1991, at Westmaas, in the Rhine-Schelde delta area. Early products include a thinnish, dry, **Koornbeurs Wit** ("Cornmarket white"). Too soon to rate.

Drie Ringen

Fruity, sweetish, ales from a micro which opened in 1989 at Amersfoort, in the central province of Utrecht. Recent products include a slightly treacly, spicy, minty, **Amersfoorts Wit**★★, made with a German Weizen yeast; a pinkish-amber **Meibock**★ (5.2, 6.5), with an intense, bittersweet, marmalade taste; and a sugary-tasting **Tripel**★→★★ (6.0, 7.5), with a hint of tropical fruits. The hoppy, honeyish, light, **Vleutens Tripel**★→★★ is made under contract for a company in that Gelderland town.

De Gans

"The Goose". Micro founded in 1988, in Goes (pronounced "goose"), Zeeland. Later moved to nearby s'Gravenpolder. Products are usually assertive, very dry, spicy and peppery, but hard to find.

Grolsche

Not only the light, fluffy, **Pils (Premium Lager)**★★, with a clean maltiness and a distinctive yeast character, but also a very sweet **Bok**★→★★ in the typically Dutch dark-brown style; a much drier, amber, **Mei Bok**★★ (16; 1064; a little over 4.8; 6.0); and **Grolsch Amber**★★→★★★, using the English spelling for something similar to an Altbier with a lightly malty start and a heartily hoppy finish. All of the beers are unpasteurized. This internationally known brewery was until recent decades a small company in the eastern towns of Enschede, in Overijssel, and Groenlo (formerly Grolle), in Gelderland. There were breweries in Grolle in the 1600s, but the present concern was formed in 1898, after which the Pilsener-style beer was launched. The beer's antiquity has been exaggerated in American advertizing by 275 years.

Gulpener

Old-established (1825), independent brewery at Gulpen, just to the southeast of Maastricht. Known especially for its **X-pert**★★→★★★ (4.0, 5.0), a super-premium Pilsener with a notably full colour and a lot of Tettnang hop in both aroma and palate. Locals often ask for a Pils with a "dash" (in Dutch, a *scheut*; in the Limburg dialect, a *sjoes*, pronounced almost the same as the German *Schuss*). Gulpener bottles a ready-mixed version of Pils and Oud Bruin, called **Sjoes**★→★★, which emerges lightly malty, smooth and dryish. Other products include an aromatically malty strong **Dort**★★ (15.5; 1062; 5.2; 6.5), the name abbreviated from the German city. The brewery has also been experimenting with a perfumy version of a Belgian-style "white" beer, called **Korenwolf** ("Hamster"). In the early 1980s, Gulpener revived a regional style of the past, with its **Mestreechs Aajt**★★★. This is a faintly herbal-tasting (gentian?) sour-and-sweet summer brew, of refreshingly low strength (2.8, 3.5), claret in colour, and made from a blend of two beers. One of the beers has a wild yeast fermentation and is aged for at least a year in unlined wood. Gulpener installed wooden tuns specifically for this purpose. This speciality is produced at a separate brewpub, called De Zwarte Ruiter (The Black Knight), at 4 Markt, Gulpen (closed Mondays). Local dishes are served as snacks.

Heineken

The most international of brewers, from a maritime country where export has always been a way of life. Half of the company's Dutch output is sent overseas, much of it to the USA, and its beers are also made by subsidiaries, associates or licensees in more than 90 breweries elsewhere. In the early 1990s, Heineken reverted to all-malt beers, abandoning the corn used by many major brewers. Despite this, **Heineken**★→★★ itself (11.4; 1045–6; 4.0; 5.0, or fractionally less) remains lighter than most German lager beers, for example, but fuller-bodied than many international brands. The beer has a touch of grassiness; a smooth, firm body; a light hop character; and spritzy finish. A version lower in alcohol is made in the British Isles and some Nordic countries. Heineken acquired Amstel in the 1960s, and later closed that brewery. In The Netherlands, **Amstel Bier**★ →★★ (4.0; 5.0) is fractionally fuller in colour, lighter in aroma, firmer in body, with more, slightly perfumy, hop flavours. Various overseas versions seem lighter and sharper. **Amstel 1870**★ →★★ is hoppier. **Amstel Gold**★ (5.6; 7.0) has some alcohol flavours. **Amstel Bock**★★ (5.6, 7.0), with a toffeeish malt character, and **Heineken Tarwebok**★★★, at the same strength but containing 17 percent wheat, are seasonal specialities for October and November. Tarwebok is silky, chocolatey, fruity and complex.

The launch of a strong (1064; 16; 5.2; 6.5), and surprisingly hoppy-tasting, Vienna-style lager called **1994**★★★ is intended to signal a regular special for December–January. At a similar strength, a creamy but slightly tart top-fermenting ale called **Kylian**★★ →★★★ is based on the George Killian "Irish Red" made at Heineken's subsidiary brewery near Lille, France. The bottom-fermenting **Van Vollenhoven's Stout**★★ (16.2; 1065; 4.8; 6.0) is creamy but lacks complexity. Heineken is headquartered in Amsterdam, and has breweries at Zoeterwoude, South Holland, and 's Hertogenbosch, North Brabant.

De Hoeksche

Micro founded in 1992, at Oud Beijerland, South Holland. Early products have included a smoky, tannic **Speciaal** (4.8, 6.0). Too early to rate.

't IJ

Under a windmill in Amsterdam (to the east of the Central Station, at Funenkade), in what was once a public bath-house, songwriter Kaspar Peterson established this brewpub in 1984/5. The bar opens Wednesday–Sunday, 3.00–8.00 pm, but the beers can be found elsewhere. The first beers were a dryish, malty-fruity, abbey-style Double called **Natte**★★ (meaning "wet") at 4.8; 6.0, and a spicy, firm, pale Triple, entitled **Zatte**★★ →★★★ ("drunk") at 6.4; 8.0.

These were followed by two yet-stronger counterparts, the pale Columbus★★★ (7.2, 9.0), with lots of malt and hop, and the dark, surprisingly dry **Struis**★★★ (8.0; 10.0), the name of which means ostrich. The brewery's symbol is an ostrich with an egg. The Dutch word for "egg" sounds like IJ, the name of the waterway on which Amsterdam harbour stands.

't Kuipertje

Tiny micro in Heukelum, Gelderland. Beers variable.

De Kroon

"The Crown". Very small independent, at Oirschot, North Brabant, not far from the Belgian border. Specialities include **Egelantier**★★, a bronze, Vienna-style, lager of conventional gravity but full body (4.0; 5.0). Also has an organic Pils, and organizes a May Bock festival.

De Leeuw

"The Lion". Independent at Valkenburg, Limburg. Specialities include a soft-tasting, all-malt, super-premium, Pils called **Jubileeuw**★★ (4.0; 5.0) and a Dortmunder called **Super-Leeuw**★★ (5.2, 6.5), with a very fresh malt character and a dry finish. Also a sweetish **Valkenburgse Wit**, with a hint of pineapple (too early to rate).

Lindeboom

"The Linden Tree". Small independent in Neer, north of Roermond, Limburg. Specialities include a bronze, malty, Vienna-style lager called **Gouverneur**★★→★★★ (4.0; 5.0) and a well-regarded Bock (not tasted).

Maasland

Micro established in 1989, in the North Brabant town of Oss, between s'Hertogenbosch and Nijmegen. Beers include **d'n Schele Os**★★→★★★ ("the cross-eyed ox"), containing rye, and spiced. This Triple (6.0; 7.5) has a fruity, sherbety, perfumy, aroma; malty sweetness, and some tart, spicy, dryness in the finish.

St Martinus

Micro established in 1992, in the northern city of Groningen. **Cluyn**★★→★★★ (7.1; 8.8) is light-heartedly intended to replicate rustic beers made in the distant past from canal water. The grist includes oats and wheat, and some of the grain is unmalted. The beer has a peachy colour, and is very fruity and grainy, with a sour edge.

Maximiliaan

Named after the Austrian Emperor who gave Amsterdam the right to display the royal crown. German-accented beers from a brewpub in a former convent just beyond the red-light district in Amsterdam's inner city (6–8 Kloveniersburgwal). The Bavarian-accented **Tarwebier**★★ (wheat beer) is slightly sweet and syrupy. A Kölsch-type named **Bethanien**★★, after the convent, is light, clean and dry, with a touch of fruit and a very good hop bitterness. A Triple called **Casper's Max**★★→★★★ (6.0; 7.5) is bronze and chewy, with lots of malt and hop. **Klooster**★→★★★ is similar, but darker, with a toffeeish malt note. There also several seasonal specials. Maximiliaan offers *cuisine à la bière*.

Moerenburg

Micro established in 1992/3, in Tilburg, North Brabant. Products have included a rather astringent **Witbier**; a summer beer, with a creamy maltiness and strawberry notes; and two strong, reddish, ales with a pleasant maltiness: **Karakter**, at 5.2; 6.5; and **Gouwe Ouwe** ("Golden Oldie"), at 6.0; 7.5; too early to rate.

Onder de Linden

Strong ales and varying specialities at a micro in Wageningen, Gelderland, in the east of The Netherlands.

Oudaen

Utrecht brewpub (99 Oudegracht). Produces a "white" beer, in cloudy and filtered forms, and seasonal specialities (not tasted).

Raaf

A farmhouse brewery dating from at least the 1700s, and defunct for 60 years, was revived in 1983 by a couple who had previously run a health-food store. Among their several products, including ales and abbey-style beers, the spicy and very tart **Witte Raaf★★** attracted the attention of Allied/ Oranjeboom, which currently controls the brewery. The Witte now dominates production, and there is a new strong ale called **Bergzicht** (too early to rate). There is a café at the brewery, open Sunday afternoons, and some weekdays in summer ☎080–581177); 232 Rijksweg, Heumen, on the N271, 5 miles south of Nijmegen, in the eastern province of Gelderland.

De Ridder

Pretty brewery, dating from 1852, on the left ̍bank of the River Meuse (Maas), in the heart of old Maastricht. De Ridder means "The Knight". Acquired by Heineken in 1982, and now specializing in an unpasteurized wheat beer, **Wieckse Witte★★★**, with a slightly grainy-mealy palate and a very late coriander finish. The brewery also has a very clean-tasting strong Dortmunder called **Maltezer★★** (16; 1064; 5.2; 6.5). As its name might suggest, this has a very creamy malt character.

Schaapskooi Trappist

The only abbey brewery in The Netherlands is called Schaapskooi ("Sheep's Pen") . It was established in 1885/6 to fund construction of the monastery itself, at a place called Koningshoeven ("King's Gardens"), near the city of Tilburg, North Brabant. An experimental Blond Trappist **Koningshoeven★★** (4.4; 5.5), was refreshing, with a dry maltiness. The older-established **La Trappe Dubbel★★→★★★** (5.2; 6.5) has a ruby colour; a yeasty fruitiness in the nose; and a complexity of pruny, sherryish, flavours. **La Trappe Tripel★★→★★★** (6.4; 8.0) is paler and drier, with notes of Goldings hops and perhaps coriander. The Dubbel has also appeared in much the same form under the Koningshoeven and Tilburg labels. The Tripel seems spicier in the La Trappe version; maltier under the Koningshoeven label; and hoppier and paler in its Tilburg form. **La Trappe Quadrupel★★★**, also introduced in 1992, has an orangey-red colour; a very fruity aroma; a distinctively smooth, syrupy, body; and lots of flavour development, towards a big, spicy (coriander again?) finish (21–22; 1084–8; 8.5; 10.0).

Us Heit

The name, meaning "Our Father", is a reference to a Frisian viceroy and hero. The brewery was founded in a cowshed in the Friesland village of Uitwellingerga ("coming out of the well"), near Sneek, by Limburger Aart van der Linde, in 1985.

He began with **Buorren★★→★★★** (4.8, 6.0), a bronze-red ale, with a dry fruitiness verging on an intentional sourness. A wide range of beers, often with this house character, has been produced since.

Zeeuwse-Vlaamse

Located in Flemish Zeeland, as the name suggests, this micro was established in Hulst, south of the River Schelde, in 1991. Early products have included a very dry, fruity, smoky, thinnish **Zeeuwsche Witte★**; a reddish, slightly sour **Zeeuwsche Bruine★★** (5.0; 6.0) in broadly the Flemish style; and oddities coloured with beetroot and chlorophyl, under the Paranoia label. Also a somewhat acidic **Sint Jan Bier** (too early to rate) produced under contract for a label in Schiedam (historically, the jenever gin capital, near Rotterdam).

De Zon

"The sun". Micro established in 1992/3 in Schaijk, near Oss, North Brabant. Early products have included a very fruity, sweet and sour, Triple called **Brabants Glorie**. Too early to rate.

BELGIUM

Belgium has long enjoyed the world's most individualistic beers but, even in the country itself, sales of speciality brews are increasing. Elsewhere in the world, helped by the introduction of beer-oriented Belgian restaurants (in Paris, London, Montreal, New York, Philadelphia, Washington ...), the appreciation of these distinctive brews is spreading fast.

Belgium's beer tradition is no Jean-come-lately. Its cidery, winey, spontaneously fermenting *lambic* family predate the pitching of yeast by brewers and its cherry *kriek*, strawberry *framboise* and spiced "white" brews pre-date the acceptance of the hop as the universal seasoning in beer. Other countries have monastery breweries but it is only in Belgium that the brothers have evolved their own collective style of beers. The country's five Trappist breweries, and their many secular imitators, have developed a distinct family of brews: always strong, top-fermenting and bottle-matured. They often have a heavy sediment and a fruity palate, sometimes evincing hints of chocolate. Within these characteristics, however, there are substantial differences between the brews, and a couple of subcategories, but that is the way of Belgian beer. Some Belgian specialities are hard to categorize, although most are top-fermenting and many are bottle-matured. No country has a more diverse range even within the bottle-matured group – the Belgians are keen on this means of conditioning and sometimes refer to it as their *méthode champenoise*.

In a Belgian café, the list of beers will identify at least one member of the *lambic* family (occasionally a sweet *faro*, often a sparkling *gueuze*); perhaps a honeyish "white" beer (*witbier* or *bière blanche*) from the village or a brown (*bruin*) from the town of Oudenaarde; a local *spéciale*; and a strong, bottle-conditioned monastery (*abdij* or *abbaye*) brew. There may also be a Belgian *ale*, as well as local interpretations of English, Scottish and sometimes German styles. This is in an ordinary café; there will be a far greater categorization in a café that makes a feature of speciality beers, listing them by the hundred. After decades of decline when they were regarded as "old-fashioned", speciality beers began to enjoy a revival in the late 1970s. They are a joy to the visiting beer-lover, although it is necessary to know what to order. A request simply for "a beer" is likely to be met by a mass-market Pilsener.

With the revival of interest in speciality beers within Belgium, more of them have also entered export markets. They present a bewildering choice. As always, the selection of beers reflects both history and geography. The influence of the brewing customs of the surrounding nations has been accepted with shrewd selectivity by the Belgians, yet they have also contrived to be conservative and inward-looking to the point that their principal regions maintain their own traditions. The country is divided not only into its Dutch-speaking north (Flanders) and French-speaking south (Wallonia) but also has a German-speaking corner in the east and a bilingual knot around the city of Brussels. Some styles of beer are perceived as belonging not to a region but to a province, river valley, town or village.

The Belgians like to talk about beer as their reply to Burgundy. They suggest that beer is to them what wine is to France. Cheese might be an even better comparison. The beers of Belgium, like the cheeses of France, are often idiosyncratic, cranky, artisanal. Some drinkers could never learn to enjoy one of the cloudy, sour specialities of the Senne Valley any more than they could acquire a taste for a smelly cheese. In both cases, the loss would be theirs. This is drink at its most sensuous. In its native gastronomy, Belgium is a land of beer, seafood and – after dinner – the world's finest chocolate. It is a land of German portions and French culinary skills. Beer may be served, with some ceremony at a family meal, and might well have been used in the cooking. Other countries have the odd dish prepared with beer, but Belgium has hundreds. The Belgians even eat hop shoots, as a delicacy, in the brief season of their availability, served like asparagus.

Beer is also a central theme in Belgium's history and culture. St Arnold of Oudenaarde (or was it Oudenburg?) is remembered for having successfully beseeched God, in the 11th century, to provide more beer after an abbey brewery collapsed. He is the patron saint of Belgian brewers, some of whom display his statue by their kettles. (French-speakers can, if they prefer, remember another beery miracle, that of St Arnold at Metz.) The 13th-century Duke Jan the First of Brabant, Louvain and Antwerp has passed into legend as the King of Beer: "Jan Primus" has been corrupted into "Gambrinus", by which name he is remembered not only in Belgium but also in Germany, the Czech Republic and far beyond. Jan Primus is said to have been an honorary member of the Brewers' Guild, although their present gilded premises on Brussels' Grand' Place were not built until 1701. Today, the "Brewers' House" is the only building on the Grand' Place still to be used as the headquarters of a trade guild. Today's Confederation has about a hundred members, and that represents roughly the number of breweries in Belgium. The figure has been declining for some years, although recently a number of new micro-breweries have opened. Many Belgian breweries are family owned, which can lead to problems when there is no clear succession. But however much the number of breweries fluctuates, the tally of beers increases, with new specialities constantly being launched. At any one time, there are probably more than 800 Belgium beers on the market.

FLANDERS

Flemish painters like Bruegel and the aptly named Brouwer depicted the people of their home stage as enthusiastic beer-drinkers. It has been like that for a thousand years. As Emperor of Europe, Charlemagne took an interest in brewing, and perhaps he brought the news from Aix to Ghent. The nationalistic Flemings might, however, secretly resent their famous artists' depiction of beery excess. They take pride in being hard-working, and the Early and Late Flemish schools of painting were made possible by the prosperity of Flanders at different times as an exporter of beer as well as textiles, and as a commercial centre. Flanders emerged as a principal component of the new Belgium in 1830, and has in recent years reasserted itself through the trading prosperity of the River Scheldt – with beer exports once again on the upswing.

As a region, Flanders stretches from the Dutch side of the Scheldt to a slice of northern France. Politically, it comprises the Belgian provinces of West and East Flanders, Antwerp and Limburg.

West Flanders, with its 15th-century canalside capital Bruges, has traditionally been known for its sour, burgundy-coloured style of beer – the classic example is Rodenbach. The province is well served by small breweries and has two of the strongest beers in Belgium, from the revivalist Dolle Brouwers and the monastery brewery of Westvleteren. East Flanders, with the proud city of Ghent as its capital, is noted for slightly less sour brown ales, produced in or near the town of Oudenaarde, which has a cluster of small breweries to the east.

The province and city of Antwerp are noted for the beauti-fully made De Koninck beer (a copper ale). The province also has the monastery of Westmalle, which created the Triple style of abbey beer, and in the south, the strong, golden ale called Duvel, the potent, dark Gouden Carolus and the well-liked Maes Pils.

Limburg has a less gilded capital, the pretty little town of Hasselt, which is known for the production of *genever* gin. It is a thinly breweried province but has the distinctive Sezoens beer from the Martens brewery; and Cristal Alken, an especially well-respected Pilsener beer.

Where to drink

There are several speciality beer cafés in Antwerp. With about 500 beers, the most famous among devotees is Kulminator, 32 Vleminckveld (opens 8.00 pm Monday; noon on other weekdays; 5.00 pm on Saturday; closed Sunday). Also highly regarded is Taverne Bierland, 28 Korte Nieuw Straat, (opens noon, closed Sunday), in the Old Town.

After Antwerp, the largest city in Flanders is Ghent, which has a popular and well-run specialist beer café called De Hopduvel ("the hop devil"), at 10 Rokerel Straat. De Hopduvel also features the growing number of Belgian cheeses.

The beautiful tourist city of Bruges has a justifiably famous beer café called 't Brugs Beertje, at 5 Kemel Straat, an alley near Simon Stevin Plein. Open 4.00 pm; closed Wednesday. A couple of doors away is the beer-and-gin bar 't Dreupel Huisje.

Elsewhere in Flanders, the Limburg town of Hasselt has 't Hemelrijk, in the street of the same name, at no 11.

Cristal Alken

The hoppiest of the principal Belgian Pilseners is **Cristal Alken★★→★★★**. This well-made Pilsener with a notably pale colour, fresh, hoppy nose; very clean, crisp palate and a smooth dryness in the finish. It is hopped principally with blossoms, including Saaz for aroma, fermented at relatively cold temperatures, lagered for a respectable period and not pasteurized. Alken and its former rival Maes are now part-owned by Kronenbourg of France.

De Dolle Brouwers

"The Mad Brewers", they call themselves. It is a typically Flemish sardonic shrug on behalf of a group of enthusiasts who rescued from closure a village brewery near Diksmuide, not far from Ostend. As a weekend project, they renovated the brewery, which dates from the mid-19th century and is a classic of its type. (Tours welcome; ☎051-502781.) They specialize in strong, top-fermenting beers, bottle-matured. The house speciality is **Oerbier★★★**, very dark and smooth, with a sweetness that is offset by licorice tones (original gravity 1100; alcohol content 6 percent by weight; 7.5 by volume). There are also several seasonal products: the brassy-coloured, honey-primed **Boskeun★★★**, an Easter beer of about 8 percent by volume; the pale, dry-hopped **Arabier★★★**, for summer, with a similar alcohol content; and **Stille Nacht★★★**, a claret-coloured Christmas brew, with hints of apple in its aroma and palate, and an alcohol content of around 9 percent. The Ostend area also has a micro-brewery called 't Steedje, producing an ale and a "Triple".

De Koninck

A classic. This perilously drinkable, copper-coloured, top-fermenting beer fits in stylistically somewhere between an English ale (a fruity "best bitter") and a smooth Düsseldorf *Altbier*. For all its complexity of character, it pursues an unassuming occupation as the local beer of Antwerp, from the city's only brewery. The company stayed with top-fermentation when other big-city breweries were switching to Pilseners. Its sole product is **De Koninck★★★**, an all-malt beer of 12 Plato, brewed by direct flame in a cast-iron kettle. It is cold-conditioned and emerges with an alcohol content of a little over 4 percent by weight and 5 by volume. De Koninck has an excellent malt character, a yeasty fruitiness and a great deal of Saaz hoppiness, especially in its big finish. Its full palate is best experienced in the draught form, which is unpasteurized. Opposite the brewery, at the Pilgrim Café (8 Boomgardstraat), drinkers sometimes add a sprinkle of yeast to the beer. In the heart of Antwerp, the beer is available at the city's oldest café, Quinten Matsijs (17 Moriaanstraat) and at Den Engel (3 Grote Markt).

Duvel

This means "Devil" and is the name of the world's most beguiling beer. With its pale, golden sparkle, **Duvel★★★★** looks superficially like a Pilsener. Its palate is soft and seductive. Beneath its frothy head, behind its dense lacework, this all-malt, top-fermenting beer has the power (6.7 percent alcohol by weight; 8.2 by volume) to lead anyone into temptation. The pale colour is achieved with the help of the brewery's own maltings; Styrian and Saaz hops are used; a very distinctive yeast imparts a subtle fruitiness (reminiscent of Poire Williams); the cleanness and smoothness is enhanced by both cold and warm maturation; and, in the classic, sedimented, version, the *mousse* develops from bottle-conditioning. Duvel is customarily chilled as though it were an *alcool blanc*. It is produced by the Moortgat brewery in the village of Breendonk near Mechelen/Malines. Other Moortgat products include tasty, abbey-style beers under the **Maredsous★★** label, for the monastery of that name. Duvel is sometimes compared with the various monastic Triple beers, but this is self-evident heresy. Duvel is lighter in body, less sweet, more delicate. It is the original, and therefore classic, example of what has become a distinct style. Broadly in this style are **Deugniet★★**, **Hapkin★★→★★★**, **Lucifer★**, and perhaps the darker **Sloeber★★**.

Gouden Carolus

This is the classic strong, dark ale of Belgium. Its name derives from a gold coin from the realm of the Holy Roman Emperor

Charles V, who grew up in the Flemish City of Mechelen (better known by its French name, Malines) where this beer is brewed. **Gouden Carolus★★★**, has a dense, dark colour, a gentle, soothing character, a hint of fruitiness in the finish and, from a gravity of 19 Plato, an alcohol content of 6 percent by weight; 7.5 by volume. A lovely after-dinner beer; or, better still, a nightcap. The brewery is now affiliated with Riva, of Dentergem. It is to be hoped that its beers can maintain their individuality.

Kwak Pauwel

The odd name derives from an antique Flemish speciality. This revival, a strong (9 percent by volume), amber-red, top-fermenting brew, is notable for its spicy aroma and palate. **Kwak Pauwel★★** is a hearty, warming brew. When it first appeared in Belgium, it won attention by being served in a "yard of ale" glass, of the type allegedly handed up to coachmen in times past when they stopped for a restorative drink.

Liefmans

This classic product is now owned by Riva, of Dentergem, in West Flanders. The mashing and brewing are carried out there, with water treated to match that of its home town of Oudenaarde, a few miles away in East Flanders. The water is low in calcium but high in sodium bicarbonate. The wort is then transferred to the old brewery in Oudenaarde, for fermentation with the house's mutli-strain "top" yeast, and maturation. The basic **Oud Bruin★★→★★★** ("Old Brown") has four to six weeks' warm conditioning. The classic **Goudenband★★★→★★★★** ("Gold Riband") is a blend of the basic beer with a slightly stronger version that has an additional six to eight months' maturation. The two beers are centrifuged, then primed, re-yeasted and given a further three months in the bottle before leaving the brewery. The Goudenband (4.8; 6) is unusually spritzy and dry for a brown ale, with a finish reminiscent of Montilla. It will continue to develop, at a natural cellar temperature, for months, and perhaps years, becoming more complex, drier and tarter. The brewery's brown ale is also used as the base for a bittersweet **Kriek★★★** and a candyish **Frambozen/Framboise★★**.

Maes

A flowery "Riesling" bouquet imparts distinctiveness to **Maes Pils★★**. This is a light, soft, dry Pilsener-style beer. The brewery is in the village of Waarloos, north of Mechelen. The company also produces two top-fermenting beers for the abbey of Grimbergen, a Flemish village near Brussels. **Grimbergen Double★★** is a dark, fruity beer, with a chocolatey palate; it has a gravity of 15.8 Plato and an alcohol content of 5.2 percent by weight; 6.5 by volume. **Grimbergen Tripel★→★★** is paler, fruity, but with a more winey character; it has a gravity of 19.6 Plato and an alcohol content of 7.2 by weight; 9 by volume. (See also Cuvée de L'Ermitage.)

Rodenbach

The unimaginative are apt to consider Rodenbach's beers undrinkable, yet they are the classics of the "sour" style of West Flanders. They gain their sourness, and their burgundy colour, in a number of ways. The sourness derives in part from the top-fermenting yeast, a blend of three strains that has been in the house for 150 years, and from cultures resident in wooden maturation tuns. The colour, too, originates partly from the use of reddish Vienna-style malts but also probably from the caramels and tannins extracted from the oak of the tuns. These vessels, made from Slavonian oak, from Poland, are uncoated. They make a remarkable sight, each tun standing vertically from floor to ceiling. The smallest contains 15,000 litres of maturing beer; the largest 60,000 litres. There are 300 in all, filling several halls, as though this were a winery or a brandy distillery. When the maturing beer has attained its typical palate, it is stabilized by flash pasteurization so does not mature in the bottle and is not intended for laying down.

The basic **Rodenbach★★★→★★★★** is a blend of "young" beer (matured five to six weeks) and "vintage" brews (matured 18 months to two years). The longer-matured beer is also bottled "straight" as **Rodenbach Grand Cru★★★★**. The basic Rodenbach has an original gravity of 11.5–11.75 Plato, emerging with 3.7 percent alcohol by weight; 4.6 volume. The Grand Cru has an original gravity of 15, but an alcohol content of only around 4.1; 5.2. The gravity is heightened by the use of non-fermented sugars and the alcohol content is diminished because some of the fermentation is lactic. There is both a sharpness and a restorative quality about these beers: perfect after a game of tennis. The Grand Cru has a slightly bigger palate and a smoother texture. Even then, some Belgians add a touch of grenadine, as though making a red *kir*. The Rodenbach brewery is in Roeselare (in French Rouliers), the centre of an agricultural area.

Several breweries in West Flanders produce beers similar to those of Rodenbach, but none with quite such a distinctive character. Perhaps the best examples are Petrus, from Bavikhove; and Ouden Tripel, from Bockor, of Bellegem.

St Louis

Using casks obtained in the traditional region of production, and containing resident wild yeasts, the Van Honsebrouck brewery, of Ingelmunster, West Flanders, has for almost 30 years made beer in the *lambic* style under the brand-name St Louis. The widely marketed examples were sweetened and rather bland. In 1993, the brewery launched **Gueuze Fond Tradition★★→★★★**, unsweetened and more traditional in style. This beer has a very refreshing acidity and a spritzy finish. Even critics of Van Honsebrouck's piratical approach are inclined to look kindly on the brewery's strong (7.2; 9) ale **Brigand**★★→★★★, bronze in colour, with lots of Saaz hoppiness and some yeast bite. In 1986, the Van Honsebrouck family bought Ingelmunster Castle, and has since been using it to bottle-condition a malty, rich, port-like **Kasteel Bier**★★★ (9.6; 11), similar in style to Thomas Hardy's Ale. The castle (3 Station Straat) has its own tavern.

St Sixtus
See **Westvleteren, Trappist Monastery of St Sixtus**.

Sezoens
While seasonal, *saison*, beers for summer are a recognized style in the French-speaking part of Belgium, they are less evident in Flemish tradition. **Sezoens**★★★ has the same connotation, but is the registered trademark of a distinctive and delightful product from the Martens brewery, in the Limburg village of Bocholt. It has a delightful label, too, showing a well-clad personification of winter handing the beer to a sunny "Mr Summer".

Sezoens is a pale, golden top-fermenting brew of 13.5 Plato, with 4 percent alcohol by weight; 5 by volume. It has a fresh, hoppy aroma, a firm, clean, notably dry palate, and plenty of hop character throughout, especially in the finish. The principal version of this beer is filtered, but there is also a bottle-conditioned interpretation, which emerges with a softer, fruitier, spicier, character. Martens also produces an amber-red counterpart called **Sezoens Quattro**★★★. This odd name is intended to suggest The Four Seasons. The beer has a touch of coffeeish maltiness, and makes a delightful apéritif.

Devotees who track these beers down to their far-flung home village should arrange in advance to visit Brouwerij Martens Museum (32 Dorp Straat, Bocholt, B3598, ☎011–461705), which is open by appointment only. In Brussels, Sezoens is the speciality of the café De Ultieme Hallucinatie (316 Konings Straat), which is in an Art Nouveau house near the Botanical Gardens.

Stropken
The first Stropken was assertively spicy, with a hint of anise, but this subsequently yielded to a more refined Grand Cru version. **Stropken Grand Cru**★★→★★★ is a well-made, top-fermenting beer, with an original gravity of 17.5 Plato and an alcohol content of around 5.5 percent by weight; 6.75 by volume. The name Stropken is an ironic Flemish reference to the halters that the rebellious Lords of Ghent were obliged to wear by Emperor Charles in the 16th century. Stropken, originally produced as the house brew at the Hopduvel specialist beer café in Ghent, is now produced under contract by the Slaghmuylder brewery also in East Flanders. Slaghmuylder produces well-made abbey-style brews.

Westmalle, Trappist Monastery

The classic example of the pale, Triple style of Belgian Trappist brew is produced by the monastery of Westmalle, a village northeast of Antwerp. The monastery, established in 1821, has brewed since its early days, though it was slow in making its beer available commercially, and remains one of the most withdrawn of the Trappist monasteries. Visits are not encouraged, though the brewery can sometimes be seen by appointment. The smart, traditional copper brewhouse is in a strikingly 1930s building. It produces three beers. The "Single", confusingly known as **Extra**, is available only to the brothers; a shame, since this pale, top-fermenting brew is a product of some delicacy. The **Double★★** is dark brown, malty, but quite dry. It has an original gravity of around 16 Plato and an alcohol content of about 5.5 by weight; just under 7 by volume. The **Triple★★★★** offers an unusual combination of features, being a strong, top-fermenting beer of pale, almost Pilsener, colour. Its mash is entirely of Pilsener malts from Germany and France but, in the classic procedure, candy sugar is added in the kettle. There are three hopping stages, using Styrian Goldings, a number of German varieties and Saaz. The brew is fermented with a hybrid house yeast, then has a secondary fermentation of one to three months in tanks, and is given a priming of sugar and a further dosage of yeast before being bottled. It is warm-conditioned in the bottle before being released from a gravity of around 20 Plato, it emerges with an alcohol content of around 7.2 percent by weight; 9 by volume. With its faintly citric fruitiness, its rounded body and its alcoholic "kick", the Triple expresses a very full character within six months of leaving the monastery, though bottles from 1927 are still in good condition. Westmalle is jealous of the individuality of its product, but several secular breweries produce beers in a similar style, using the designation Triple (in Flemish, Tripel). Good examples include Vieille Villers Triple from Van Assche; Witkap from Slaghmuylder and the slightly fuller-coloured Affligem from De Smedt.

Westvleteren, Trappist Monastery of St Sixtus

One of Belgium's strongest beers comes from by far the smallest of the country's five monastery breweries. This is the monastery of St Sixtus, at the hamlet of Westvleteren, in a rustic corner of Flanders, near the French border and between the coast and the town best known by its French name Ypres (Ieper in Flemish). Although it overlooks a hop garden, the monastery produces beers in which malty sweetness is the predominant characteristic, with spicy and fruity tones also notable. There is no Single, and the basic beer, with a green crown-cork, is called **Double★★**. Then comes the **Special★★** (red crown-cork), drier, with hints of vanilla and licorice, a gravity of around 15 Plato and an alcohol content of about 4.8 percent by weight; 6 by volume. The **Extra★★** (blue) has more fruity, acidic tones and some alcohol character

(20 Plato; 6.4; 8). Finally, the strongest beer in the monastery (and the country) is the **Abbot★★★★** (yellow), very full-bodied, creamy, soft and sweet. This is sometimes known as a 12-degree beer, its gravity in the Belgian scale. That works out at about 30 Plato (1120) and the beer has around 8.48 percent alcohol by weight; 10.6 by volume.

These beers can be bought by the case at the monastery and sampled next door in the Café De Vrede, but they are less easy to find elsewhere. For many years, the abbey permitted a nearby secular brewery to use the name St Sixtus on a similar range of beers. This agreement has now been terminated. The secular brewer has responded by dropping the "Saint" but retains the "Sixtus". The brewery is itself called St Bernard and is in Watou, near Poperinge. Its local rival Van Eecke produces a similar range of tasty yeasty, abbey-style brews, and a hoppy speciality called **Poperings Hommelbier★★→★★★**.

BRUSSELS AND BRABANT

Within the extraordinarily colourful tapestry of Belgian brewing, the most vivid shades are to be found in the country's central province, Brabant, and especially around the capital city, Brussels. If the Germanic north of Europe and the Romantic south intertwine in Belgium, it is in the province of Brabant and the city of Brussels that the knot is tied. As the nearest thing Europe has to a federal capital, Brussels has some lofty French kitchens, but it also takes pride in the heartier *carbonades* of what it terms "*cuisine de bière*", in which several restaurants specialize. On its Gallic avenues, it has some splendid Art Nouveau cafés, but the Grand' Place and the older neighbourhoods are Flemish in flavour and so is the beer.

To the east, the Flemish village of Hoegaarden is the home of the Belgian style of "white" beer. Louvain (in Flemish, Leuven) is the home of Stella Artois and the biggest brewing city in Belgium. The greatest splash of colour by far is, however, Brussels. Although it has one conventional brewery, Brussels is the local market for the *lambic* family, the most unusual beers in the world, with palate characteristics that range from a hint of pine kernels to a forkful of Brie cheese. *Lambic* is produced in the city itself and, in great variety by a cluster of specialist brewers and blenders in the Senne Valley.

The Senne is a small river that runs diagonally, often underground, from northeast to southwest through Brussels. There used to be *lambic* breweries on both sides of the city and even today *lambic* is served as a local speciality on the eastern edge of the city at Jezus-Eik. South of Brussels it is served at Hoeillaart-Overijse, where Belgium's (dessert) grapes are grown. However, it is on the western edge of Brussels that production is concentrated today spreading out into the nearby scatter of farming villages collectively known as Payottenland. Traditional *lambic*-makers brew only in the winter, and the number in production at any one time varies. So does the extent to which traditional methods are still used.

There are a couple of *lambic* breweries within the western boundary of Brussels itself and a further eight or nine active ones in Payottenland. Also, four or five companies contract or buy brews which they then ferment, mature or blend in their own cellars. A further two or three breweries beyond the traditional area also produce beers of this type (notably St Louis and Jacobins, both from West Flanders). With a dozen or more houses producing *lambic* beers to varying degrees of authenticity, and seven or eight derivative styles, some available in more than one age, there are usually about 100 products of this type on the market, though many are obtainable only on a very limited scale and in specialist cafés.

The *lambic* family are not everybody's glass of beer, but no one with a keen interest in alcoholic drink would find them anything less than fascinating. In their "wildness" and unpredictability, these are exciting brews. At their best, they are the meeting point between beer and wine. At their worst, they offer a taste of history, as though one of those stoneware jars of beer had been lifted from the canvas of a Bruegel or Brouwer.

The basic *lambic* is a spontaneously fermenting wheat beer, made from a turbid mash of 30–40 percent wheat and the rest barley, The barley is only lightly malted; the wheat not at all. The boil can last three to six hours and the brew is hopped very heavily but with blossoms that have been aged to reduce their bitterness. The hops are used for their traditional purpose as a preservative; their bitterness is not wanted in a fruity wheat beer. In the classic method, the brew is taken upstairs to the gable of the roof, where vents are left open so that the wild yeasts of the Senne Valley may enter. The brew lies uncovered in an open vessel, and consummation takes place. The brew is allowed to be aroused in this way for only one night, ideally an autumn evening, and only the wild yeasts of the Senne Valley are said to provide the proper impregnation. After its night upstairs the brew is barrelled in hogsheads, where primary and secondary fermentations take place, further stimulated by microflora resident in the wood. For this reason, *lambic* brewers are reluctant to disturb the dust that collects among the hogsheads, which are racked in galleries with no temperature control.

Brewers outside the traditional *lambic* area who wish to make a beer of this type have been known to acquire a barrel of a Senne Valley vintage to use as a starter. In the classic method the brewer never pitches any yeast. No doubt is was originally just a question of supply, but some barrels used in the maturation of *lambic* originally contained claret, port or sherry – the last reminiscent of whisky-making in Scotland. Like the whisky-maker, the *lambic*-brewer wants his barrels to respond to the natural changes in temperature.

The primary fermentation takes only five or six days, the secondary six months. If a brew of less than six months is made available for sale, it is customarily identified as young (*jong*) or "fox" (*vos*) *lambic*. The classic maturation period, however, is "one or two summers" and occasionally three.

Terminology is imprecise, not least because of the two languages in use (and Flemish manifests itself in several dialects). *Lambic* may appear as *lambiek* and both the beer and yeast are said to derive their name from the village of Lembeek, in Payottenland. In its basic form *lambic* is hard to find, but it is served on draught in some cafés in the producing area. The young version can be intensely dry, sour, cloudy and still, like an English "scrumpy" or rustic cider. The older version will have mellowed, settled, and perhaps be *pétillant*.

A blended version of young *lambic* sweetened with dark candy sugar is known as *faro*. If this is then diluted with water, it becomes *mars*. Sometimes cafés provide sugar and a muddler. If the sugared version is bottled, it is effectively chaptalized and develops a complex of sweetness in the start, fruity sharpness in the finish. If young and old versions of the basic beer are blended in the cask to start yet further fermentation, the result, sparkling and medium-dry, is known as *gueuze-lambic*. This term is also sometimes used to describe a version that is blended and conditioned in the bottle, though such a product is properly known simply as *gueuze* and is the most widely available member of the family. The bottle-conditioning may take three to nine months, though the beer will continue to improve for one or two years after leaving the brewery and will certainly last for five. Until recent years, small *lambic* brewers did not use labels. They simply put a dab of whitewash on each bottle to show which way up it had been stored. Now labels are required by law but some of the old whitewashed bottled are still in the cellars of cafés. They are likely to contain vintage beers, made at a time when all aspects of production were more traditional.

The version of lambic in which cherries have been macerated in the cask is known as *kriek*. If raspberries are used, its is called *frambozen* or *framboise*. In recent years some very untraditional fruits have also been used. The cherry version is a very traditional summer drink in the Brussels area, and the original method is to make it with whole fruit, which ferment down to the pits. Another technique is to macerate whole fruit in juice and add the mixture to the brew. The original beer is brewed from a conventional gravity of 12–13 Plato (1048–52), though the density and alcohol content varies according to dilution, blending and maceration. A basic *lambic* has only about 3.6 percent alcohol by weight; 4.4 by volume. A *gueuze* might have 4.4; 4.5. A *kriek* can go up to 4.8; 6.

Even with all of these variations at their disposal some cafés choose to offer their own blend, perhaps to offset the sourness of a young *lambic* with fruitiness of a mature one. Such a blend may be offered as the *panaché* of the house. These beers are sometimes accompanied by a hunk of brown bread with cheese, onions and radishes. A spready *fromage blanc*, made from skimmed milk, is favoured. Or a salty *Brusselsekaas* might be appropriate. The beers are served at a cool cellar temperature of around 50°F (10°C).

As if such colour were not enough, there are also a number of ale breweries in Brabant, especially northwest of Brussels.

Where to drink

One of the newest speciality cafés, on the main thoroughfare of Brussels, is Beer Street (it is named in English), at 119 Bvd Anspach, opposite the Stock Exchange (La Bourse, in French). Beer Street has more than 70 Belgian brews on tap.

Behind Beer Street is the St Catherine's quarter, with bars, restaurants and a street market. At 1 Place du Jardin aux Fleurs is In 't Spinnekopke, where it is possible simply to drink, but also to dine on *cuisine à la bière*. (On Saturdays, this bar-restaurant opens only in the evening, and is closed on Sundays.)

On the streets that frame the Stock Exchange are two famous Art Nouveau bars, Cirio and Falstaff. Behind the Stock Exchange is Rue Tabora; at No 11, down an alley, is A La Bécasse, serving sweetish *lambics* from Timmermans and De Neve, and hearty local snacks. Worth a visit for its "Dutch kitchen" style. Just beyond Rue Tabora is the Grand' Place, with several terrace cafés. A short walk from Grand' Place, at 7 Rue Montagne aux Herbes Potagères, is the 1920s café Mort Subite, serving the beer of that name. This café inspired a ballet by Maurice Béjart.

A lightly fruity "White" beer and a rich dark ale are made at the brewpub Le Miroir (24 Place Reine Astrid) in the Jette district. Le Miroir is also a speciality beer café, and offers beer-friendly hot food.

De Neve Lambic and **Girardin Gueuze** can be sampled in the region of production at In De Rare Vos (22 Markt Plaats), Schepdaal. Tiny bar at the front, dining rooms behind, and meals from mussels to horse (closed Tuesday, Wednesday; open noon other days). In the aptly named village of Beersel, the café Drie Fonteinen (3 Herman Teirlinck Plein) blends its own **Gueuze** and has a stylish kitchen. The nearby In de Drie Bronnen (31 Hoog Straat) blends its own **Kriek**. (Closed Monday and Tuesday.)

In Brabant's big brewing town of Louvain/Leuven, the Domus Taverne (8 Tiense Straat) makes its own "White" beer and a honey brew. Gambrinus (13 Grote Markt) is worth a visit for its 1890s interior.

There are many delightful places in which to drink beer in Brussels and other Belgian cities and towns, and these are described in a regularly updated guide by the local branch of the Campaign for Real Ale (Box 5, 67 Rue des Atrebates, Brussels, Belgium B1040).

Artois

A major European brewing company that is the biggest in Belgium. The name derives from a family, not the region of northern France. **Stella Artois★★** is a Pilsener-style beer with a hint of new-mown hay in the nose. Artois, based in Leuven, also produces a "Danish"-style premium lager called **Loburg★**. Products of its subsidiaries include **Vieux Temps★** and **Ginder★**, both Belgian-style ales, and the **Leffe★★** abbey-style ales. Stella and its erstwhile rival Jupiler now form a joint company called Interbrew.

Belle-Vue

In so far as the phrase mass-market can be applied to *lambic* beers, it describes the relatively mainstream products of Belle-Vue, which is owned by Interbrew. These bland, sweetened, blends have always contained a proportion of the excellent traditional *lambic* from the company's older brewery, in the Brussels district of Molenbeek. This brewery, at 43 Quai du Hainaut, can now be visited (☎Brussels 410–19–35 for details). Its sample room offers an unsweetened **Gueuze**, with much more attack and dryness, called **Séléction Lambic★★→★★★**. This version can also be found in some favoured cafés. Interbrew/Belle Vue also owns the De Neve brewery, in Schepdaal. It no longer brews, but continues to ferment, mature and blend, at least for the moment. The *lambics* made at Molenbeek are quite hard, with a touch of oakiness, while those from Schepdaal are fresher, crisper and more lemony-tasting.

Boon

A well-respected brewer and blender of *lambic* beers, Frank Boon (pronounced "Bone") has contributed much to the revival of interest in *lambic* styles since he started to blend his own products some years ago at the former De Vit brewery in, appropriately, Lembeek. **Boon's Lambic★★★★** beers are aromatic, very lively, fruity and dry. He makes a speciality of offering a variety of ages and even of *caves*. His speciality blends are labelled **Mariage Parfait★★★→★★★★**. Apart from cafés, the only pure blender still operating is Hanssens, of Dworp. Its fruity, rhubarby, blends are well worth seeking out.

Cantillon

Tiny, working "museum brewery" producing robustly authentic *lambic* beers in Brussels. Well worth a visit at 56 Rue Gheude, Anderlecht (☎5214928). Its beers are smooth, with a sustained head, assertively dry and with a sharply fruity finish. Its vintage-dated **Lambic Grand Cru★★★→★★★★** and **Framboise Rosé de Gambrinus★★★★** are classics.

Girardin

Growing its own wheat, and grinding some of it between stones, Girardin is indeed a traditional enterprise, though one so conservative that it does not readily accept visitors to its farm and brewery, at St Ulriks Kapelle. None of its **Gueuze** is filtered, and the version with a black label is not centrifuged, either. **Gueuze Girardin★★★★** is immensely complex, with suggestions of apples, sherry, wood (cedar?) and hay.

Haacht

Beyond its everyday beers (usually on the malty side), this brewery, in Boortmeerbeek, has made some effort to promote a **Gildenbier★★★**. This is an unusual, Belgian style of top-fermenting dark brown beer that is notable for its rich sweetness. It may have limited application – as a restorative perhaps – but is a part of tradition. This example has a hint of iron in the nose and licorice-toffee tones in the finish. The style was originally local to Diest, not far away on the northeast border of Brabant.

Hoegaarden "White"

Hoegaarden is a village in the far east of Brabant that is famous for cloudy "white" wheat beers. There were once 30 breweries in the area producing beers in this style. The last closed in the mid-1950s and a decade later a revivalist brewer recommenced production on a small scale. This unlikely venture has proved to be both a critical and commercial success. The brewery is called De Kluis and the beer **Hoegaarden**★★★→★★★★. This brew is produced from equal proportions of raw wheat and unmalted barley. It is spiced with coriander and curaçao, both of which were more commonly used before the universal adoption of the hop as a seasoning. A top-fermenting yeast is used and there is a further dosage in the bottle, with a priming of sugar. The nature of the grist and the use of a slowly flocculating yeast in the bottle help ensure the characteristic "white" cloudiness. The beer has a conventional gravity of 12 Plato, and emerges with an alcohol content of 3.84 percent by weight; 4.8 by volume. As it ages, it gains a refractive quality known as "double shine", and its fruity sourness gives way to a honeyish sweetness.

A similar beer, aromatic and pale but stronger (18.4 Plato. 7;8.7) and made exclusively from barley malt, is called **Hoegaarden Grand Cru**★★★. As its name suggests, a beer of nobility and complexity.

Meanwhile, the Hoegaarden brewery's taste for experimentation is unquenchable. Another of its products is called Forbidden Fruit. **Verboden Vrucht**★★→★★★ (Le Fruit Défendu) is a claret-coloured, all-malt, strong ale of 19.5 Plato (7.2; 9), which combines a spicing of coriander with a hefty helping of Challenger and Styrian aroma hops. The spicy, sweet fruitiness is very evident in the aroma, and the earthy hoppiness in the palate. A very sexy strong ale, as its label implies. There are several further colourful specialities. In funding its growth the brewery sought partners, and is now owned by Interbrew. As production has grown the beer has lost some of its complexity. The original is now challenged by the "White", made by founder Pierre Celis at his new brewery in Austin, Texas.

Lindemans

This classic Brabant farmhouse brewery in *lambic* country at Vlezenbeek seems an unlikely location from which to attach world markets. Nonetheless, its craftsman-made **Faro**★★, **Gueuze**★★, **Kriek**★★→★★★ and **Framboise**★★→★★★ are variously well known in The Netherlands, France and the USA. In gaining popularity, they have become much sweeter. Now a more traditional range is to be launched under the rubric **Cuvée René** (the proprietor's Christian name). This is eagerly awaited.

Mort Subite

A dice game played in the bar gave its name to the famous Café Mort Subite, in Brussels, and to the house's *lambic* beers, which are made in Kobbegem. The name may mean "Sudden Death", but *lambics* are too light to be lethal.

The brewery in Kobbegem was established by the De Keersmaeker family, beer-makers since the 1700s, and they have in recent years run it as part of the Alken-Maes group. Its herbal-tasting **De Keersmaeker Faro★★★** (actually a *lambic*) can be found in cafés in the area.

The unfiltered **Gueuze Mort Subite★★★** is labelled to indicate re-fermentation in the bottle. The filtered version is sweeter and less interesting.

The De Keersmaekers also produce a *lambic* that is fermented and matured in the old Eylenbosch brewery, at Schepdaal. This has a nuttier character.

Palm

Typically Belgian ales are produced by this medium-sized family brewery in the hamlet of Steenhuffel, to the northwest of Brussels. In Belgium a top-fermenting beer of no regional style is often identified simply as a "special" to distinguish it from a Pilsener. Hence **Spéciale Palm★★**, exported to the USA under the more precise name Palm Ale. It has an original gravity of around 11.25 Plato and its yeast is a combination of three strains. Palm Ale has a bright, amber colour; a light-to-medium body; a fruity, bitter-orange aroma and a tart finish. Other products include the dry-hopped, bottle-conditioned **Aerts 1900★★★**, an outstanding example of the style.

Timmermans

Widely available *lambic* beers made at Itterbeek in Payottenland. Timmermans' **Lambic★★→★★★**, **Gueuze★★→★★★** and **Kriek★★→★★★** are fruity and acidic but all three are easily drinkable.

De Troch

Very small *lambic* brewery in Wambeek, still using a coal-fired kettle. It still produces an unfiltered **Gueuze★★★**, on the dark side, full-bodied, with lots of apple-like notes, but finishing light. Its more commercial fruit beers are easier to find.

Vanderlinden

Lambic beers, produced at Halle in Payottenland. Vanderlinden's **Vieux Foudre Gueuze★★→★★★** has a full colour, a dense, rocky head and a palate that is smooth and dry, with a sour-apples tartness. **Vieux Foudre Kriek★★→★★★** is lively, with lots of aroma, starting with hints of sweetness and finishing with a dry bitterness. The brewery also has a fruity **Framboise★★→★★★**. Its house speciality **Duivel★★★** is an odd combination of a *lambic* with a conventional top-fermenting beer.

Vandervelden

Piney-tasting Oud Beersel★★★ *lambics* from a museum-style brewery and café in Beersel (232 Laarheid Straat).

FRENCH-SPEAKING BELGIUM

Perhaps it is the softness of the language: summer beers called *saisons*, winter-warmers like Cuvée de l'Ermitage and Chimay Grande Réserve, apéritifs like Abbaye d'Orval. Or maybe the rolling, wooded countryside, occasionally hiding a brewery in its folds. The French-speaking south seems a restful, contemplative place in which to drink. Just as there are fewer people in the south, so the breweries and beer styles are thinner on the ground, but they are rich in character.

When, as sometimes happens, a beer menu in Belgium lists "Wallonian specialities" (in whichever language), it is referring to *saisons* and monastery beers from four provinces. Among these, the province of Hainaut (with interesting industrial archaeology around the cities of Mons and Charleroi) has the most breweries, including the celebrated one at the abbey of Chimay. The province of Namur, named after its pleasant and historically interesting capital city, has the Rochefort monastery brewery. The province of Liège, also named after its principal city, has the Jupiler brewery, producing the biggest-selling Pilsener in Belgium.

Where to drink

The best base for an exploration of Wallonia is the handsome and historically interesting town of Namur, on the River Meuse. This has an outstanding beer-bar called L'Eblouissant, at 27 Rue de l'Armée Grouchy. Open noon; 7.00 Saturday. Closed Sundays except for performances of folk music, often Irish. The town also has a beer shop, La Table de Wallonie (6 Rue de la Halle).

Other recommended cafés in French-speaking Belgium include: in Charleroi, Beau Lieu (3 Rue du Commerce); in Liège, La Vaudrée, 149 Rue St Gilles; in Mons, L'Alambic (25 Place du Marché aux Herbes) and La Podo (43 Rue de la Coupe).

Bush Beer

This distinctive and extra-strong brew takes its name from that of the family Dubuisson (*buisson* means "bush") by whom it is made, in the village of Pipaix in the province of Hainaut. The family renamed the beer Scaldis for the American market, to avoid conflict with the US brewers Busch. Scaldis was the Latin name for the River Scheldt.

Under either name, **Bush Beer/Scaldis★★★** might be more accurately described as an ale. It has a copper colour, a gravity of 24.5 Plato (1098) and an alcohol content of 9.6;12. Produced with a top-fermenting yeast and filtered but not pasteurized, it emerges with a chewy, malty, perhaps nutty, palate and with a hoppy dryness in the finish. A Christmas version is dry-hopped.

Chimay Trappist Monastery

The best-known and biggest monastery brewery in Belgium. Its products are, in the monastic tradition, top-fermenting strong ales, conditioned in the bottle. Within this tradition, the Chimay beers have a house character that is fruity, both in the intense aroma and the palate. Beyond that, each has its own features. Each is distinguished by its own colour of crown cork (*capsule*). The basic beer, **Chimay Red★★★**, has a gravity of 6.2 Belgian degrees, 15.5 Plato, 1063, with 5.5 percent alcohol by weight; 7 by volume. It has a full, copper colour, a notably soft palate and a hint of blackcurrant. The quite different **Chimay White★★★** has a gravity of 7 Belgian degrees; 17.35 Plato (1071) and an alcohol content of 6.3; 8. It has a firm, dry body, slender for its gravity, with plenty of hop character in the finish and a quenching hint of acidity. This noble beer is very highly regarded by the brewery, but it does not have the most typically Chimay character. A return to type is represented by the **Chimay Blue★★★★**, which has a gravity of 8; 19.62 (1081) and an alcohol content of 7.1; 9. This has, again, that characteristically Chimay depth of aromatic fruitiness – a Zinfandel, or even a port, among beers. Chimay Blue is vintage-dated on the crown cork. If it is kept in a dark, cool place (ideally 65°F/19°C, but definitely not refrigerated), it will become markedly smoother after a year and sometimes continues to improve for two or three, drying slightly as it progresses. After five years, it could lose a little character, but some samples have flourished for a quarter of a century. A version of Chimay Blue in a corked 75cl bottle is called **Grande Réserve**. The larger bottle size and different method of sealing seem to mature the beer in a softer manner. With different surface areas and air space, a slightly larger yeast presence and the very slight porosity of cork this is not fanciful.

The full name of the abbey is Notre Dame de Scourmont, after the hill on which it stands near the hamlet of Forges, close to the small town of Chimay in the province of Hainaut. The monastery was founded in 1850, during the post-Napoleonic restoration of abbey life. The monks began to brew not long after, in 1861–62. They were the first monks in Belgium to sell their brew commercially, introduced the designation "Trappist Beer" and in the period after World War II perfected the style.

La Chouffe

Visitors to the Ardennes love calling in at this farmhouse site for a beer and a meal at La Chouffe micro and pub. It is at Achouffe, in a spectacular valley near Houffalize, just north of Bastogne. The chief beers, both with a clean, soft, lightly malty fruitiness, are the pale **La Chouffe** (6.4; 8) and the darker, winier, **McChouffe**, which is of Scottish inspiration.

Cuvée de l'Ermitage

Hermitages were the first homes of monks in the western world and there were many in the forests of Hainaut in the early Middle Ages, but no one is certain which of two sites gave their name to this brew. It is certainly worthy of being enjoyed in a reflective moment, though not necessarily to the ascetic taste. **Cuvée de l'Ermitage★★★** is a very dark and strong all-malt brew of 18.7 Plato, with an alcohol content of 6 percent by weight; 7.5 by volume. It is produced from three malts and heavily hopped with an interesting combination of Kent Goldings and Hallertaus (both for bitterness) and North-ern Brewer and Saaz (both for aroma). It has a distinctively creamy bouquet, a smooth start, with hints of sweetness, then a surprising dryness in the finish – almost the sappiness of an Armagnac. Cuvée is the local speciality of the old Union brewery at Jumet, on the edge of Charleroi. The brewery produces a range of top-fermenting beers of its parent, Maes.

Jupiler

The biggest-selling Pilsener beer in Belgium takes its name from Jupille, near Liège, where it is produced by a brewery that for many years rejoiced in the odd name Piedboeuf. In recent years, the company itself has become known as Jupiler. Although it has lost some of its hoppiness, **Jupiler★** remains dry and soft and is a pleasant enough mass-market beer.

Orval Trappist Monastery

There is a purity of conception about both the brewery and the monastery of Orval. The brewery provides its own distinctive interpretation of the monastic style and offers just one beer: **Orval★★★★**. This brew gains its unusual orangey colour from the use of three malts produced to its own specification, plus white candy sugar in the kettle; its aromatic, apéritif bitterness derives from the use of Hallertau and (more especially) Styrian Goldings, not only in the kettle but also in dry-hopping; its characterful acidity comes from its own single-cell yeast in its primary and bottle fermentations and a blend of several bottom cultures in its secondary. As to which of these procedures is most important in imparting the *goût d'Orval*, there may be some debate. The triple fermentation process is certainly important, but the dry-hopping is perhaps the critical factor. The beer has an original gravity of 13.5–14 Plato (1055+) and emerges with an alcohol content of more than 5.0 percent by weight, around 6.2 by volume. Its secondary fermentation lasts for five to seven weeks, at a relatively warm temperature of around 60°F (15°C). Its bottle-conditioning, regarded by the brewery as a third fermentation, lasts for two months, again at warm temperatures. The beer should be kept in a dark place, ideally at a natural cellar temperature. If it was bought in a shop, give the beer a few days to recover its equilibrium and pour gently. It should improve for about a year and, although its character may then diminish, it could keep for five years.

This is a short period in the life of an abbey that was founded in 1070 by Benedictines from Calabria, rebuilt in the 12th century by early Cistercians from Champagne and sacked in several conflicts along the way, in the 17th century leaving most of the ruins that stand today. From the 18th century, there are records of brewing having taken place in the restored abbey, which was then sacked in the French Revolution. The present monastery, with its dramatic, dream-like purity of line, subsumes Romanesque-Burgundian influences in a design of the late 1920s and 1930s. The monastery makes its beer, crusty brown bread and two cheeses, of the Port Salut and (in a somewhat distant interpretation) Cheddar types, and sells them to tourists in its gift shop.

Meanwhile, in its corner of the province of Luxembourg, not far from the small town of Florenville, the "valley of gold" dreams. Legend says that Countess Mathilda of Tuscany lost a gold ring in the lake in the valley. When a fish recovered the ring for her, the countess was so grateful that she gave the land to God for the foundation of the monastery. The fish with the golden ring is now the emblem of Orval and its beer.

No other beer can be said to match the character of Orval but there are secular products in a broadly similar style. One example from this part of Belgium is the beer of the micro-brewery at Montignies sur Roc. And from Flanders, there is Augustijn, produced by the Van Steenbergen brewery.

Rochefort Trappist Monastery

Perhaps the least known of the Trappist breweries, but one that has gained in reputation in recent years. The monastery's name is Notre Dame de Saint-Rémy, and it is at Rochefort, east of Namur. The beers are identified by their gravity in Belgian degrees. **Rochefort 6★★→★★★** (6; 7.5) has a russet colour and a slightly herbal palate. **Rochefort 8★★★** (7.3; 9.3) is tawnier and fruitier, with a suggestion of figs. **Rochefort 10★★★→★★★★** (9; 11.3) is dark brown and rich, with depths of fruity and chocolatey flavours.

Saison 1900

Its date recalling its brewery's height of production, during the digging of huge quarries nearby, this is a splendidly quenching beer. **Saison 1900★★★** is full-bodied, well-hopped, and very evidently spiced with ginger. It is produced by the coal-fired brewery Lefèbvre, at Quenast, just across the border from Hainaut into Brabant.

Saison Dupont

Farmhouse brewery specialising in variations on the Saison theme, at Tourpes, near Leuze, in the province of Hainaut. Its principal product, **Saison Dupont★★★** has a big, rocky, creamy head; a sharp, refreshing attack; and a long, notably hoppy, dry finish.

Saison de Pipaix/Brasserie à Vapeur

Steam-powered brewery, operated at weekends by school-teacher Jean-Louis Dits and his wife Vinciane Corbisier, at

Pipaix, also near Leuze. **Saison de Pipaix★★★ →★★★★**, which has a very fresh, orangey, character, contains six "botanicals", including anise, black pepper and a medicinal lichen. Such experiments have extended even to the use of ash leaves, as prescribed by the Benedictine Abbess Hildegarde (1098–1179).

Saison Régal

From a relatively rustic brewery, but middle-sized by Belgian standards, at Purnode, in the province of Namur. **Saison Régal★★** is firm, well attenuated, with a teasing balance between aromatic hoppiness and fruitiness.

Saison de Silly

Farmhouse brewery at the village of Silly, in Hainaut. Its **Saison de Silly★★★** is notable for being aged in the traditional way, in metal tanks for about a year. This imparts a distinctive wineyness and tartness. Unfortunately, this example is not bottle-conditioned.

THE GRAND DUCHY OF LUXEMBOURG

Although it shares its name with a province of Belgium, and has economic ties with that country, the Grand Duchy of Luxembourg is a sovereign state. In the matter of beer, the Grand Duchy leans in the other direction, towards Germany. It even claims that its Purity Law is similar to Germany's, though it does, in fact, permit adjuncts. The typical range of a Luxembourgeoise brewery includes a relatively mild Pilsener; a slightly more potent brew, perhaps in the Export style; and a bottom-fermenting strong beer, some-times seasonal.

Luxembourg has five brewing companies, each with just one plant. The biggest, just, is Diekirch, which has a fairly big-bodied, clean-tasting, all-malt **Pils★★**, with a good hop aroma. There have also been occasional sightings of a stronger (4.9 by weight; 6.1 by volume) pale, bottom-fermenting beer called **Premium★★** from Diekirch.

The second largest brewery is Mousel et Clausen, with the Royal-Altmünster brand. Then Brasserie Nationale, of Bascharage, with the Bofferding and Funck-Bricher labels. The small Simon brewery, of Wiltz, produces some excellent beers. So does the tiniest of them all, Battin, of Esch, with its Gambrinus label.

FRANCE

Being true lovers of food and drink, the French enjoy not only wine but also beer. They have two brewing regions: the North, especially French Flanders, around the city of Lille, specializes in *bières de garde*, similar in style to some Belgian ales; and the East, centred on Strasbourg, makes a lighter interpretation of German lagers. Breweries in both traditions have in recent years begun to produce malty *bières de mars* – seasonal March beers – which are something of a new fashion.

The national brewers are Kronenbourg/Kanterbrau (with the same parent), along with Mützig, 33 and Pelforth (owned by Heineken), but there are also 20-odd smaller companies, ranging from sizable independents to the tiny Brasserie Bobtail, which makes yeasty Anglo-Belgian specialities at St Séverin, in the Périgord. There are also about 15 brewpubs. A pioneer was Les Brasseurs, making Belgian-accented beers on the railway station square in Lille; one of the more recent is the Frog and Rosbif, producing English ales at 116 Rue St Denis, Paris.

Annoeullin
Family-owned brewery at the town of the same name, between Lille and Lens. Produces **Pastor Ale**★★→★★★, which, despite its name, is a spicy, fruity, *bière de garde*; and **L'Angélus**★★★, a perfumy wheat beer.

Bailleux/Au Baron
Brewpub on the Belgian border at Gussignies, N of Bavay. Its **Saison Médard**★★→★★★, beautifully balanced and long, might better be described as a *bière de garde*.

Castelain
Sweetish *bières de garde* under the name Ch'ti (local patois for a Northerner), from a brewery at Bénifontaine, near Lens. **Ch'ti Brune**★★→★★★, with port-like notes, is the best balanced. The fruitier **Saint Arnoldus**★★★ (6; 7.5) is bottled *sur lie* (on a yeast sediment).

La Choulette
Farmhouse brewery making *bières de garde* at Hordain, S of Valenciennes. **Sans Culottes**★★★→★★★★ has a yeasty note like that of champagne. The darker **La Choulette**★★★ is softer. **Brassin Robespierre**★★★ is golden, smooth and strong.

De Clerck
Flemish-sounding brewery in Peronne, Picardy, producing the dryish, fruity, *bière de garde* **Pot Flamand**★★→★★★.

Duyck
This family brews France's best-known *bière de garde*, **Jenlain**★★★, at the hamlet of the same name, near Valenciennes. The beer is notably spicy, with suggestions of vanilla and anise.

Enfants de Gayant
The malty **Lutèce Bière de Paris★★** and the strong, golden **Bière du Démon★★→★★★** (9.6; 12) are produced by this brewery at Douai.

Fischer/Pecheur
Sizable independent lager brewery near Strasbourg; also owns Adelshoffen. Very commercially inclined. Products include **Adlescott★★→★★★**, a lightly smoky *bière au malt whisky*, and a peatier version called **Adelscott Noir★★★**.

Meteor
Independent lager brewery at Hochfelden, 20 miles from Strasbourg. Products include a copper-coloured Vienna-style lager called **Mortimer★★→★★★** (6.4; 8), very smooth and malty but well balanced.

Pelforth
Once called the Pelican brewery (the suffix was added to imply *fort*, meaning strong). Produces the aromatically malty dark lager **Pelforth Brune★★→★★★** (5.2; 6.5); a roastier **Porter★★**; and the top-fermenting French version of **George Killian★★★** (5.2; 6.5) "Irish Red Ale". The brewery, near Lille, is owned by Heineken.

Réserve du Brasseur
The brand-name of this lightly malty *bière de garde* is better known than its brewer. **Réserve du Brasseur★★** is made by the St Arnould group, of St Omer.

St Sylvestre
Classically artisanal brewery at St Sylvestre, between Steen-voorde and Hazebrouck, near the Belgian border. Its **Trois Monts★★★★** is a top-fermenting *bière de garde* with a slightly sour, winey, character. **Bière des Templiers★★★→★★★★**, served *sur lie*, is fruity, creamy and sappy. Both have around 6.0 percent alcohol by weight; 8.5 by volume.

Schutzenberger
Independent lager brewery in Strasbourg. Products include a pleasantly hoppy strong golden lager called **Jubilator★★** (5.6; 7) and a smooth, fruity-malty, yet-stronger, Vienna-style, lager called **Cuivrée★★★** (6.4; 8).

Septante Cinq
Liqueur-ish *bière de garde* made by the 1896 Grande Brasserie Moderne, at Roubaix. The name **Septante Cinq★★→★★★** is an allusion to the alcohol content of 7.5 by volume.

Theillier
Husband-and-wife brewery in a house at Bavay dating back to 1670. Making a rich, sweet, malty, *bière de garde* called **la Bavaisienne★★★**.

THE BRITISH ISLES

Speciality brews have a higher share of the market in Britain and Ireland than in any other nation. Britain's specialities are ales, most famously Bitter. Ireland's are stouts, in varying degrees of dryness. In each case, the national style has about half the market, the rest going mainly to undistinguished local interpretations of international lagers.

Even to the British, ale can be an acquired, adult, taste. The writer Graham Greene, whose own family had a renowned brewery, recalls in his autobiographical volume *A Sort of Life* that he "hated" his first pint but that when he tried a second, he "enjoyed the taste with a pleasure that has never failed me since". The delights afforded by the classic draught ales of Britain might be compared to the pleasures offered by the red wines of Bordeaux. Both have a subtlety of colour; a fresh fruitiness; dashes of sweetness and counter-strokes of dryness; and sometimes a hint of oak.

The dry stouts of Ireland have the qualities ascribed by Hugh Johnson in his *World Atlas of Wine* to true Amontillado sherries: "Dry and almost stingingly powerful of flavour, with a dark, fat, rich tang."

The British term "real ale" implies a secondary fermentation or maturation on yeast, either in the bottle or, more often, in the cask in the cellar of the pub. Bottle-conditioning or cask-conditioning require cellar temperatures typically in the lower to mid-50s°F; 11–13°C. Cask-conditioned ales are to British brewing what château-bottled wines are to Bordeaux.

The brewers

Britain has about 250 breweries. Its biggest brewing company is Bass, with a wide variety of ales, lagers and brand-names, produced in half a dozen towns and cities.

Allied Breweries, owner of the famous ale-producer Tetley's, established in 1993 a joint venture with Carlsberg, of Denmark. This grouping has a similar number of breweries. Courage, which in 1992 acquired the former Watney's breweries, and owns John Smith's, is itself controlled by Foster's, of Australia. Watney's Red Barrel is produced only for export.

Whitbread, which owns Boddington's, of Manchester, is wholly British, though it has long-established trading relationships with Heineken, of The Netherlands, and Artois (Interbrew), of Belgium.

Scottish & Newcastle Breweries was formed by the merger of McEwan's and Younger's on one side of the border with the famous brown ale specialists on the other. It also owns Theakston's, in Yorkshire, and Home, of Nottingham. Together, the nationals have about two dozen breweries.

The famous ale-producer Ruddles, of Rutland, is owned by Grolsch, of The Netherlands; and Cain's, of Liverpool, by the Danish brewers Faxe and Ceres. There are another 50-odd old-established independents, some owning more than one brewery; well over 100 micros; and more than 60 brewpubs. While the micros and brewpubs often produce characterful brews, regrettably few of them make speciality styles.

Where to drink in Britain

Britain has about 80,000 full bar licences. Some are for hotels or restaurants, but the majority represent pubs, and more than half of those serve cask-conditioned ale. Standards of cellaring and service vary greatly. The 5,000 pubs chosen each year for *The Good Beer Guide* are nominated by members of the consumerist Campaign for Real Ale, CAMRA (34 Alma Rd, St Albans, Herts AL1 3BW ☎0727 867201). The guide, which is also available from bookstore chains, additionally identifies which pubs offer accommodation.

Most visitors to Britain arrive in the capital, where out-of-town beers can be expensive and badly kept. In fairness, cask beers prefer not to travel too far. A much more satisfying experience may well be obtained if the drinker does the travelling, whether for a long weekend or for a browse of two or three weeks around the British Isles. Starting in London, the review below takes an anti-clockwise tour of the British Isles.

LONDON AND THE SOUTH

Perhaps because the most renowned hop-growing county, Kent, is in the Southeast, many of the Bitters brewed in this part of the country have traditionally been on the dry side. Kent is especially noted for Goldings hops, which impart an aromatic, resiny, dryness. This hoppy dryness is best tasted if the beer is served with an especially light carbonation, though this southern practice is diminishing in face of competition from the maltier, nuttier, northern ales, which are customarily presented with a creamy head.

Where to drink in London

The capital is lucky enough to have two world-class local breweries, Fuller's and Young's, and they have some of the best pubs. In Central London, The Guinea, in Bruton Place, a mews hidden off the northeast corner of Berkeley Square, is a delightful Young's house, dating from the 1400s; equally elusive and worthwhile is The Star, 6 Belgrave Mews West, for Fuller's ales. In the museum country of Kensington/ Chelsea, The Anglesea, on Onslow Gardens, offers ales from five brewers. Further west at Parson's Green (close to its Tube station), The White Horse has the classic Highgate Mild, London's best-kept **Draught Bass** (sometimes dry-hopped on the premises), guest taps, and it hosts beer events.

The overseas fame of **Sam Smith's** leads some visitors to hunt it in London: the Cheshire Cheese, at 145 Fleet Street, is among several famous London pubs to serve this northern brew.

Among the most central brewpubs is The Orange, 37–9 Pimlico Road; noted for its **Porter★★**. More adventurous drinkers will visit The Greyhound, 151 Greyhound Lane, in Streatham, a South London neighbourhood; try **Pedigree Mild★★**.

Shop: The Beer Shop, 8 Pitfield St, near Old St Tube station has a wide selection of British, Belgian and German brews.

Days out/weekends

Along the Thames Valley, where every brewery offers good, country ales. Go via the regatta town of Henley (Brakspear's at many pubs; try The Anchor, Friday St); Abingdon (Morland's at The Brewery Tap, Ock St), to Oxford (Morrell's fruity **Varsity★★**, at lots of pubs; try The Old Tom, 101 St Aldates). Venture further north to Banbury, for Hook Norton's dry, hoppy, ales at The Coach and Horses, Butchers' Row, or return via the B474 to visit The Royal Standard of England (for **Marston's Owd Roger**), at Forty Green, near Beaconsfield.

South to the sea, via Horsham (King and Barnes at The Stout House, 29 Carfax) or lovely Lewes (**Harvey's**, at the Lewes Arms, off the High St), to Brighton (to the Hand in Hand brewpub at 33 Upper St James St, Kemptown; or sample the wares of brewpub pioneer David Bruce, at the Hedgehog and Hogshead, Goldstone Villas, Hove).

East, via Kent hop country around Faversham, where the local Shepherd Neame ales are well presented at The Crown and Anchor and many others at The Elephant, both on The Mall.

On to Canterbury, where The Tales (opposite the Marlow Theatre) offers very dry ales from the Goacher's micro-brewery, of Maidstone, as well as Belgian specialities. Return via Tunbridge Wells, stopping at The Beacon, Tea Garden Lane (off the A264), for a fruity pint from Larkins, of Chiddingstone.

Brakspear

Rhymes with Shakespeare. Contemporary playwright John Mortimer deems it his favourite brewery. Its gently drinkable, dryish, beers have become even better in recent years. The typically hoppy accent (East Kent Goldings, Hereford Fuggles) is most evident in the "ordinary" **Bitter★★★★**, which has 38 EBU (9 Plato; 1035; 2.7; 3.4). The **Special Bitter★★★** with 48 EBU but a higher gravity (1043) is beautifully balanced. A modestly stronger (4.0; 5.0) newcomer called **Oh Be Joyful** (not tasted) reportedly has a more resiny hop character. Pretty brewery, at Henley-on-Thames.

Fuller's

London brewery (see it on the road from Heathrow airport) that consistently wins awards. The flowery, hoppy, **Chiswick Bitter★★★** is a light delight at 2.8; 3.5. **London Pride★★→★★★** (3.3, 4.1) seems to have lost some of its fruit, but is still a very complex brew. **Extra Special Bitter★★★★** (4.4, 5.5) is hugely so. **Golden Pride★★★** is a honeyish, but quite dry, pale barley wine (22; 1088; 7.4; 9.2).

Gale's

The corked and bottle-conditioned **Prize Old Ale★★★→★★★★** (23.5; 1094; 7.2; 9.0) has such a dry fruitiness, and alcoholic warmth, as to be reminiscent of a Calvados. This fruitiness, and lots of sappy, aromatic, bitterness, characterize the range. The handsome brewery is on the edge of Portsmouth.

Harvey

Victorian-Gothic brewery which in February/March 1993, launched a seasonal, bottle-conditioned, **Porter★★★→★★★★** with yeasty flavours that challenge Dublin Guinness. In summer, there is a dry-hopped **Thomas Paine Ale★★→★★★** (named for the political philosopher, who lived in Lewes, the brewery's home town). Winter's fruity **Elizabethan★★★→★★★★** is magnificent (22.5; 1090; 6.7; 8.3).

King and Barnes

Enjoys a growing reputation, especially for its **Festive★★★**, with a very hoppy, herbal, aroma and a big, smooth fruitiness (12.5; 1050, 3.6; 4.5). Available bottle-conditioned. Old-established, country brewery, with modern equipment, in Horsham, Sussex.

Morland's

Georgian landscape painter George Morland (1763–1804) was a member of the family. The beers tend to be malt-accented, with a touch of yeasty dryness, as typified in **Old Speckled Hen**★★ (12.5; 1050; 4.1; 5.2). Morland's home is in Abingdon, Oxfordshire, an old malting and brewing town, but this beer is named after a famous MG car made there.

Shepherd Neame

A wine-grower as well as Britain's oldest brewery (founded 1698), in the heart of East Kent hop country. Local hops are featured, but not with sufficient emphasis. The "ordinary" bitter, **Masterbrew**★★ →★★★, is well balanced, with good hop flavours and bitterness. The bottle-conditioned **Spitfire**★★★ is dry-hopped with East Kent Goldings. **Bishop's Finger**★★ →★★★ is maltier (12.5; 1050; 4.1; 5.2). A **Porter**★★★, containing licorice root, has the bouquet of a well-sherried malt whisky.

Whitbread

Founded in London, and historically known for porters and stouts. Today, its revivalist **Porter**★★★, lightly smoky, fig-like, and hopped entirely with Goldings, is made in the north, at Whitbread's brewery in Castle Eden, County Durham. Its Mackeson **Stout**★★★, originally from Hythe, Kent, also now emerges from the north, at Samlesbury, Lancashire, an odd home for a beer that tastes like sweetened espresso. This brewery also now produces the fruity (apricot, anise?) **Gold Label**★★★, which pioneered pale barley wines. The winey, bottle-conditioned **Celebration Ale**★★★★ made for Whitbread's 250th anniversary is now a collector's item.

Young's

A live ram is the mascot; geese guard the brewery; and there are two dozen dray-horses … all in an inner London neighbourhood, where the River Wandle meets the Thames. The **Bitter**★★ →★★★ is famously dry, but not as assertive as it once was. The **Special**★★★ is very well balanced. **Ramrod**★★ →★★★ is more malt-accented. **Winter Warmer**★★★ is dark, luscious, fruity, but surprisingly dry (13.5; 1055; 4.0; 5.0). Young's Export Special **London Ale**★★★ →★★★★ has, when it is fresh, a wonderful hop aroma (16; 1062–4; 5.l; 6.4). **Old Nick**★★★ →★★★★ (21; 1084; 5.7; 7.2) is a classic dark barley wine, with some liqueur-ish fruitiness (a hint of banana?). The more recent **Oatmeal Stout**★★ →★★★ is light but very smooth, with a touch of oily dryness.

EASTERN ENGLAND

From London, it is only 30 or 40 miles to the rustic countryside of East Anglia, the region that grows the biggest share of England's malting barley. This is also a region that historically enjoyed much Flemish influence; is it fanciful still to find that in the yeasty fruitiness of some local beers?

In Essex, the first stop, north of Chelmsford, might be The Compasses, at Littley Green, for Ridley's full-flavoured, hoppy ales. This area also has hoppy-fruity brews from the micro Crouch Vale.

Across the county line in Suffolk, the micro Mauldon's, of Sudbury, makes malty brews including the spicy-tasting stout **Black Adder★★→★★★**. The county's several other micros include, in nearby Clare, Nethergate, whose iron-tinged **Old Growler★★→★★★** has occasionally been brewed in special editions with coriander and bog myrtle. Earl Soham, near Woodbridge, has the reputedly hoppy **Albert Ale** (not tasted), at the Victoria brewpub. No visitor should miss the time-warp resort of Southwold, to taste Adnams' on its home ground.

In Norfolk, the micro Woodforde has a brewery tap called The Fur and Feather, at Salhouse, near Norwich. The city itself has ales full of flavour at the Reindeer brewpub, Dereham Rd.

Return via Cambridge for the brewpub Ancient Druids (Napier St), which also has Charles Wells' slightly sulphury **Bombardier★★**. The Cambridge Blue, in Gwydir St, has Nethergate ales.

Adnams

Noted wine merchants as well as brewers. It seemed like a Scotch whisky allusion, too, when British beer-writer Roger Protz observed that he found a salty, tangy, "seaweedy" character in the complex ales of this harbourside brewery. The outstanding Bitter is **Adnams' Extra★★** (a similar beer is bottled and canned as **Suffolk Strong**), with a dry, flowery, piney, resiny aroma of finest Fuggles hops. The full-bodied pale ale **Broadside★★★** blends hoppy, almondy, dryness with oily, treacly, maltiness. A draught version has 12.5; 1049; 3.6; 4.7; a stronger, bottled counterpart 17; 1069; 5.2; 6.3. The aromatic, toffeeish, barley wine **Tally-Ho★★★** is available on draught at Christmas.

Elgood

A Georgian mill and granary in the Cambridgeshire town of Wisbech became a brewery in 1795, and should have a museum and visitor-centre in time for its bi-centenary. Products include the contract-brewed **Original Viking Ale★★★**, a yeasty, fruity, spicy, toffeeish speciality created by brewing scientist Keith Thomas. The yeast used in secondary fermentation was obtained from farmhouse brewers in western Norway.

Greene King

Graham Greene, in celebration of his 80th birthday, mashed a special "edition" of the family brewery's **St Edmund Ale★★→★★★**, a malty but crisp barley wine (15; 1060; 5.2; 6.5). This independent, but large and commercially aggressive, brewery is in the town of Bury St Edmund's, Suffolk. Its most interesting beer is **Strong Suffolk★★★→★★★★**, a dark blend, a proportion of which is aged in unlined oak for between one and five years – a technique better known across the water in Flanders (14.5; 1058; 4.8; 6.0). The result is oaky, winey and iron-like. Greene King's products are in general on the fruity, dry, side, notably the well-known **Abbot Ale★★→★★★** (12.5; 1049; 4.0; 5.0). The brewery is near the ruins of an abbey that grew up on the site of St Edmund's murder.

McMullen

The Irish family McMullen came to the malting and brewing town of Hertford in 1827, and in 1832 launched a beer called **AK★★★**. The origin of the name is the constant subject of speculation, but the beer is a classic pale Mild, full of flavours: dry maltiness, leafy hoppiness, and refreshing acidity (9.0; 1033; 3.1; 3.8). Other products include limited editions under the rubric Special Reserve; the fresh-tasting, crisp, fruity, bottled, **Castle Pale Ale★★→★★★**, in the bottle; and bottle-conditioned contract-brews such as chocolatey, spicy, **Black Russian★★★**.

Woodforde

On a farm at Woodbastwick, near Norwich. Outstanding micro, whose products include **Mardler's Mild★★→★★★**, which is toffeeish but smooth and firm, finishing with a touch of apple-like tartness; **Wherry Best Bitter★★→★★★**, hoppy and dry, with a refreshing sharpness in the finish; and an Old Ale called **Norfolk Nog★★** which, again, starts malty but finishes with a touch of sharpness.

YORKSHIRE AND THE NORTHEAST

England's biggest county considers itself a nation in its own right, and steadfastly protects its customs. Its brewing tradition of using double-deck "Yorkshire Square" fermenters leaves it with a family of yeasts that are as headstrong as Yorkshiremen. Perhaps that is why the character of its creamy, yeasty, nutty, ales has been better sustained than that of the counties further north, clustered around the city of Newcastle. Traditionally, this creaminess and nuttiness is enhanced by the serving of the beer through a tight tap to create a dense head.

In the old steel city of Sheffield, the Frog and Parrot brewpub (Division St) produces from malt extract an immensely potent (31; 1125; 13.5; 16.9), but still soft and smooth, winter ale called **Roger and Out★★★→★★★★**. Ward's, a sturdy Victorian brewery owned by Vaux, produces distinctively malty ales, including a **Mild★★→★★★** with a dash of dark candy sugar.

Leeds, the commercial capital, is famous for Tetley's and handy for Timothy Taylor's. Nearby brewing towns include Wakefield (with a wide selection of full-flavoured, hoppy-flowery, ales from the micro Clark's); Huddersfield (with robust, fruity, ales at the Sair Inn, a revived brewpub, at Lane Top, Linthwaite); and Halifax (with light, faintly oily, ales from Webster's, owned by Courage). There are several other micros, including the new Rudgate, which makes the firm, dry and hoppy **Battleaxe★★** at Tockwith, between Harrogate and York.

The Viking and Roman city of York is a better base from which to explore rural brewing towns like Tadcaster and Masham. The first is known for pale ales, thanks to water with a dash of calcium sulphate. The second may owe its brewing tradition to the abbeys of the Yorkshire Dales.

Micros to the east include Old Mill, making dry, hoppy, almost herbal, ales at Snaith; Hull Brewery, noted for its well-rounded **Mild★★**; and Malton, in the town of the same name, whose products include the coffeeish **Pickwick Porter★★**.

Handsome Newcastle has hoppy ales from Big Lamp, and dry, fresh-tasting, examples from Hadrian, both micros, as well as the faintly winey **Brown Ale★★★** from its famous big brewer. Across the River Tyne, the Federation Brewery, owned by working men's clubs, has the sweeter, buttery **High Level Brown Ale★★**. In adjoining Sunderland, Vaux makes the characteristically smooth brown ale **Double Maxim★★→★★★**. In Hartlepool, Cameron's makes nutty ales. At Bishop Auckland, the Butterknowle micro produces complex, well-balanced, beers. At Berwick, the last town in England, the revived Border micro makes very fruity brews.

Black Sheep

Paul Theakston left the family brewery some years after it lost its independence, and in 1992 started this tiny rival in the same town, Masham (population 2,000), near Ripon. Black Sheep is in buildings dated from the mid-1800s of a brewery that was taken over by Theakston's in 1919. In its revived form, the brewery uses stone (slate) "Yorkshire Square" fermenters. This malty, yeasty, dryness, which is typical in traditional Yorkshire ales, is notably evident in the **Special Bitter★★★**.

John Smith

Magnificent Victorian brewery, with small museum, in Tadcaster, near York. No longer uses "Yorkshire Squares", but there is still some local character in John Smith's **Bitter★→★★** and the sweeter **Magnet★→★★**. The brewery is owned by Courage, and produces the famous **Imperial Russian Stout★★★**, with flavours reminiscent of fruit cake, burnt currants, dark sherry, chocolate and coffee (24–27; 1098–1107; 7.6–8.5; 9.5–10.5). For decades, this was the only brew to use the term "Imperial Stout".

Samuel Smith

The two Smith breweries are next door. This branch of the family remains robustly independent, and still has "Yorkshire Squares" (slate), not to mention wooden casks. The cask-conditioned **Museum Ale★★★**, malty and rounded, is the basis for the bottled **Pale Ale** (chic in the USA); **Strong Brown★★★** is the maltiest, nuttiest example of its style. It is marketed in the USA as **Nut Brown**. What the Americans know as **Samuel Smith's Porter** is marketed in Britain under the delightful name **Nourishing Strong Stout★★★**. The silky **Oatmeal Stout★★★★**, launched in the 1980s, was the first revival of this style. All of these beers are around 12.5; 1050; 4.0; 5.0). The powerful, estery, **Imperial Stout★★★→★★★★**, launched in the 1980s, helped create new interest in this style (18; 1072; 5.6; 7.0). **Winter Welcome★★★**, a wonderfully winey strong ale, is also a relatively new brew.

Tetley

The classically creamy, nutty, Yorkshire ale is Tetley **Bitter★★→★★★**. Other products include a distinctively rummy **Mild★★→★★★**. No other single site produces as high a volume of cask-conditioned ale as Tetley's brewery in Leeds. It ferments in Yorkshire Squares, made from stainless steel.

Theakston

Tiny brewery famous for its **Old Peculier★★★**. This soft and fruity dark brew, with its intentionally archaic spelling, is a classic Old Ale (14–15; 1057; 4.2; 5.6). Theakston products also include a yeastily dry **Best Bitter★★** and stronger **XB★★**. The family lost financial control of the tiny brewery in the 1980s, but it still operates. Theakston ales are also produced in the parent company's brewery in Newcastle.

Timothy Taylor

In Brontë country at Keighley. Revered for its **Landlord★★★**, one of England's finest bitters, with a superb interplay of juicy maltiness; hard, Dales water; and a flowery, almost heathery, hop character.

SCOTLAND

A colder country that specializes in rich, sweetish, malty, warming ales, often tawny or dark and sometimes strong. These are often identified, in ascending order of strength as Light, Heavy, Export and Wee Heavy (the last implying an ale so strong that it can be offered only in a small serving). Or 60/-, 70/-, 80/-, 90/-, etc. (The symbols refer to shillings, an old unit of currency.)

Scotland was a great brewing nation until the takeovers and mergers of the 1960s, and in recent years Edinburgh has become a lively city in which to drink good beer.

Among British giants, Bass owns Tennent's, mainly known for its lager, in Glasgow. In the old brewing town of Alloa, Carlsberg-Tetley produces various lagers and **Archibald Arrol's 80/-★★**, malty, dryish and faintly medicinal. This company also owns Edinburgh's Rose Street brewpub, which makes malty ales from extract. The West Highland brewpub makes hoppy ales in a railway station at Taynuilt, near Oban. In 1992/3, the Tomintoul micro opened in the mountain village of the same name, in the heart of Speyside whisky country.

Where to drink

Edinburgh: The Guildford, 1 West Register St; The Cumberland, on the street of the same name, in the Georgian "New Town"; The Bow Bar, Victoria St; Bannerman's, Cowgate; Bennet's, next to the King's Theatre. The Bank is a bar and hotel at 1–3 South Bridge (☎031–556–9043). T.G.Willis, at 135 George St, is a food hall with an upstairs bar that serves breakfast from 7.00 and beer from 8.00 am.

Glasgow: The Boswell, cask ale bar, restaurant and hotel, 27 Mansion House Road (☎041–632–9812).

Aberdeen: Betty Burke's, 45 Langstane Place; Carriages, 101 Crown St. The Ale Cellar, 114 Rosemount Viaduct, is a shop.

Belhaven

With monastic beginnings in its harbour village of Dunbar, between Edinburgh and the border, Belhaven has always had romance. It has also had classic Scottish ales. After constant changes of ownership, it is to be hoped that the integrity of these products is finally safe with the management buyout of 1993. The **70/-★★→★★★** typifies the complexity and depth of the Belhaven ales. **Sandy Hunter's★★★**, named after a great Belhaven brewer, has a delightfully light touch of malt. **St Andrew's★★→★★★** is remarkably soft. The **90/-★★★** is a classic strong Scotch Ale (17.5; 1070; 5.9; 7.3). A similar brew appears as a bottled "Wee Heavy" under the Belhaven and Fowler's names.

Borve House

Eccentric micro/brewpub at Ruthven, near Huntly, north-west of Aberdeen. Products have included the sweetish **Cairm Porter★★→★★★**, made with licorice, and the smoky **Borve Extra Strong★★★**, which has some of its primary fermentation and all of its secondary in casks that have been used first to mature bourbon and then Scotch (21; 1085; 8.0; 10.0).

Broughton

Novelist John Buchan was born at Broughton, near Biggar (between Glasgow and the border). Hence the local micro-brewery's **Greenmantle Ale★★**, with an interesting balance of malt and hop. **Special Bitter★★** is a dry-hopped version. **Merlin's Ale★★** is golden and dry. **Old Jock** is dark, malty and very tasty, despite a name that could have sweaty undertones. **Scottish Oatmeal Stout★★→★★★** is a lightly silky interpretation.

Caledonian

With its open kettles, fired by direct flame, Caledonian is the crucible of Edinburgh's brewing traditions. Managing director Russell Sharp once worked for Chivas, and his ales are the maltiest in Scotland. The lightly malty **Caledonian 70/-★★→★★★** evokes memories of the Heavy from the long-gone Bernard's brewery. Another deceased brewery is honoured by the name Deuchar's, on the hoppy **IPA★★→★★★**. The **80/-** is beautifully balanced. **Double Amber★★★→★★★★** is full of Golden Promise maltiness, and reminiscent of the ales from Campbell, Hope and King. **Merman★★★** is a dark malty ale for winter. **Edinburgh Strong Ale★★★**, which has been reduced slightly in strength (16; 1065; 5.2; 6.5), is the basis for MacAndrew's in the USA. Caledonian holds an annual festival in early June (☎031–337–1286).

Harviestoun

Farmhouse micro-brewery at Dollar, near Stirling. A wide range of interesting ales includes the nutty-fruity **70/-★★**.

McEwan/Younger

The sweetish McEwan's **80/-★→★★**, a cask-conditioned ale, and a similar canned product called **Export** have some following in Scotland. The darker Younger's **No 3★→★★** has become hard to find. All of these beers have gravities of just above 10.5; 1042; 3.3; 4.4. In the Americas, **McEwan's Scotch Ale★★★** packs a more obvious punch (22; 1088; 6.4; 8.0). A similar beer is marketed in Belgium as **Gordon's** and in France as **Douglas**.

Maclay

New ownership has given fresh life to this Victorian brewery in Alloa. The bronze-coloured **70/-★★→★★★** has a clean, sweet, maltiness; the darker **80/- Export★★** has a hint of caramel. The **Scotch Ale★★→★★★** has lots of malty-fruity character for a modest gravity of 12.5; 1050 (4.0; 5.0). **Old Alloa Ale★★★** is full-bodied, with flavours reminiscent of candy sugar (17.5; 1070; 5.2; 6.5). **Oat Malt Stout★★★** is made with that version of the grain, rather than the rolled form. It has a touch of sweetness, suggestions of dark chocolate, and a long finish. There is an occasional brew flavoured with local raspberries. Maclay's has also contract-brewed the gingery, perfumy, oily, dry, **Leann Fraoch★★★** (Scottish gaelic for heather ale).

Orkney

In a former schoolhouse, in the windswept hamlet of Quoyloo, on the largest of the Orkney Islands. Beers include the chocolatey **Dark Island★★★** (11.3; 1045; 3.7; 4.6) and the sweeter, winier **Skullsplitter★★★** (20; 1080; 6.8; 8.5).

Traquair

A manor house (or castle?) in which Bonnie Prince Charlie once took refuge, near Peebles, in the Borders. Like any other large residence, it had its own brewery, enterprisingly put back into operation by the Laird (lord of the manor) in 1965. At his death in 1990, his daughter Catherine, then in her mid-twenties, took over, and has since expanded the brewhouse. Uncoated wooden fermenters are used, and **Traquair House Ale★★★★** has a touch of oaky earthiness to balance its dark-malt nuttiness (18.5–21; 1074–82; a little over 5.6; 7.0). Special editions have been produced at various gravities, and there is a **Bear Ale**★★→★★★ of a more conventional strength (12.5; 1050; 4.0; 5.0). The house can be visited, and has a beer festival at the end of May (☎0896–830323).

THE NORTHWEST

The Lake District, Lancashire, and the Manchester–Liverpool area are dotted with breweries. The beers of the northwest tend to be dry, though there is no obvious reason for this accent.

The Northern Lakes have fruity-tasting ales (including an occasional bramble brew) from the micro Yates, of Westnewton, and spritzy ones from the Old Crown brewpub at Hesket Newmarket.

No visitor to the Southern Lakes should miss The Mason's Arms, Strawberry Bank, Cartmel Fell, near Windermere. This pub has a huge selection of brews, and makes its own, including a **Damson Beer**★★★ which is full of fruit and flavour.

Manchester has a remarkable collection of old-established breweries, but their beers are hard to find in the city centre. The eccentric West Coast micro, produces its own tributes to world-famous beers (**Guiltless Stout**, for example), and serves them at The King's Arms, Helmshaw Walk, Chorlton-on-Medlock, Manchester.

Boddington

Manchester brewery known for its distinctively pale **Bitter**★. This has lost much of its assertive dryness over the years, especially since the brewery (now owned by Whitbread) began to emphasize the creamy head.

Cain's

A Victorian landmark in Liverpool. After decades as Higson's, the brewery in 1991 re-established the name of its founder, Robert Cain, a swashbuckling immigrant from Cork, Ireland. Its **Traditional Bitter**★★→★★★ is packed with flavour: soft maltiness; spicy, hoppy, dryness; and banana-like fruitiness. **Formidable Ale**★★ is hoppier and drier.

Holt

Unpretentious to the point of being taciturn, but famous among beer-lovers in Manchester. Distinctive notes of black malt, high hop rates and the dry fruitiness of the house's hybrid yeast in a roasty, dry, **Mild**★★★ and an intense, austere, **Bitter**★★★. The brewery tap is The Derby, 95 Cheetham Hill Rd.

Hyde

Country-style brewery in the urban heart of Manchester. Not to be overlooked. Its **Bitter**★★→★★★, with a malty texture, a clean fruitiness, and a long, hoppy, finish, is a particular delight. The beers can be found at The Jolly Angler, Ducie St, behind Piccadilly Station.

Jennings

Rural independent at Cockermouth, Cumbria. Noted for its hoppy, fruity, **Bitter★★→★★★**.

Lees

Dry, malty, ales from a respected brewery among the cotton towns on the edge of Manchester. Noteworthy for its strong **Harvest Ale★★★→★★★★**, made each year from the new season's malt (Maris Otter, Yorkshire) and hops (Goldings, East Kent), and released in late November, with a vintage date. This pale brew has a warm, fruity (lemony?), aroma; a smooth palate; and a lot of hoppy dryness in the finish (30; 1120; 9.2; 11.5).

Mitchell's

Lancaster brewery noted for its very dry (almost sharp), malty, **ESB★★**. A "winter warmer" (not tasted) is called Single Malt. The barley for this is malted in Scotland.

Moorhouse's

Noted for its **Pendle Witches Brew★★**, named after a local hill that has associations with devil-worship. This robust ale counterpoints sweet maltiness and herbal-tasting dryness. The brewery is in the old cotton town of Burnley, Lancashire, and originally made a hop-flavoured soft drink.

Robinson's

Sizable independent in Greater Manchester. Products include a bronze-coloured **Best Mild★★→★★★** that is a very good example of the style; a pale, dryish Bitter★★; and the fruity **Old Tom★★★**, with a warming dash of alcohol (20; 1080; 6.8; 8.5).

Thwaite's

Noted for its complex **Best Mild★★★** among a range of nutty-tasting ales. Thwaite's is in the old brewing town of Blackburn, Lancashire.

BURTON AND THE MIDLANDS

The brewing capital of Britain is Burton-on-Trent, a small town between the West Midlands city of Birmingham and the East Midlands cities of Derby and Nottingham.

Benedictine monks are said to have brewed in Burton as early as the 1200s. The water of the Trent Valley has a calcium sulphate content that favours pale, firm-bodied beers, helps to highlight the hop character, and makes for good keeping qualities. Hops, notably Fuggles (known for their soft, aromatic, bitterness), are grown not far away in Hereford and Worcester.

Via the rivers Trent and Humber, the town became a major exporter of beer to continental Europe and the British Empire, especially of Pale Ale to India.

Burton has the principal Bass brewery, with an award-winning museum (☎0283–42031); Carlsberg-Tetley (producing eight or nine cask ales that are local to the Midlands and the South); Marston's (a large independent); Burton Bridge (a micro); and Heritage (which has not brewed in recent years, but has long-term plans to become a working museum).

Shropshire and the "Black Country" of the West Midlands have a tradition of sweetish ales, and have managed to retain several very old brewpubs, though some have faltered in recent years. The revived Beacon Hotel brewery, 129 Bilston St, Sedgley, Dudley, is a fine example of a Black Country brewpub, with its rich, smooth, complex, **Sarah Hughes Ruby Mild★★★**. In nearby Brierley Hill, Batham's is a classic small Black Country brewery, producing a **Bitter★★→★★★** that subtly balances maltiness of palate with light hoppiness of finish. The brewery tap is The Vine (locally known as The Bull and Bladder), Delph Rd, Brierley Hill. Its local rival in Dudley is Holden's, with a characteristically malty range. The Enville Brewery, on the Earls of Stamford estate, near Stourbridge, is a promising newcomer. Its soft, smooth, flowery, **Enville Ale★★★** is primed with honey from the estate.

The biggest city of the East Midlands, Nottingham, also on the Trent, has sweetish ales from the independent Hardy and Hanson, and well-rounded brews from Home, which is owned by the distant Scottish & Newcastle. In Nottinghamshire, the Mansfield brewery has ales with something of an across-the-county line Yorkshire taste. Leicester has Everards, with malty but dryish ales. Leicestershire embraces Rutland, where Ruddles produces a hoppy **Best Bitter★→★★** and the malty **County★**.

Banks

A cult following attends the malty, tasty, medium-dark, **Mild★★★** that is the principal product of this sizeable independent in the West Midlands.

Bass

The classic ale under the Bass name is cask-conditioned, and therefore available only in Britain. **Draught Bass★★★** lost some of its fruity delicacy when the brewery foolishly abandoned the "Burton Union" system of linked wooden fermentation vessels, and has ceded more character by ceasing to dry-hop. Its bottled big brother, **Worthington White Shield★★★→★★★★** also lost some character when its yeast was "cleaned up", but the company deserves praise for its marketing effort with this speciality. A small Bass brewery at Walsall, in the West Midlands, produces **Highgate Dark★★★**, a classic Mild, with a smooth complex of maltiness and fruitiness, and a touch of iron. **Highgate Old★★★** is a fuller-flavoured and strong winter brew (14; 1055.5; 4.2; 5.3).

Bateman

Renowned for a successful battle to remain independent in the mid-80s. Classic country brewery in vegetable-growing country at Wainfleet, near Skegness, Lincolnshire. Its "Good, Honest Ales" are all smooth, firm, malty and beautifully balanced, sometimes with a spicy hint of anise and lots of flavour development. The premium Bitter **XXXB**★★★ is rightly celebrated.

Burton Bridge
Micro with adjoining pub, at 24 Bridge St. Wide selection includes a dry and coffeeish **Porter**★★★ that is available bottle-conditioned.

Ind Coope
Burton brewery of Carlsberg-Tetley. Noted for its cask-conditioned **Burton Ale**★★★, with a great depth of flavour and a big hop character. A similar beer, filtered and pasteurized, is marketed in the USA under the Double Diamond name.

Marston
Heroically, and expensively, extended its Burton Union system (see Bass) to ensure the clean, dry, gently fruity (Cox's Orange Pippin?), nutty, character of its **Pedigree**★★★★, described as a Bitter, but surely the classic Burton Pale Ale. The creamy, fruity, **Owd Roger**★★→★★★ (20; 1080; 6.1 7.6) tops a range that also includes some adventurous special editions under the title Head Brewer's Choice.

Titanic
Micro in Stoke-on-Trent, birthplace of the vessel's captain. Beers have wry names like **Lifeboat**★★→★★★ (a soft, sweetish, aromatic Bitter).

WALES
The Welsh had a recognized national style of beer in the 8th century, according to Brian Glover in his book *Prince of Ales*. His interpretation of records from that time is that Welsh ale, laced with honey, cinnamon, cloves and ginger, was sweeter, spicier and thicker than English brews. Today, Wales has no distinct style, but its ales do still lean towards a slightly sticky sweetness.

Traditional, farmhouse, brewing survived longest in the mountainous north and rural west, areas where there are now a number of newish micros. The north has Dyffryn Clwyd, at Denbigh; and Plassey, at Eyton. The northwest has the Snowdonia brewpub, at Gellilydan, Blaenau Ffestiniog.

The handful of older-established independent breweries all grew up with the coal and steel industries on the more cosmopolitan south coast. That stretch also has a micro, Bullmastiff, in Cardiff.

Brain's
Cardiff brewing company established by Joseph and Samuel Brain in 1882. Known for its slogan, "It's Brain's you want". Its **S.A.**★★★ ("Special Ale") is smooth, malty, dryish and

delicious, arguably the Welsh classic. Brain's **Dark★★→★★★**, a relatively full-bodied Mild, is also recommended.

Crown Buckley

Malty-fruity ales, notably **Reverend James Bitter★★**. Reverend James was a Methodist minister who married into the Buckleys. The brewery is at Llanelli, a steel and Rugby Union town west of Swansea, and not far from Laugharne, setting for Dylan Thomas's "Under Milk Wood".

Felinfoel

Also in Llanelli, whose local industry pioneered the canning of beer for Felinfoel. Noted for its nutty **Double Dragon ★★→★★★**, marketed in the USA as Welsh Ale.

THE WEST COUNTRY

The most westerly brewery in Britain is also one of the strangest. It is The Bird in Hand brewpub, in Paradise Park, at Hayle, Cornwall. The name derives from the fact that Paradise Park is a garden in which rare birds are bred. It supports itself by attracting visitors – and by selling them a choice of three hearty ales in its pub.

With monastic origins in the 1400s, The Blue Anchor, at Helston, Cornwall, is Britain's oldest brewpub, noted for a range of strong ales under the name **Spingo**.

The Redruth Brewery, in the town of the same name, produces the light, dry, **Cornish Original★→★★**. The St Austell brewery, in that town, has the well-balanced, but hop-accented, **Tinners' Bitter★★**, honouring Cornwall's mining industry.

Devon's oldest surviving brewery is Blackawton, a micro founded in 1977 and producing sweetish ales, but this county is rich in younger breweries. Across the county line in Somerset, the village of Wiveliscombe even has two: Cotleigh (founded in 1979), producing hoppy ales; and Golden Hill (1980), making the more malty (but well-balanced) **Exmoor Ales**.

In the county of Avon, the historically interesting cities of Bath and Bristol are dotted with good pubs. Bristol has a wonderfully refreshing, cleansing, dry, **Bitter★★** from the Butcombe micro (1978) and soft, malt-accented, ales from Smiles.

Across the county line in Gloucestershire is the Uley micro, producing hoppy ales in Dursley. The handsome Cotswold town of Stow has Britain's prettiest brewery, Donnington, making malt-accented ales of great subtlety.

A more southerly exploration would sample the brews of Dorset: lightly hoppy ales from the partly thatched Palmer's, of Bridport; the magnificently tasty, hoppy, **Tanglefoot★★→★★★**, from Hall & Woodhouse, of Blandford Forum; and the delights of Eldridge Pope (see entry).

In Wiltshire, Salisbury has the old-established Gibbs Mew (noted for **Bishop's Tipple★★→★★★**, an intense, dry, dark, strong ale: 16.5; 1066; 5.2; 6.5) and the micro Hop Back (with its flowery, resiny, fruity, **Summer Lightning★★→★★★** and a **Wheat Beer★★→★★★** with a hint of apricot). Nearby at Netheravon, the micro Bunce's makes a hoppy but well-balanced **Best Bitter★★**, the more aromatic **Pigswill★→★★**; the winey **Old Smoky★★** and an apple-tinged **Wheat Beer★★★**. Devizes has Wadworth, and Swindon accommodates both the old-established Arkell's (noted for its complex, assertive, **Kingsdown★★**) and the micro Archer's, which makes clean, fruity, ales.

Courage

The cask-conditioned ales under the Courage name are produced at the company's brewery in Bristol. The best-known is the full-bodied, hoppy **Directors' Bitter★★**. Courage's Reading brewery makes the fruity **Bulldog Pale Ale★★**, now reduced in strength to 4.0; 5.0.

Eldridge Pope

The famous, vintage-dated, **Thomas Hardy's Ale★★★★** is produced by this fine brewery in Dorchester. The Victorian poet and novelist Thomas Hardy lived in the town, and set most of his work in the area. He knew the owners of the brewery, and wrote lyrically of the local beer. This strong (30-plus; 1125; a little over 9.6; 12.0), dark ale was originally produced for a festival to commemorate Hardy, and is now made in regular, dated, batches. New "vintages" are very sweet and sticky, but it is bottle-conditioned and becomes drier with age, gaining sherryish notes. Other products include the dryish, malty-fruity **Thomas Hardy Country Bitter★★→★★★** (available bottle-conditioned), the soft, fresh, fruity, **Royal Oak★★→★★★**; and the magnificently hoppy **Goldie★★★**, a pale barley wine.

Ringwood

The godfather of new, small breweries in many parts of the world is Peter Austin, who in 1977/8 established the pioneering micro Ringwood in the Hampshire town of that name, in the New Forest. As a consultant, he has since helped many others in four continents to do the same. Ringwood's ales have a firm body, a dry maltiness, lots of hop character, and a syrupy fruitiness. The brewery is noted for its pale **Old Thumper★★★** (15; 1060; 4.8; 6.0).

Wadworth

Towering 1890s brewery, with earlier origins, in the country town of Devizes, Wiltshire. Its famous **6X★★** drinks bigger than its gravity (10; 1040; 3.4; 4.3) would suggest, with a Cognac-like fruitiness and a touch of hoppy acidity. **Farmer's Glory★★→★★★** (11.5; 1046; 3.6; 4.5), darker and earthier, is replaced in winter with the more malty **Old Timer★★→★★★** (14; 1055; 4.6; 5.8). Green hops, straight from the harvest, are used to make a brief seasonal brew in mid-September; **Malt and Hops★★★** (11; 1043; 3.6; 4.5) is full of the cleansing floweriness of Herefordshire Fuggles.

IRELAND

The land of dry stout. While the best-known examples are produced by Guinness, of Dublin, the style is also upheld by Murphy and Beamish – both of Cork, second city of the Republic.

Beamish

Beamish Genuine Stout★★→★★★ is creamy, chocolatey and delicious – least dry of the style (9.75; 1039; 3.4; 4.2). The site of production, at the south end of town, may have had a brewery since the 1600s. Messrs Beamish and Crawford, who established the present company in 1792 to make porter, were Scottish-Irish Protestant landowners. The brewery is now owned by Foster's, of Australia.

Guinness

Richard Guinness was an estate manager for a clergyman, and made beer for his boss's table. The rector left £100 to Richard's son Arthur, who in 1759 bought a disused brewery near an abbey in Dublin. Over the years, Guinness's various Stouts have lost some of their fruity, earthy, intensity, but they are still the driest and most complex of the style. The bottle-conditioned **Guinness Extra Stout★★★★** sold in Ireland best expresses the character (9.75; 1039; 3.4; 4.2). **Draught Guinness★★★** in Britain, Ireland and the USA has a similar specification but less complexity, and a nitrogen-induced foam. The same is true of "draught" Guinness in a can. The bottled Guinness in the USA is stronger (4.8; 6.0) and versions in some parts of continental Europe and the Tropics yet more potent (6.0; 7.5). Tropical countries served from Dublin get an especially complex, winey, blend that is a classic in itself.

Other Guinness products include several typically Irish, reddish, buttery, ales and a tasty barley wine, under the **Smithwick's/Kilkenny★★★** name, from a subsidiary brewery in that handsome town; similar ales at Cherry's, in Waterford; and the slightly darker, drier, **Macardle's★★** ales, made in Dundalk. There are also several versions of **Harp★→★★**, a lager of no especially Irish character, produced in various breweries.

Hilden

Lonely cask ale brewery at the Georgian Hilden House, at Lisburn, County Antrim. **Hilden Ale★★★** is a splendidly hoppy Bitter.

Murphy

Murphy's **Irish Stout★★→★★★** is a distinctively toasty-tasting, malty, interpretation of the style. The brewery, at the north end of town, originally took its water from a well consecrated to Our Lady. The brewery dates from the 1850s, and was founded by a family who also made whiskey. It is now owned by Heineken.

SOUTHERN EUROPE

The fastest-growing consumption of beer in Europe is in Italy, where the bright young things of prosperous northern cities like Milan regard wine as a drink for their parents. Brewers in other European countries have poured their most sophisticated beers into the Italian market, and now local companies are responding with their own specialities.

One of the more interesting Italian breweries (with its "moustachioed man" trademark) is Moretti, headquartered in Udine, north of Venice. In winter, the restaurant adjoining its offices serves a yeastily unfiltered version (ordered as *integrale*, meaning "whole") of the basic **Moretti★★** beer, which in its normal form is a clean and lightly spritzy Pilsener. Moretti is also very proud of its export-style **Sans Souci★★** (15 Plato; 1060; 4.5; 5.6), which has a flowery hop aroma and a smooth, malty finish. The brewery also has a higher-gravity (16; 1064; 5; 6.25), all-malt version of a Münchener dark, called **Bruna★★ →★★★**. Its most specialized beer, however, is the deep red **La Rossa★★★** (18; 1072; 6; 7.5), that is also all-malt, as evidenced by its rich aroma and palate. Sad to say, Moretti is no longer family owned. A controlling share is now held by Labatt, of Canada, which also owns Prinz Bräu in Italy.

The smallest brewery in Italy is Menabrea. The largest is Peroni, producer of **Nastro Azzuro★ →★★★**, and the very similar **Raffo★ →★★**, both well-balanced Pilseners in the light Italian style.

A beer in the style of a "red ale", **McFarland★★ →★★★** (13.5; 1054; 4.4; 5.5) is made by Dreher (now owned by Heineken). The most exotic speciality, a deeper copper-red in colour, is **Splügen Fumée★★★**, made with medium-smoked Franconian malts, by Poretti (in which Carlsberg has a share).

Elsewhere in Southern Europe, Spain has some pleasantly dry Pilseners and a good few stronger lagers in broadly the Dortmunder Export and Bock styles. On Malta, the top-fermenting specialities of the **Farsons★★★** brewery are all worthy of attention: a genuine **Milk Stout** (1045); a darkish Mild ale, **Blue Label** (1039); a very pale, dry ale called **Hop Leaf** (1040); and a darker, fuller-bodied ale, **Brewer's Choice** (1050). Greece has now relaxed its Beer Purity Law, which dated from its royal family's historic links with Germany. The former Yugoslavia, on the other hand, is hop-growing country, so that ingredient tends to be emphasized by brewers in Slovenia. Some, like Karlovačko in Croatia, also have a bottom-fermenting **Porter★★★** (1064).

CANADA

In some countries, beers from Canada have enjoyed a fashionability based on images of mountains, forests, wildlife and lakes. To drape all this behind names like Labatt and Molson, mass-market brewing companies based in big cities, is to stretch a point. Nor has the Canadian identity of either Labatt or Molson been sharpened by their international relationships with other brewing companies.

Canada grows a great deal of six-row barley, the tougher husk of which can impart a "rougher" texture than the two-row varieties used elsewhere. This might give a slight local accent to some of the country's mass-market brews, though six-row barley is by no means unknown in the USA. Canadian mass-market beers were once slightly hoppier than their counterparts in the USA, but that difference is less evident today. The difference in strength between the mainstream beers of the two countries is often exaggerated by misunderstanding. While most everyday beers in the USA have between 3.2 and 3.9 percent alcohol by weight, the standard in Canada is just one notch higher, at 4.0. However, 4.0 by weight is the same as 5.0 by volume and the latter, larger-sounding, measure is used in Canada.

As elsewhere, many of the most interesting beers are produced by micros and brewpubs. Some of the best, and most accessible, brewpubs are discussed here. Canada seems to be especially prone to brewpubs that use extract and produce standard lagers. Predictably, these come and go in the blink of an eye.

Where to drink

In Montreal, l'Ile Noire (342 Ontario St E) tries to feature all of Quebec's micros. In the same city, Le Sergent Recruter (4650 Bvd St Laurent), which opened in 1993, makes its own own hoppy ales, and offers those from local micros. Near Montreal is the tiny brewpub/micro Mon Village, at St Lazare (2760 Côte St Charles). Quebec City has the brewpub L'Inox (37 Rue St André).

Toronto has one or two bars with notable selections, including C'est What (67 Front St) and Allen's (143 Danforth Ave). Also in Ontario, in the whisky- and beer-making town of Waterloo, the Huether Hotel (59 King St N) had a brewery in the late 19th century and has once more. Its Lion Brewery offers a tasty lager, and ales in the Canadian and British styles. Near Waterloo, in Mennonite country, Heidelberg has an eponymous brewpub (2 King St).

Regina, Saskatchewan, has several brewpubs, including the Barley Mill (6807 Rochdale Bvd), Bonzzini's (4634 Albert St S), the Bushwakker (2206 Dewdney Ave), and Brewsters (see entry). Saskatoon has Cheers (2105 8th St E); Clark's Crossing (3030 Diefenbaker Drive); and The Fox & Hounds (7 Assiniboine Drive). A branch of the Bushwakker is planned for Winnipeg, Manitoba. In Alberta, Calgary has a Brewsters, and Buzzard's (140 10th Ave SW) has a good selection by Prairie standards.

In the west, Fogg n' Suds is a small chain of speciality beer-bars, headquartered in Vancouver.

Algonquin

Marketing-oriented micro on the site of a famous old brewery (1870–1971) in Formosa, Ontario. A wide range includes **Country Lager★→★★**, sweetish and flavourful, with a faintly astringent finish; and a pleasant but mild **Special Reserve Ale★★**, with a fuller colour and a fruity, tart, palate.

Amsterdam

Toronto's first brewpub (133 John St) changed hands in late 1993. It had previously worked in partnership with the Rotterdam (see entry). Developments are awaited with interest.

Arctic

New (1993) micro, making fruity-tasting ales, in Yellowknife, Northwest Territories.

Big Rock

In the foothills of the Rockies, at Calgary, Alberta. This micro is getting bigger at a remarkable rate. Its well-made brews, unpasteurized but tightly filtered, have included the perfumy, malty, dry **XO Lager★★★★**; the hoppy **Royal Coachman Dry Ale★★**; a dry, malty, very smooth, golden **Pale Ale★→★★**; the slightly hoppier **Albino Rhino★★**; a straw-coloured Bitter called **Classical Ale★★→★★★**, malty in the palate and nicely hoppy in the finish; an amber-red, malty-fruity **Traditional Ale★★→★★★**, with a dryish finish; a smooth, sweetish, light-tasting brown ale called **Warthog★★**; the malty-buttery **McNally's Extra★★★** (5.6; 7.0), a classic Irish-style ale; the confusingly named **Springbok Ale★★** (4; 5), with a bronze colour, a flowery aroma, a light start and a dry finish; a coffeeish, creamy, **Porter★★**; and the stronger (4.8; 6), richer, **Cold Cock★★→★★★** winter porter.

Boréale

Punning brand-name of Les Brasseurs du Nord, a micro at St Jérôme, just N of Montreal. Brewer Laura Urtnowski produces a spritzy, dry, slightly tannic, **Blonde★→★★**; a sweet **Rousse★★**, with a touch of cough syrupiness; and a creamy, coffeeish, **Noire★★**.

Brasal

Brasserie Allemande in full, though the founders are actually Austrians. This well-equipped micro, emphasizing the German Beer Purity Law, is in Montreal. Products include a light lager, **Legère★**; the smooth, dry, **Hopps Bräu★★→★★★**, in broadly the Pilsener style; and a dark, malty-fruity, **Bock★★★**.

Brewsters

Small chain, with two brewpubs in Calgary and a couple in Saskatchewan, at Regina and Moose Jaw. Products include several undistinguished lagers; the light but smooth **Wild West Wheat★→★★**; a hoppy, herbal-tasting, **Bitter★★**; a buttery **Brown Ale★★**; a spicy, maple-tasting, **Barley Wine★★**; and a dryish, coffeeish, **Stout★→★★**.

Brick

Pioneering, now sizable, micro. Founded by Jim Brickman in the brewing and distilling town of Waterloo, Ontario. Principal products are the very light, fresh-tasting, **Red Baron★→★★**; and the all-malt **Brick Premium Lager★★**, sweetish, firm-bodied, with some dryness in the finish. Seasonal specials have included a tawny, malty-roasty, **Brick Bock★★→★★★** (5.2; 6.5).

La Cervoise

Looking like a 1950s coffee-bar, this brewpub (4457 Bvd St Laurent) is on the main thoroughfare that divides Montreal. Products include **La Main★→★★**, a sweetish, amber-red, ale; **Good Dog★★**, a fruity, golden ale; and **Obelix★★**, a light, smooth, very dry, stout. Production has been from extract, but the brewery can now make small batches from full grain.

Le Cheval Blanc

An old, Formica-clad, tavern that has crammed a brewhouse into its tiny quarters (809 Ontario St E, Montreal). Beers vary, but have included a dry, thinnish, **Blonde★**; a light but chocolatey **Ambrée★→★★**; a coffee-tasting **Brune★★**; and a slightly tannic **Weissbier★→★★**. There are occasional bottle-conditioned editions. **Tord Vis!★★** (a Quebecois exclamation) turned out to be a smoky-tasting, golden ale made with a dash of maple syrup. A toffeeish, fruity, **Scotch Ale★★★** was very enjoyable.

Conners

Pioneering micro that has undergone changes not only of ownership but also of location. It is now at the former Sculler brewery, in St Catherine's, Ontario. Products have included a fruity-hoppy **Ale★★**; a more malty **Bitter★★** and a roasty, dry but smooth **Stout★★→★★★**.

Creemore Springs

Spring water is taken two miles by tanker to the brewery, in the town of Creemore, 80-odd miles NW of Toronto. Creemore was a railhead for an agricultural region, and now has second homes for Toronto weekenders. The brewery is in an 1890s hardware store. The only product, **Creemore Springs Premium Lager★★★**, has a dense head; a light, Saaz-accented, hoppiness in the aroma; a firm, malty body; a soft, hoppy palate; and an elegant, light but lingering, hoppy finish. It is not pasteurized.

Denison's

Wheat beers and lagers from a Toronto brewpub with its own restaurant complex (75 Victoria St). Products have included a very sweet, fruity **Weizen★★**; a sweetish, soft **Lager★★**; a firmer, Export-style, golden **Spezial★★**; the chocolatey **Royal Dunkel★★**; and a malty-fruity **Märzen★★★**.

Drummond

In Red Deer, Alberta. Products have included **Wolfsbräu Amber Lager★★**, lightly aromatic, firm-bodied, on the dry side.

GMT
Unimaginatively named micro in Montreal (after founders Gravel, Martineau and Thibault). Products have included two golden lagers: light **Tremblay★→★★** and the maltier, smooth **Belle Gueule★★**.

Granite
Now in Toronto (245 Eglington Ave E) as well as Halifax, Nova Scotia (1222 Barrington St). Brewpubs owned by brothers Ron and Kevin Keefe. Products include a flowery **Summer Ale★★** and a malty, buttery, **Best Bitter★★→★★★**. The latter is also available dry-hopped under the name **Special★★★**, cask-conditioned and served on hand-pump. A deep, amber-brown, ale of 4.5, 5.6, called **Peculiar★★★**, is clean, soft and fruity. This is a classic old ale, though slightly lighter in body than its Peculier (*sic*) inspiration in Britain. Also on Eglington Ave E are two unrelated brewpubs, The Spruce Goose (at 130) and the sardonically named Vinifera (at 150).

Granville Island
Pioneering, sizable, micro in a trendy-touristy shopping area of Vancouver. Products have included a **Lager★★**, with a good dash of hop character, a smooth body and a dry finish; an amber-red **Märzen★★★** with a dry, malty start and a long, hoppy finish; and **Island Bock★★★**, with an amber-brown colour, a smooth body and touches of chocolate in its warming finish.

Great Lakes
This name occurs in several places in the N American brewing industry. This micro, originally in Brampton, Ontario, is now in Etobicoke, in the Toronto metro area. **Great Lakes Lager** was at first soft and sweet, drying in the finish, and has since been reformulated for "more commercial appeal". (New version not tasted.)

Great Western
Regional brewery making lightish lagers in Saskatoon.

Hart
In the Ottawa Valley, at Carleton Place. Micro producing the beautifully balanced **Hart Amber Ale★★★**, with a rocky head; creamy malt aroma and palate; lots of American hop aromas and flavours; and a clean, refreshing, fruitiness towards its dry finish.

Horseshoe Bay
The first micro in Canada when it was founded in 1982, and still very small. Its amber-red, malty, dry **Horseshoe Bay Ale★★→★★★** can be found bottle-conditioned.

Labatt
National giant, which also owns Rolling Rock, in the USA, and Moretti, in Italy. Labatt, headquartered in London, Ontario, is partly controlled by a splinter of the Bronfman (Seagram's whisky) family. Its beers lean towards perfuminess, new-mown hay, and sweetness. Its biggest-selling brand is the bland

Labatt's Blue★, a pale lager. **Labatt's Classic★→★★** is all-malt and *kräusened*, but still very light in character. **Labatt 50★** is a lightly aromatic golden ale. The company's golden **IPA★★** is less distinctive than it was. A red ale called **Duffy's★★** has a hint of aromatic fruitiness. The company's **Porter★→★★** is sweet and thin, with a hint of roastiness in the finish. Local brands include the sweetish **Schooner★** (in the Maritimes) and the drier **Kokanee★→★★★** (in the west). **Labatt Ice Beer★★**, introduced in 1993, is carbonic, with a curiously tongue-drying texture (if a beer can be crisp, may it also be crunchy?).

Lion D'Or

English-style ales at a brewpub in Lennoxville (6 College St, near Bishop's University), in the townships to the E of Montreal. Products include the beautifully balanced **Lion's Pride★★→★★★**, clearly inspired by the similarly named ale from Fuller's, of London, England.

McAuslan

On Rue St Ambroise (reputedly named after a monk who was the first brewer in Montreal), near the district of Griffin Town. This micro produces under the St Ambroise name a clean, appetizing, **Pale Ale★★★**, with a very good hop character from nose to finish, and a smooth, dry, roasty, robust **Oatmeal Stout/Bière Noire★★★**. Under the Griffon name, it has a lightly hoppy-fruity **Extra Pale Ale/Bière Blonde★★** and a malty, nutty, but beautifully balanced **Brune/Brown Ale★★→★★★**.

Molson

National giant which also owns Carling of Canada. A minority share in Molson is held by Miller of the USA, and a substantial stake by Foster's of Australia. In 1993, the "Molson Signature" series of all-malt speciality products was introduced. Early examples, tasted while still in development, included a peachy-coloured **Cream Ale★★★**, soft, smooth and fruity, with a touch of hop in the finish; and a chewy, malty **Amber Lager★★→★★★**. Also in 1993, the company announced that it was no longer using preservatives. The regular range of Molson ales includes **Golden★**, light in both palate and body; the carbonic, fruity, **O'Keefe★**; the well-known **Export★→★★**, lightly fruity and spicy; **Stock Ale★★**, with more hop character; **Rickard's Nutbrown★★**, thinnish in body, with caramel and coffee flavours; and **Brador★★→★★★**, an ale-like malt liquor (5; 6.2). Lagers include **Molson Canadian★**, clean and well-balanced but rather bland; the slightly tart **Carling Black Label★**; the sweetish **Old Vienna★**; and the very perfumy, fruity, crisp **Molson Ice★★**, introduced in 1993.

Moosehead

Sizable regional brewer, in New Brunswick, exporting widely. Moosehead's beers have a delicate hop character, firm body, and grassy yeastiness. Its local brew, **Alpine★→★★**, has a little more character than **Moosehead Canadian Lager★**, which is marketed in the USA. **Moosehead Pale Ale★→★★** is drier. **Ten Penny Stock Ale★★** is slightly more characterful.

Niagara Falls Brewing

In the town of Niagara, on the Canadian side of the Falls. As several of the local vineyards make Eiswein, this micro, established in July 1989, produced in November of that year an Eisbock, certainly the first commercially made "ice beer" in the Americas since Prohibition, and probably the first ever in the New World. **Niagara Eisbock★★★→★★★★** (15.3; 1060–62; 6.4; 8) has a peachy colour and palate; a light, soft, maltiness; a smooth body and palate; and a dry, estery, finish. The brewery's other products include the hoppy **Trapper Premium★★**, a conventional lager; **Maple Wheat Strong Beer★★★** (6.8; 8.5), in which the defining ingredient is very evident among nutty flavours and cracker-like crispness; the caramelly, grainy, **Gritstone Premium★★→★★★** (4.7; 5.8), something between an English Brown Ale and a stronger Belgian dark brew; the soft, slightly syrupy, **Olde Jack★★→★★★** (5.8; 7.2), which sounds like an old ale, is billed as an extra-strong bitter and might best be styled as a barley wine; and the very rich, tar-like, complex **Brock's Extra Stout★★★** (4.7; 5.8).

Nelson

Micro in a 19th-century brewery building in Nelson, British Columbia. Produces ales (not tasted).

Northern

Former Carling breweries in N of Ontario, now owned by employees. Making mainstream beers.

Okanagan Spring

Expanding micro in the Okanagan Valley, at Vernon, British Columbia. Products have included a light but flowery **Pilsner★★**; a **Premium Lager★★**; still on the light side, but well rounded; **Old Munich★★★**, a dark wheat beer with a light, fruity, tartness, now with the clovey-notes of a Bavarian yeast; **Extra Special Pale Ale★★**, clean and rounded, only lightly fruity (it is made with a bottom-fermenting yeast), but with a good touch of hop in the finish; **St Patrick Stout★★→★★★**, dense, creamy and full of dark chocolate character; and **Old English Porter★★★** (6.8; 8.5), rich with coffee and oloroso sherry flavours.

Pacific Western

Regional brewery in Prince George, British Columbia, producing mainstream lagers and a bland, reddish ale, **Canterbury Dark★**.

Prairie Inn

Roadhouse-sports bar brewing from extract, N of Victoria, British Columbia (7806 E Saanich Rd). **English Gold★→★★** (more bronze-coloured) is fruity, but lacking in hop. **Black Bitter's★** (*sic*) tastes of caramel. **Fruit Lager★→★★** is light, honeyish; a hint of strawberry.

Rotterdam

Flavoursome beers at a Toronto brewpub (600 King St W). Regulars include clean, sweetish **Lager★★**, with a mildly dry finish; and aromatically hoppy **Pilsener★★ →★★★**. Specials have ranged through a very hoppy strong pale lager, **Doppelpils★★★**; earthy **Weiss★★★** with a lactic fermentation; and a malty, buttery, **Scotch Ale★★★**.

Shaftebury

Named after the town in Dorset, England, but with its spelling amended to make it more proprietary. English-style ales, with a smooth, dryish, house character, from a micro in Vancouver. Products include a malty, nutty, brew in broadly the style of a strongish (4.0; 5.0) Dark Mild, oddly named **Cream Ale★★★**; and a firm, fruity, slightly tart **ESB★★ →★★★** (4.4; 5.5).

Sleeman

Having brewed in Cornwall, then in Guelph, Ontario, from the mid-19th century, the Sleeman family lapsed from the industry before World War II, then returned to start this sizable micro in the same town in 1988. Products include dryish **Silver Creek Lager★★**; and **Sleeman Cream Ale★★**, with a perfumy, sweetish, bouquet and a slightly tart, fruity, flavour development. The latter is to some extent based on an original Sleeman formulation.

Spinnakers

The first brewpub in Canada (308 Catherine St, Victoria, British Columbia) in 1984. Still producing some excellent ales, with casks on the bar for as long as they last on Thursday, Friday and Saturday evenings. Products have included: a superbly refreshing **Hefe-Weizen★★ →★★★** (sometimes rendered Heffe-), spiced with coriander and laced with peach juice; a big, toasty, **Dunkelweizen★★**; **Doc Hadfield's★★**, a very fruity and dry golden ale; **Mount Tolmie Dark★★**, malty and coffeeish and somewhere between a Mild and an Old Ale; **ESB★★★** (4.4; 5.5), full of earthy hop character and bitterness; the strong (5.0; 6.2) **Ogden Porter★★ →★★★**, creamy, roasty and hoppy; and the very soft **Empress Stout★★ →★★★** (4.3; 5.2). **Eau de Tabernac★★★** was a medicinal-tasting beer made with maple syrup and aged in the style of *Rodenbach*. **Unusual★★★** was an acidic blend of aged beers in the style of a *lambic*. This was also used as the basis for a light but syrupy, fruity-tart **Pêche**.

Swan's

Second brewpub in Victoria (506 Pandora St), with bedrooms. Products include: a malty **Bavarian Lager★★ →★★★**; a coffeeish, long, **Dark Lager★★ →★★★**; a flowery, heathery, (American-style) **Wheat Beer★★**; a honeyish **Pale Ale★★**; a hoppy, dry, **Bitter★★★**; a smooth, malty-fruity, **Scotch Ale★★ →★★★**; nutty **Appleton Brown Ale★★ →★★★**; a light but oily, roasty, **Porter★★**; and a relatively light, sweetish, **Oatmeal Stout★★**.

Thames Valley

Newish micro producing lager in London, Ontario.

Unibroue
In the Montreal suburb of Chambly, a micro whose share-holders include rock singer Robert Charlebois and Belgian brewery Riva. Products include the very pale, heavily sedimented, candyish **Blanche de Chambly★★**, a Belgian-style "White"; the medicinal, spicy, peppery **Maudite★★→★★★** ("Damned"), a Belgian-style strong (6.4; 8) russet ale; and **La Fin du Monde★★→★★★**, a very pale, slightly stronger brew with suggestions of honey and anise.

Upper Canada
Interesting, well-made brews from a sizable micro in Toronto. Its flagship **Dark Ale★★→★★★** is malt-accented, with a soft fruitiness and a dry, hoppy, finish. The pleasant, easy-to-drink, **Publican's Bitter★★** is actually on the sweet side, but with some tartness and hop in the finish. The **Wheat Beer ★★→★★★** is golden and bright, very refeshing, slightly tart. The **Lager★★→★★★** is soft, clean and spritzy, with good hop character in both the bouquet and finish. **Rebellion★★** is a malty, substantial, strong, golden lager. **True Bock★★→★★★** has a good malt character, a warming finish, and a full amber colour.

Vancouver Island
On the island, near Victoria. This early micro produces a soft, lightly malty, **Premium Lager★★→★★★**, with a touch of hoppy dryness in the finish; the Kulmbacher-style Hermann's **Dark Lager★★★**, with a very good bitter-chocolate character; a sweetish, fruity, spritzy, top-fermenting, **Piper's Pale Ale★★**; and an aromatic, spicy, **Victoria Weizen★★★**, made with a Bavarian yeast.

Wellington County
English-style ales, sometimes cask-conditioned, from a classic micro in the old brewing town of Guelph, in a region with connections with the British brewing family Arkell. Hence **Arkell Best Bitter★★★** (3.2; 4.0), which has in its cask form an earthy aroma of Goldings hops; a deft balance of malty dryness and restrained fruitiness; and a long, hoppy, finish. A good, honest ale. The same beer filtered for the bottle tastes slightly less hoppy. **Wellington SPA★★** (Special Pale Ale), at 3.6; 4.5, is sweeter and fruitier. **County Ale★★★** (4; 5) is bigger-bodied, complex, well-rounded, with a very hoppy finish. **Iron Duke★★★** (5.3; 6.5) is malt-accented but beautifully balanced, with great depth of flavour and a dry finish. **Imperial Stout★★★** (6.4; 8) is roasty, chocolatey, syrupy, alcoholic and warming. **Wellington Premium Lager★★** (3.6; 4.5) rounded and flavoursome.

Whistler
A mountain known as Whistler gives its name to a ski resort 80-odd miles N of Vancouver. The resort's micro produces, among other beers, the light, soft, smooth, **Whistler Premium Lager★★**; and the malty, slightly roasty, coffeeish, but light-bodied, **Black Tusk Ale★★**.

THE UNITED STATES

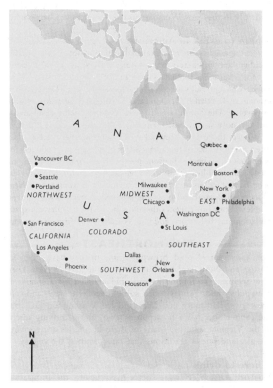

CANADA

Vancouver BC

Quebec •
Montreal •
Boston •

• Seattle
• Portland
NORTHWEST

Milwaukee
•
Chicago •

MIDWEST

New York •
EAST • Philadelphia

U

S

A

Washington DC

• San Francisco
CALIFORNIA

Denver •
COLORADO

• St Louis

SOUTHEAST

Los Angeles

Dallas
•

• Phoenix
SOUTHWEST

New
Orleans

Houston •

N
↑

The surge of brewpubs, micro-breweries and "niche market" beers from regional and national producers means that the United States now has a more comprehensive range of specialities than any other country.

The number of brewing companies in the USA has grown from around 40 to almost 400 in under two decades. Even the national brewers have experimented (Anheuser-Busch, producers of Budweiser, with a Pilsener and a Märzenbier; Miller with an ale and a stout; Coors with an "Irish Ale" a wheat beer, a Vienna-style winter brew and an Eisbock; Stroh's with a wheat beer and a Doppelbock; Heileman with local versions of an "Amber", for example), but the smaller companies are setting the pace. Between them, they are producing everything from abbey-style ales, barley wines and cranberry beers to India pales, "Russian" stouts, Dortmunder lagers and smoked beers.

The diversity of brewing traditions implanted by the first European settlers were lost between Prohibition, two world wars, the uniformity of the 1950s and the heyday of mass-marketing on network television – now, they are being rediscovered.

Often, the European inspiration is exceeded by the new generation. Some of the born-again styles, especially the very hoppy ales, belong as firmly in the New World as an oaky California Chardonnay.

Where to drink in America

Several speciality beers are available nationally, but a greater number are marketed only locally. They are easily found in, for example, the cities and hinterlands of Boston, New York, Chicago/Milwaukee, Minneapolis/St Paul, Denver, San Francisco, Portland, Oregon, and Seattle, but far more elusive in parts of The South, small-town America, many rural areas, and the hottest, dustiest, states.

Where there are brewpubs or speciality beer bars, they often carry stocks of the various free newspapers produced for beer-lovers. These "brewspapers" cover the fast-changing scene, and publish comprehensive listings of local breweries, beer bars, tastings and festivals. In the East, *Yankee Brew News* reports on Boston and New England; *Ale Street News* is centred on New York but covers other Northern cities; *Barleycorn* spans Philadelphia, Baltimore and the Washington/Virginia region.

THE NORTHEAST

The most sure-footed brewpubs and micros have been in Boston and New England, but the city and state of New York now seems to be finding its way. Philadelphia has a couple of brewpubs, and Pennsylvania some excellent new and old breweries. Baltimore and Maryland led Washington DC, but the capital now has a brewpub or two, and a thriving micro in the Virginia suburbs. Many of these breweries are reviving the ales and porter traditions that once typified the region.

Where to drink

Boston: Less beer-aware locals may suggest the inspiration of TV's *Cheers*, The Bull and Finch (84 Beacon St) or the city's oldest tavern, Jacob Wirth (31 Stuart), but enthusiasts will want a sampling from the 70-odd draughts and American cuisine at The Sunset Grill (130 Brighton Ave, Allston). Ambience and beer selection are excellent at Doyle's (3484 Washington St, Jamaica Plain), splendidly multi-cultural despite rooms devoted to the Kennedys and Michael Collins. At the Back Bay Hilton Hotel, Boodle's Bar has a notable selection. The area has several beer festivals, the biggest in May.

New York: The oldest saloon, McSorley's, the Rabelaisian Belgian café Burp Castle and speciality beer-bar Brewsky's (with a Ukrainian flavour) are all on the short stretch of 7th St between 1st and 2nd Aves, in the East Village. Also in the Village, the Peculier Pub (145 Bleecker and W Broadway) is Tommy Chou's pioneering beer-bar. In the West Village, Chumley's (86 Bedford, at Barrow) has a political and literary history and American microbrews. The same beer policy obtains at The American Festival Café (Rockefeller Center, 20 W 50th, Midtown). The Waldorf-Astoria Hotel's Bull and Bear pub (Lexington and 49th) has a well-chosen international beer selection. At South

Street Seaport, The North Star specializes in British ales and single malt Scotches. New York has a growing roster of beer festivals, the biggest under Brooklyn Bridge in late September. **Philadelphia**: The Irish-spelled Bridgid's (726 N 24th and Meredith, Fairmount) is a Belgian-owned restaurant with appropriate beers. The White Dog is a politically aware cafe in the university district (3420 Sansom) with a good selection of American brews; Stoudt's beers are featured. Other bars with good selections include Copa, Too! ("Avenue of the Arts", S Broad St), Khyber Pass (54 S 2nd) and Tangier Cafe (18th and Lombard). There are plans for a brewpub in the Manayunk Farmers' Market.

Baltimore: Beer-lovers head for Fell's Point: Bertha's (734 S Broadway); Duda's (1600 Thames St); The Horse You Came In On (1626 Thames St).

Washington, DC area: The Brickskeller (1523 22nd NW, on the fringes of Georgetown) has the biggest selection in the US and regular tutored tastings. In the near suburbs Arlington has Bardo Rodeo (2000 Wilson Bvd), a neo-psychedelic beer-bar with plans to brew; and Alexandria has several less eccentric establishments within walking distance, including Hard Times (1201 King St), King Street Blues (112 N Saint Asaph) and Union St Public House (121 S Union).

Arrowhead
Red Feather Pale Ale★★, light, dry, firm, hoppy and fruity, was the launch brew in 1991 from this micro in Chambersburg, Pennsylvania.

Baltimore Brewing Company
A member of the Grolsch family privately launched this establishment, making and serving lagers, unfiltered but bright, in what was once the brewery neighbourhood (104 Albemarle). Fresh, malty **Helles★★**; soft, smooth, hoppy **Pils★★★**; coffeeish **Dunkles★★→★★★**. See also entry for Sisson's. A third brewpub, The Wharf Rat (204–8 West Pratt) brews robust ales (not tasted).

Boston Beer Works
Industrial chic brewpub (61 Brookline Ave), handy for Fenway Park and the Red Sox. Wide range includes **Boston Red★★**, a very full amber colour, with a sweetish fruitiness enwrapped in an earthy hop to start and finish; the flavourful, flowery **Beantown Nutbrown★★→★★★**; the perfumy, very hoppy and dry **Back Bay IPA★★★**; and a smooth, chocolatey, roasty **Oatmeal Stout★★→★★★**. See also Cambridge and Commonwealth.

Boston Brewing (Samuel Adams)
Relentlessly publicized, but deservedly successful on merit. Specialities are made in a micro at the 1865 former Haffenreffer brewery (tour and sample: ☎617-522-9080), near Doyle's pub, at Jamaica Plain. These include: the draught version of **Boston Stock Ale★★★**, oily and perfumy, dry-hopped

with Goldings and cold-conditioned (the bottled counterpart is made under contract at F. X. Matt); a rich, chocolatey, **Cream Stout**★★→★★★; a lightly fruity, smooth and tart, wheat-based, **Cranberry Lambic**★★→★★★ (a misnomer, since all the yeast is pitched); a lightly clove-ish **Wheat**★★→★★★; a firm, fruity, **Dunkelweizen**★★→★★★; a remarkably malty, long, **Doppelbock**★★★ (21; 1084; 6; 7.5); and an occasional **"Triple Bock"**★★★→★★★★ (really a barley wine, made with champagne yeast), the ascending strength of which reached a world record 17.5 in 1993. The alcoholic attack of this highly distinctive brew is softened by maple syrup, one of the sugars that helps it reach that potency. It is further rounded out by sugar-maple charcoal and vanilla notes emerging from the Tennessee whiskey casks in which it spends three months maturing.

The company's principal product, in broadly the Pilsener style, is **Samuel Adams Boston Lager**★★★. This has a flowery aroma; a gold-to-bronze colour; a soft, malty, palate; and Hallertau Mittelfruh hop flavours in the dry finish. Despite the Bostonian name, this is produced in Pittsburgh and Portland, Oregon. The company also has a Samuel Adams brewpub in Philadelphia (above The Oyster House at 1516 Sansom). This produces a fruity, hoppy, **Amber Ale**★→★★ and a **Porter**★★ with a touch of treacle-toffee, both from extract.

Brooklyn Brewery
The dry-hopped, fresh, flowery, firm, flavourful, **Brooklyn Lager**★★→★★★ started well, in 1988, and has gained in character since. It is fermented with the yeast of Schaefer, which departed in 1976, leaving Brooklyn without a brewery. **Brooklyn Brown**★★★ is a hoppy, relatively strong (13.5–14; 1054–6; 4.8; 6.0) and more complex counterpart to the Northern English style. Despite its name, Brooklyn has its beers brewed under contract at F. X. Matt. Brooklyn also distributes for other American micro-brewers.

Buffalo Brewing Company
First there was a brewpub, using extract with some grain, at 6861 Main and Transit, Williamsville. The Buffalo Brewpub made the first **American Oatmeal Stout**★★, light, smooth and dry. That still operates, but there is also a full-grain brewery, with beer-hall, at 1830 Abbot Rd, in the old steel-industry neighbourhood of Lackawanna. Products include a grassy-tasting **Lager**★→★★ (also brewed, for bottling, by F. X. Matt), a flowery, dry, **Pils**★★, a coffeeish, smooth, **Blizzard Bock**★★; a spicy, buttery, **Weisse**★→★★; and a very sweet **Limerick's Irish Red Ale**★→★★.

Cambridge Brewing Company
From downtown Boston, head across the river to 1 Kendall Sq, at Broadway and Hampshire, Cambridge. Conservatory-style bar-restaurant. Sweetish, fruity, **Golden**★→★★ ale; hoppy **Pale**★★; spicy **Amber**★★; very fruity, leafy, **IPA**★★; **Porter**★★

with notes of treacle-toffee and roasted chocolate beans; and some characterful seasonal specialities. There is a newer, unconnected brewpub called John Harvard, at 33 Dunster St, Cambridge (beers not tasted).

Capitol City
In Washington, DC, at restored Art Deco bus station (110 New York Ave NW and H St, near Metro Center subway). Brewpub/grill, opened in 1992. Early offerings have included a butter-fruity **Pils★**; a malty-fruity, perfumy, **Alt★★**; and other styles not tasted.

Catamount
The classic example of a regular golden ale in the East Coast tradition comes from this Vermont micro. **Catamount Gold★★★** (10.5; 1042; 3.6; 4.5) has a good American hop character in both bouquet and finish, between which is a clean, lightly malty, palate, with flavour development towards fruity notes. **Catamount Amber★★ →★★★** (12; 1048; 4.0; 5.0) is more assertive all round, with a polite nod towards an English Pale Ale. **Catamount Porter★★★** (13; 1052; 4.2; 5.3) is remarkably smooth, creamy and chocolatey. The outstanding porter on the East Coast. Catamount, at White River Junction, makes several products under contract for other brewers.

Chapter House
Student pub in Cornell University's home town of Ithaca (400 Stewart Ave), in central New York state. After a sabbatical, brewing recommenced in 1993. Early brews included a nutty **Märzen★★**; a very malty **Vienna Amber★★ →★★★**; and a **Moravian Porter★★ →★★★**, with notes of coffee and figs.

Commonwealth
Original Burton Unions decorate this pioneering brewpub in Boston (138 Portland and Merrimac) between Boston Gardens (home of the Celtics) and the Faneuil Hall tourist area. Products include **Best Burton Bitter★★★**, with plenty of hop in its aroma and long finish; the soft, sweetish **Amber Ale★★**; the complex, rummy, **Stout★★ →★★★**; and seasonal specialities that include a faintly medicinal **Porter★★ →★★★**; and a winey **Winter Warmer/Special Old Ale★★★**.

Dock Street
Much mentioned in a popular TV series, *Thirty-Something*. "Brasserie" food and an astonishingly varied, ever-changing, range of well-made beers in a chic brewpub at 2 Logan Square (18th and Cherry), Philadelphia. Products have included: a soft, aromatic, **Bohemian Pils★★ →★★★**; a hoppy **German Pils★★**; a slightly chocolatey **Oscura★★ →★★★**, based on the Mexican dark type; a lightly malty **Dunkel★★**; a very malty **Bock★★**; a lightly spicy **Hefe-Weisse★★**; a grainy **Rye Beer★★ →★★★**; a lightly chocolatey **Mild★★ →★★★**; a soft, lightly fruity, **Amber★★** ale; a dryish **Pale Ale★★**; a very

fruity, slightly winey, **Bitter★★**; an **IPA★→★★** somewhat lacking in hop; an oily, firm, **Irish Red Ale★★→★★★**; a chocolatey **Stout★★**; and a rich **Barley Wine★★★→★★★★** with an astonishingly spritzy finish. Bottled products are made under contract at F. X. Matt. Dock Street also has a branch planned for Washington, DC (at 13th and Pennsylvania, in the restored Warner Theater).

Geary
Highly regarded micro in Portland, Maine. The Anglo-American accent of its ales echoes the early traditions of East Coast brewing. **Geary's Pale Ale★★→★★★** (12; 1048; 3.6; 4.5) is a New England classic: copper-coloured, dry, clean, crisp, with lots of late-hop taste, in an appetizing complex with ale fruitiness (from old Hampshire's Ringwood yeast). **Hampshire Special Ale★★★** (17.5; 1070; around 5.6; 7.0), tawny, bittersweet, drying to a tremendous hop finish, is produced for winter.

Genesee
The name of the river on which stands the city of Rochester, New York, home of America's biggest regional brewery. Creditably, for a brewery so large, it specializes in ales. Sad to say, neither its **Twelve-Horse Ale★★** (3.8; 4.7) nor its **Genesee Cream Ale★→★★** (3.7; 4.6) has much character. Both have a sweet, creamy, palate, balanced by a lightly fruity tartness in the finish. Genesee also produces **Michael Shea's Irish Amber★→★★**, with a touch of malty sweetness.

Gritty McDuff's
Brewpub in the Old Town area of Portland, Maine (396 Fore St). Products include a well-balanced **Bitter★★★**; a **Brown Ale★★→★★★**, the palate on the light side, but with some maltiness; a coffeeish **Stout★→★★**; and many seasonal specials.

Hartford
Brewpub in town of same name (35 Pearl St, in a former ice-cream parlour in the financial district). Lively-tasting brews include the unfortunately named **Pitbull Gold★★**, a fruity, perfumy, hoppy, dryish, ale; **Arch Amber★★** (named after a Civil War memorial), sweeter, but well balanced. Specials have included a **Brown Ale★★→★★★** which is chocolatey, but again very well balanced.

Ipswich
Earthy, hoppy, fruity **Ipswich Ale★★**, from a micro in the town of the same name, in Massachusetts. The brewery also has a fruity, slightly tannic, brown ale called **Pilgrim★→★★**.

Jones
A rock-like Welshman named "Stoney" Jones founded this brewery in 1907, at Smithton, Pennsylvania, where coal from

nearby mines was loaded on to the railroad to Pittsburgh. Beers include the tart **Stoney's★**; the crisp **Esquire Extra Dry★**; and the hoppier **Fort Pitt★★**.

Lion
Old-established brewery in the former coal town of Wilkes-Barre, Pennsylvania. Products include **Stegmaier 1857★★**, malty but dryish, with a good hop note in the finish; and **Stegmaier Porter★★→★★★**, dry, firm, chocolatey, slightly oily, and now an all-malt brew. Stegmaier was once a rival brewery across town.

McNeill's
Cask-conditioned ales at a brewpub in Brattleboro, Vermont (90 Elliot St). Robust, malty and sometimes with Madeira notes. A sweetish, creamy, golden, **Bitter★★**; a fuller-coloured, hoppier, **Special★★**; a dryish, tasty, **Nut-brown★★**; a flavour-packed **Double Brown★★★**; and hugely aromatic **IPA★★★**. Products have also included a soft, pale **Bock★★**, with a good malt character.

Manhattan Brewing Company
A stylish, young, beer-maker, Garrett Oliver, has brought new life to this pioneering brewpub since it reopened in 1993. Products include a fresh-tasting, crisp, dry, hoppy, **Gold Ale★★**; a nutty, flowery, British-style, **Amber Ale★★→★★★**; a fruity, dryish, strong, **IPA★★**; and a smooth, creamy, chocolatey, **Extra Stout★★★**. Character-ful seasonal specials include a soft, malty, **Märzen★★→★★★** and a spicily refreshing **Bavarian Wheat★★→★★★**. The brewpub is housed in a former power station, at 42 Thompson St and Broome (between 6th Ave and W Broadway), SoHo.

Mass Bay
Abbreviated micro on Boston Harbor, Massachusetts Bay. Principal product is **Harpoon Ale★★**, fruity, with a firm, cookie-like maltiness and a perfumy, hoppy finish. Bottled beers brewed at F. X. Matt.

F. X. Matt
From the Black Forest, the Francis Xavier Matt family emigrated to the Mohawk River valley and built a brewery in Utica when upstate New York was still famous for its ales. Today, the fourth generation of the Utica Matts works in the company. Its many products include the hoppy, dry, Pilsener-type **Saranac 1888★★→★★★**, a fruity, toffeeish, **Porter★★**, a smooth, tasty, **Black and Tan★★**, and bottled editions for many draught-only micros and brewpubs.

Middlesex Brewing Company
Micro established in 1993 in the high-tech town of Burlington, near Boston, Massachusetts, Early products include the

chocolatey, dark, **Middlesex Brown Ale★★→★★★** and an **Oatmeal Stout** (not tasted).

The Mountain Brewers
Near skiing country, at Bridgewater, Vermont. Micro making **Long Trail Ale★★**, light, soft, fruity, with a gentle bitterness in the finish.

Mountain Valley
In the Ramapo Mountains, at Suffern (122 Orange Ave), on the New York side of the border with New Jersey. This brewpub produces a well-balanced **India Pale Ale★★→★★★**, closer to the British than the American interpretation; a **Porter★★→★★★** with treacle-toffee notes; a **Rauchbier★★★** that starts soft but finishes with an emphatically smoky dryness; and a **Blonde Double Bock★★★** full of malty flavours (20; 1080; 6.2; 7.75).

New Amsterdam
New Amsterdam Amber★★ is a fruity lager/ale hybrid. A hoppier version is called **New Amsterdam Ale★★→★★★**. These were briefly brewed in Chelsea, Manhattan, but are now made under contract at F. X. Matt.

New England Brewing Company
Micro in Norwalk, Connecticut. Products include **Atlantic Amber★★→★★★**, a medium-bodied, malt-accented, creamy, earthy, fruity brew; **Gold Stock Ale★★★**, with an oily-malty body, lots of flavour development and a long, hoppy, finish; and a dry, firm, smooth, palate-arousing **Oatmeal Stout★★→★★★**.

New Haven Brewing Company
In the home town of Yale University, formerly also noted for its elm trees. **Elm City Connecticut Ale★★★** has a full, amber-brown, colour; a clean malt emphasis; and a lightly dry, fruity, finish. **Blackwell Stout★★★** has a teasing balance of roasted coffee and syrupy sweetness. **Belle Dock Barley Wine★★★** has a huge hop aroma, a beautifully balanced palate and a touch of warming alcohol in the finish. This micro is in a building that once housed a power plant for what the Americans call trolleys, the British trams.

New York Harbor
New York Harbor Ale★★ is golden in colour, starting soft and malty, but with a crisp, hoppy, almost tart, finish. **New York Harbor Porter★→★★** is a light, well-balanced, coffeeish, interpretation of the style. These beers were created by New Yorker Sal Pennachio, and are brewed under contract at Stevens Point, Wisconsin.

Northampton Brewery
Bar and grill making lagers and ales, at Brewster Court, Northampton, Massachusetts. Products have included a Saaz-

accented Pilsener called **Gold★★**; a relatively light Vienna-style **Amber★★**; and some excellent seasonal specials, including a dark, smooth, **Bock★★→★★★**.

Old Dominion

Virginia, the first English colony, is sometimes known as the Old Dominion. This sobriquet was taken as a corporate name by a micro established in 1990 in the Virginia suburbs, near to Washington's Dulles Airport. The "old" is dropped in the name of the beers. Early examples have included **Dominion Lager★★→★★★**, broadly in the Dortmunder style, with a touch of new-mown hay and a good malt character when served fresh; the hoppier, more herbal-tasting, unfiltered, **Victory Amber★→★★**; a spicy, clovey, **Summer Wheat★★★**; **Blue Point Ale★★→★★★**, accented towards hop aroma; and a creamy **Stout★★→★★★**.

Olde Heurich

Washington, DC, once had a brewery called Christian Heurich (pronounced High Rick). The proprietor's grandson now has a contract brew called **Olde Heurich Maerzen★★**. This has a full gold colour; a malty palate, and an elegantly hoppy finish. Made by F. X. Matt.

Old Marlborough

Creators of a fruity, dry, hoppy, ale called **Post Road Pale★★**. The company is in Framingham, near Marlborough, Massachusetts; the beer is made under contract at Catamount.

Old Newbury

Commercial home-brewery in Newbury, on the North Shore of Massachusetts. **Yankee Ale★★** is soft and sweetish, with a good hoppy dryness in the finish. It is marketed unfiltered.

Oxford Brewing

A Briton founded this micro, in Baltimore. Its **Oxford Class★★→★★★** is a very English-tasting ale, malt accented but very well balanced. Sometimes found cask-conditioned as Oxford Real Ale. Also a smooth, chocolatey **Porter★★→★★★**.

Pennsylvania Brewing

Handsome beer-hall, making its own, excellent, products in the 1880 Eberhardt & Ober brewery building in the "German town" of Pittsburgh (800 Vinial St, at Troy Hill, Allegheny). Products include a clean, malty, Helles, called **Penn Light Lager★★→★★★**; a hoppy **Kaiser Pils★★★**; a fuller-coloured, maltier, smooth, **Penn Pilsner★★** that is more in the style of a Dortmunder; the Munich-style chocolatey, slight roasty, **Penn Dark★★**; an aromatically malty, smooth, **Märzen Fest★★★**; and a very malty, delicious **Bock★★→★★★**. Penn Pilsner is made for bottling at the Jones Brewery.

Portsmouth Brewery
Brewery-restaurant in Portsmouth, New Hampshire (56 Market St). Products include the malty, fruity (figgy?) ale **Old Brown Dog★★→★★★**.

Potomac River
Micro established in Chantilly, Virginia, in 1993. First product, adopting an earlier spelling, was **Patowmack Ale★★**, with a firm body and a touch of maltiness in the finish. Also a fruity **Red★★** and a medium-dry chocolatey **Porter★★**.

Rochester
The Rochester Brewpub (800 Jefferson Rd, Henrietta) was established as a spin-off from the one in Buffalo. A newer, unrelated, brewpub, Rohrbach (315 Gregory) produces the tasty **Highland Amber★★**, with notes of toffee and chocolate. Elsewhere in Rochester, The Old Toad Pub (277 Alexander St) cask-conditions ales from Manhattan Brewing and Geary.

Rolling Rock
A long-established light American lager with its own cult following, though it has no great character beyond a touch of new-mown hay. **Rolling Rock★→★★** and a thinnish **Bock★→★★** are made in the old monastery town of Latrobe, near Pittsburgh, Pennsylvania. The brewery is owned by Labatt, of Canada.

Sisson's/South Baltimore Brewing
Well-regarded brewpub (and excellent restaurant), for which reservations are recommended. Opposite Cross Street Market. Hugh Sisson's refreshing, aromatic, golden **Marble Ale★★→★★★** and a less distinctive, amber, **Stockade Ale★★** are heartily dry-hopped. Even the **Stout★★** has a lot of hop aroma before it moves from licorice sweetness to spicy dryness. Seasonal specials have included a tart but smooth **Dunkel Weizen★★★**.

Stoudt
Not a style but a surname. Mrs Carol Stoudt's brewery constantly wins awards, confirming its status as one of the finest in the East. Products include a **Pilsener★★★** with a delicate bouquet, good hop flavours and a dry finish; a well-balanced **Export Gold★★★** with a superbly aromatic malt character; a creamy, floral, **Adamstown Amber★★**; a nutty, sweet, clean **Märzen★★→★★★**; a clean, soft, malty **Festbier★★★**; several seasonal interpretations of malty Bocks (one with clover honey) and spicy wheat beers, as well as more Anglophone top-fermenting styles such as a hoppy **IPA★★→★★★**. There has even been a creamy, medium-dry, **Stout★★**. The brewery is at Adamstown, Pennsylvania, between Reading and Lancaster, on Route 272. There is a steak restaurant, beer garden, and Sunday antiques market.

Spring Street

New York company with beer called **Wit★★**, an orangey interpretation of the Belgian "White" style. This light-tasting beer is produced at Stevens Point, Wisconsin.

Straub

Smallest of the old-established breweries in the USA. Family-owned and a part of the local folklore in St Mary's, in the Allegheny Mtns, 100 miles N of Pittsburgh. **Straub Beer★→★★** has a sweet aroma and palate, a light body and a dry finish.

Sunday River

Ski resort brewery and restaurant, at Sunday River, near Bethel, Maine. Well-made beers include a malty but well-balanced **Alt★★→★★★**; the sweeter, fruitier, hoppier, **Redstone Ale★★**; the slightly syrupy **Barons Brown Ale★★→★★★**; and **Black Bear Porter★★**, coffeeish, liqueur-like, and perhaps more of a sweet stout.

Vermont Pub and Brewery

A respected author of books on brewing, Greg Noonan, creates his own products in this vaguely Irish pub in an Italianate restaurant (144 College St) in downtown Burlington (a college town and tourist spot on the US side of Lake Champlain. A wide and constantly changing range has included a full-bodied but dry **Kellerbier★★→★★★**; the sweetish, perfumy, **Burly Irish Ale★★**; a hoppy **Winter Ale★★**; and a very dry **Smoked Porter★★★**, the latter made at various times with maple, hickory or applewood.

West Side

Old-established neighbourhood pub, now brewing its own, at 340 Amsterdam Ave and 76th, on the west side of Manhattan. Brews have included a sweetish, lightly fruity, **Wheat Ale★→★★**; a lightly hoppy **Blond Ale★→★★**; a firmer, drier, **Pale Ale★★**; an **ESB★→★★**, somewhat lacking in bitterness; and a syrupy **Red★→★★**.

Wild Goose

The geese that give their name to this micro visit its home turf each October, and take their chance with hunters. The brewery is at Cambridge, Maryland. Its **Amber Beer★★** has a malty start, with hoppy dryness in the finish. Its **Porter★★→★★★** is full of flavour, with fruit, chocolate, vanilla, and Bourbon-like notes.

Woodstock

The festival was not quite in Woodstock, and neither is this micro, though the owner lives there. The Woodstock Brewing Company is nearby, in the Hudson Valley town of Kingston, once the state capital of New York. It began in 1992, with the spicily malty **Hudson Lager★★→★★★**. An ale (not tasted), a tasty **Porter★★→★★★** and seasonal specials have followed.

Yuengling

The oldest brewery in the United States, and thriving. Yuengling, founded in 1829 and still owned by the family, is best known for its **Porter★★**, which has a soft, medium, body, a hint of licorice and a dash of roasty dryness. **Lord Chesterfield Ale★→★★** is light, but with a nice touch of hops.

Zip City

The name derives from Sinclair Lewis's novel *Babbitt*, and the brewpub is in a building that once housed the Temperance Society, in the Flatiron district of Manhattan (3 W 18th St and 5th Ave). It opened in 1991, and beers have included a soft **Helles★★→★★★**; a dryish **Pils★★**; a sweetish **Vienna★★★**; a toffeeish **Dunkel★★→★★★** and some smooth variations on the Bock theme. The beers are served unfiltered.

THE SOUTHEAST

The Old South is beginning to gain some new brewers, despite the heat that favours beer as simply a cold, quenching commodity; social attitudes that deem anything but Budweiser or Schlitz un-American; and religious fundamentalists who prefer their counties dry.

In Tennessee and Alabama, for example, brewpubs are legal only in certain counties. In South Carolina, Georgia and Mississippi, they are illegal. Florida, a more dynamic state, is dotted with brewpubs, but many seem more driven by short-term commercial razzmatazz than by the love of interesting beer; light refreshers do better than specialities in family resorts, retirement communities and rum-and-Coke territories. Louisiana, with some of America's most liberal laws on drink, also has the odd brewpub and micro, though in New Orleans some drinkers may be equally tempted by the cocktails.

Where to drink

North Carolina has, apart from those detailed below, brew-pubs at Greensboro (Loggerhead, 2006 W Vandalia) and Spring Garden (714 Francis King); Raleigh (Greenshield's, 214 E Martin) and Boone (Tumbleweed, 122 Blowing Rock Rd).

In Florida, the Sarasota brewpub, in the town of the same name (6607 Gateway) has attracted good reports for its wide range of beers. Other places with brewpubs include Gainesville (Market St Pub, 120 SW 1st Ave); Jacksonville (River City, 835 Gulf Life Drive); Key West (Kelly's, 301 Whitehead); and Walton Beach (Santa Rosa, 54 Miracle Strip Parkway).

Tennessee has the Big River brewpub, 222 Broad St, Chattanooga. Alabama has the Port City Brewery, 225 Dauphin St, Mobile. In Louisiana, the city of New Orleans has two pubs notable for their ranges of beers. Carrollton Station (8140 Willow St), is the place for the serious devotee, though Cooter Brown's (509 S Carrollton) has the bigger selection.

Southern Draft, the region's brewspaper, is published in Casselberry, Florida.

Abita

The sulphur spring at Abita, Louisiana, was once thought to offer protection against yellow fever. Today, the town of Abita Springs is little more than a crossroads in swampy country, wooded with pecans, magnolias and sweet gum trees, across Lake Ponchartrain from New Orleans. Its modern-day claim to fame is an isolated micro-brewery producing lagers: a dry, malty, **Golden★★**, with some flowery hop character, a sweeter **Amber★★** and seasonal specialities such as the tawny, grainier, **Turbodog★★→★★★** (15; 1060; 5; 6.25) and the stronger (20; 1080; 7.0; 8.75) **Andygator★★→★★★**, bronze, with a lot of malt, hop and alcohol taste. New Orleans itself also has the Crescent City brewpub, making a range of German-accented lagers (not tasted), at 527 Decatur St.

Beach Brewing

Micro opposite Universal Studios, Orlando, Florida. Sweetish **Red Rock★→★★** and tawnier, nuttier, **Magic Brew★→★★**. Part of the Mill group (see entry).

Birmingham Brewing Company

Micro in Birmingham, Alabama. Products include the malty, fruity, slightly tart **Red Mountain Red Ale★★**.

Bohannon/Market Street

Lindsay Bohannon's family was in the tobacco business, but he prefers beer. His micro-brew is in what were the elegant offices and warehouse of the long-defunct Green Briar whiskey distillery, on 2nd Ave (formerly Market St), Nashville, Tennessee. The brewery's **Pilsener★★→★★★** is smooth and dry, with a spicy hop finish; its **Wheat★★** soft and fruity; its **Golden Ale★★** fruity and sweetish. Among seasonal specialities, the **Oktoberfest★★** (15; 1060; 4.5; 5.6) has a beautifully sustained aromatic hop character but perhaps too roasty a malt note.

Bosco's

A stone beer, based on the old technique of heating the brew with hot rocks, has been experimentally produced at this pub and pizza kitchen, at Germantown (7615 W Farmington), E of Memphis. Other products have included the very light **Tennessee Cream Ale★★** and a thinnish **Germantown Alt★→★★**.

Dilworth

Brewpub in Charlotte (1301 E Bvd), N Carolina. Products include **Albemarle Ale★★**, bronze, buttery, and slightly sharp in the finish, and a malty, grainy, very sweet, **Scottish Ale★★→★★★** and a coffeeish **Porter★★**.

Dixie

New Orleans colourful survivor. This much-loved 1907 brewery, with its domed building and cypress fermenters, now makes a far greater range of beers. The basic **Dixie Beer★★** is a light lager with a touch of malt character. A belated "Cajun" brew, **Blackened Voodoo Lager★★→★★★** has a deep, tawny colour and a malty, treacly, palate (4.3; 5.4); really a respectable Kulmbach-style lager? Newer specialities include a smoked beer, a porter, an ale and a chocolate brew (not tasted).

Hops
Brewpub in Clearwater, E of Tampa, Florida. Very light, sweetish, **Golden★** and malty, well-balanced, **Hammerhead Red Ale★★**.

Irish Times
Mock-Irish pub with brewery, in Palm Beach Gardens (9920 Alternate A-I-A), Florida. Products include a sweet, toffeeish, **Irish Red Ale★→★★**.

McGuire's
Brewpub in Pensacola (600 E Gregory), Florida. Principal product is a malty, buttery, vanilla-scented, **Irish Red★★**. A grainier, fruitier, version called **Irish Ale** is produced by Oldenberg for bottling.

Mill Bakery and Brewery
Small brewpub chain with branches in Charlotte, N Carolina, and Fort Myers and Winter Park, both in Florida. Beers, typically sweet and buttery, include the amber **Red October★→★★** and **Hornet Tail★→★★**, broadly in the style of a brown ale.

Oldenberg
A Southern brewery by virtue of its location in Fort Mitchell (400 Buttermilk Pike), Kentucky, but just across the river from the Midwestern city of Cincinnati. It looks authentically like a German brewery of the 1880s, but actually built in the 1980s, with its own entertainment hall and pub-restaurant.

Oldenburg's chief product is a soft, aromatically malty pale lager **Premium Verum★★**. Seasonal specialities have included a tawny, smoky **Bock★★**; a faintly medicinal **Stout★★** and a sour-mash **Summer Beer★★→★★★**. The fruity **Vail Ale★★** is brewed under contract for a company based in Colorado.

Ragtime
Brewpub and seafood grill, in Atlantic Beach, Florida (207 Atlantic Bvd). Products include **Redbrick Ale★★**, light, soft and malty-fruity.

Silo
The silo is a grain elevator next to this brewpub in Louisville (630 Barret Ave), Kentucky. Beers include the syrupy, fruity, **Red Rock Ale★★** and the thinnish **Derby City Dark★→★★**. Louisville also has the Bluegrass brewpub, at 3929 Shelbyville Rd (products not tasted).

Weeping Radish

Large, black-skinned radishes accompany every beer-snack in Bavaria. They are peeled and salted, and must begin to "weep" before they are eaten. Bavarian Uli Bennewitz chose this name for his brewpub on Roanoke Island, in North Carolina. Its regular beer is a sweetish, unfiltered, easily drinkable **Lager★★**.

THE MIDWEST

The Midwest has long ceased to be America's brewing capital in terms of volume or variety, but Milwaukee, along with some other cities, is fighting back.

The Milwaukee brewer Miller, infamous for Lite, has launched a fruity Amber Ale and a chocolatey stout, and even Pabst has promoted its Old Tankard Ale (very similar to the current version of Ballantine's IPA). Milwaukee also has colourful micros, including Sprecher and Lakefront.

Chicago, which was briefly without a brewery, now has two or three micros and four or five brewpubs. In Minneapolis/St Paul, one old brewery has been revived, there a couple of micros, and brewpubs are burgeoning.

The region's brewspaper is *Midwest Beer Notes*, published in Clayton, Wisconsin.

Where to drink

Chicago:The Great Beer Palace, boasting 24 taps, is a newish place at 4128 N Lincoln Ave. Quenchers, at Fullerton and Western Ave, is a more established speciality beer-bar. A former brewing family owns The Berghoff (17 W Adams and State St, in The Loop), perhaps the best of the surviving old beer taverns in the USA; it is well-run, with a carefully chosen, if limited, selection of beers, and its lunch counter's halibut sandwiches are justly famous. For German nationalism and beers to match, try Resi's, on Irving Park Rd, W of Lincoln. Among stores, Sam's (1000 W North, at Clybourn) has an excellent selection of beers and alcoholic esoterica. Every beer-lover visiting Chicago should pop into the Goose Island brewpub (see entry); the Weinkeller (see entry) now has a second branch, and there are brewpubs further out at South Barrington (see Mill Rose) and Naperville (Taylor Brewing, 200 E 5th Ave), producing ales from extract; not tasted.

Milwaukee: It sounds ironic, but the Water Street brewpub takes its name from the thoroughfare on which it stands, at number 1101, one block N of the Performing Arts Center. The brewery makes commendable ales from extract. At the former Schlitz brewery tap, the Brown Bottle (221 W Galena Court), there is a long beer-list, and a splendid 1930s interior.

No city has as many famous old German restaurants. These include the grand, vaulted dining rooms of Maders (1037–41 3rd Ave), with a long list of beers and a museum of steins. Drinking vessels also form part of the lavish decor at Karl Ratsch's (320 E Mason). The less elaborate Kalt's (2858 N Oakland, on the east side) has a good selection of beers and a collection of breweriana. Don't leave town without dipping into the cosmopolitan selection at The Port of Hamburg (5937 S Howell), just outside the airport.

Adler of Appleton

A 1858 brewery in Appleton, Wisconsin, converted into a mall that accommodates two restaurants served by a single small brewhouse (1004 S Old Oneida). Products, which seem somewhat variable, have included a sweetish **Amber★** and a rich **Bock★→★★**. A pumpkin beer (not tasted) has won plaudits.

Anheuser-Busch

The world's biggest brewing company, headquartered in St Louis, Missouri, and producing some 90 million barrels a year, shared between a dozen plants across the nation. Anheuser and Busch were related by marriage, and the company – dating from 1860 – is still controlled by the family. The beer called simply **Busch★** was once the most local and traditional of the company's products but is now a light, low-priced, brand. Bohemia's royal court brewing town, Budweis, inspired the name of the first beer in the world to be consciously mass-marketed. America's **Budweiser★** is light and sweetish, with a touch of apple-like fruitiness. A careful blend of famous hop varieties is used, but in such small quantities in recent years that their influence is barely perceptible. A Bohemian brewing town also inspired the name of the "super-premium" **Michelob★★**, which is fractionally fuller-bodied (a higher malt-to-rice ratio) and better balanced. **Michelob Classic Dark★→★★** is a pleasant enough beer, but has less character than it promises. It is a shame that the brewery has not persisted with its experimental Pilsener and Märzen under the Anheuser name, but there will no doubt be further essays into the speciality market. The flagship beers are fined by maturation over beechwood chips, a very old Bavarian technique.

Barleyhoppers

Located in Moscow, Idaho (507 S Main). Brewpub whose products include the smooth, firm, dry **McGinty's Irish Stout★★**.

Boulevard

Micro in Kansas City, Missouri, producing a dry, clean, peachy-citric, refreshing **Wheat Beer★★→★★★**; a **Pale Ale★★→★★★** with a rounded, fruity, palate, moving to a hoppy finish; and **Bully!★★→★★★**, a chocolatey, fruity, roasty, earthy, dry porter.

Brewmasters Pub

Housed in a former monastery building in Kenosha (4017 80th St), between Milwaukee and Chicago. **Kenosha Gold★** is a sweetish lager; **Amber Vienna Style★★** has a touch of malt; **Royal Dark★★** is malty and pruney; while

Maibock★★ is rich and malty. **Nort's Cream Ale★→★★** has the appropriate tartness. **Johnson's Honey Lager★★** is very sweet. This brewpub has also made beers flavoured with chocolate and coffee.

Broad Ripple

Brewpub in the Broad Ripple entertainment district of Indianapolis (840 E 65th St). The owner, John Hill, is from Yorkshire, England. Products have included an **IPA★★→★★★** with a sharp smack of hop in the finish; a British-accented **ESB★★★**, with lots of flavour development; and a light, smooth, malty-coffeeish **Porter★★**. There is also a **Kölsch★★→★★★**, quite big-bodied for the style.

Capital

Its beer-garden gave the rubric Garten Bräu to beers from this micro in Middleton, which adjoins Madison, state capital of Wisconsin. At their best, the beers are very good. They include a malty **Lager★★** broadly in the Munich Helles style; a hoppy Pilsener called **Special★★→★★★**; a malty, coffeeish, slightly oily **Dark★★**; an enjoyably spicy **Weizen★★★** (served with yeast) and seasonal specials.

Cherryland

Close to the cherry-growing country of Door County, Wisconsin, this micro is in a turn-of-the-century train station, at Sturgeon Bay. Its malt-tinged **Golden Rail★** and hoppier **Silver Rail★** are brewed from extract. Both are thinnish, with a touch of fruitiness. The brewery also makes cherry and apple beers.

Chicago Brewing Company

Born in a former pickle factory in 1989. Aggressive micro producing **Legacy Lager★★★**, starting firm and malty and becoming perfumy and hoppy; **Legacy Red Ale★★**, its syrupy maltiness balanced by a touch of tart hoppiness; **Big Shoulders Porter★★**, with a suggestion of licorice; and **Heartland Weiss★★→★★★**, with a hint of clove.

Cold Spring

Very old plant in Cold Spring, Minnesota. Its **Cold Spring Export★** originally had some Dortmunder character, but that is long gone.

Columbus

Promising ales, made with a mix of whole grain and malt extract, at a very small micro in an old brewery complex in Columbus, state capital of Ohio. Products include a hoppy, perfumy, **Gold★★**, reminiscent of a Kölsch; a **Pale Ale★★★** in very much the British style; a **Nutbrown Ale★★→★★★** with a malty palate and a "winter warmer" character; and a sweetish **Black Forest Porter**. The beers are available at the adjoining Gibby's Tavern and Hagen's, a restaurant serving hearty American food.

Crane River

Brewpub in Lincoln, Nebraska (200 N 11th). Products include the somewhat roasty **Sod House Altbier★→★★**.

Detroit and Mackinac

Echoing the whimsical name stretching from Detroit, Michigan, to the far north of the state. This micro, in the city, has produced the sweetish **Mackinac Gold★★**, with a good malt character; a nutty **Irish Red Ale★★→★★★**; a very hoppy **IPA★★→★★★**; and the roasty, wheaty, grainy **Mackinac Black★★→★★★**.

Firehouse

In the 1915 firehouse of Rapid City, S Dakota (610 Main St). Products have included a very hoppy **Bitter★★** and a very sweet **Barley Wine★★**.

Frankenmuth Brewery

"Franconian Courage" is the translated name of a town in rural Michigan, a couple of hours north of Detroit. It was settled in 1845 by Franconians, and there has been brewing on the present site since 1862. In 1986, new owners rebuilt the brewery, with kettles brought from Franconia. The brewery is run by Fred Schumacher, of the Düsseldorf Altbier family. It is a popular tourist attraction in this "old German" town. Products include a delicate, well-balanced, **Pilsener★★**; a smooth, dryish, **Dark★★→★★★**; a lightly malty **Oktoberfest★★**; a firm, malty, sweetish, warming **Bock★★★**; a refreshing **Weisse★★★**, with a sweet-apple fruitiness and some tartness; and a fruity, dryish, amber ale, **Old Detroit★★**. An organic beer (a malty, slightly buttery, sweetish, Vienna-style lager called **Perry's Majestic★★→★★★**) is made under contract for a company in New York. Also produces the house beers at Franklin St Brewing, a bar-restaurant in Detroit.

Free State

Between Kansas City and Topeka, the town of Lawrence was associated with the anti-slavery Free State Party. Today, it is the home of a well-regarded brewpub in an old trolley depot (tram-shed) at 636 Massachusetts, just north of Liberty Hall Opera House. Products include a hearty **India Pale Ale★★★** with excellent hop flavours.

Golden Prairie

Tiny micro in old tannery in Chicago. Began in 1992 with an Alt-like **Golden Prairie Ale★★**. This beer starts malty, then becomes fruity, finishing hoppy. It has clear, bold, flavours and a firm body. In spring, there is a honey-ginger ale (not tasted).

Goose Island

The name refers to a neck of land near Chicago's Halsted nightlife area. This pubby establishment (1800 N Clybourn) has produced a wide range of excellent beers. They include the lightly hoppy **Golden Goose Pilsener★★→★★★**, with lots of Saaz aroma; something between a Vienna and a Munich Dark, called **Lincoln Park★★★**, with a toasty malt character; a creamy, chocolatey **Mild★★★**; an aromatic **Best Bitter★★★**; **Honker's Ale★★→★★★**, with a faintly buttery Irish character; a sweetish, winey **Winter Warmer★★→★★★**; an oily **Oatmeal Stout★★★**; a dense **Imperial Stout★★★**; and many seasonal brews.

Great Lakes

In an 1860s saloon (complete with genuine bullet holes), Jungian academic Patrick Conway and his brother Dan established Cleveland's first brewpub, with a modestly serious restaurant downstairs (2516 Market St). Early products were a soft, perfumy, dryish Dortmunder named after footballer **John Heisman★★→★★★**; and a rounder, deeper, Vienna-style lager named after local gangbuster **Eliot Ness★★→★★★**. Additions include a beautifully balanced hoppy-fruity bitter called **Moondog Ale★★★**; the bravely named (after an incident in local folklore) **Burning River Pale Ale★★→★★★**, full of malt and hop flavours, with a long finish; the aromatic, hoppy, fruity **Commodore Perry IPA★★→★★★**; and very dark, dense, coffeeish but dry and clean **Porter★★→★★★** that might better be termed a stout.

Heileman

National brewer, headquartered in La Crosse, Wisconsin. Products include **Old Style★**, a rather limp beer with a lot of corn in the palate, and **Special Export★→★★**, which has a hint of hop and bears better witness to the company's much-vaunted *kräusening*. **Windy City Amber★★** is pleasant, if undistinguished.

Hoster

Revival of old brewery name, near its original premises, in Columbus, Ohio. The new Hoster's is an excellent brewpub, in an old trolley barn (tram-shed), at 550 S High St. The delicate hop character in **Double X★★→★★★** is reminiscent of that in some Pilseners from the Rhineland; the **Export-style Gold Top★★★** is firm-bodied and well-balanced, with a malt accent; **Amber Lager★★** has a nicely malty finish. Bologna sandwiches are recommended.

Huber

This old-established family brewery in Monroe, Wisconsin, includes in its portfolio beers originally made for the Berghoff tavern, in Chicago. **Berghoff Beer★★** has perhaps a dash more malt and hop than some American golden lagers. **Berghoff Dark★★** has a syrupy touch of chocolate. The brewery began in 1993 to feature a golden lager brewed under licence from the abbey of Andechs in Bavaria. Early brews have been variable but always robust.

Hudepohl-Schoenling

Merger of two old-established breweries in Cincinnati, a town that once had 30. Hudepohl brought into the partnership its "super-premium" **Christian Moerlein★★**, a creamy, sweetish lager in broadly the Munich Helles style, brewed according to the Reinheitsgebot, but still not as characterful as it might be. **Christian Moerlein Double Dark★★→★★★**, with a good dose of black malt, has more character. **Christian Moerlein Bock★★** is toffeeish, grainy, and slightly winey. **Little Kings Cream Ale★★→★★★**, a classic example of this American style, is made by bottom-fermentation but gains some of its distinctive aromatics from the use of Belgian-grown Hallertau hops.

Indianapolis Brewing Company

In German immigrant days there was a brewery of this name, using the brand Duesseldorfer. The name is reminiscent of Altbier, but the new micro has revived the name for several ales. These include a pale, perfumy, malty **Amber★★** and a thinnish but smooth and roasty **Dark★★**.

Jones Street

New brewpub in the old beer-and-brewing neighbourhood of Omaha, Nebraska (1316 Jones). Products include **Ryan's Irish Stout★★→★★★**, smooth, with treacle-toffee and burnt flavours.

Kalamazoo Brewing Company

Talented brewer Larry Bell makes tasty, fruity brews in his tiny micro at Kalamazoo, Michigan. These have included the peachy, soft **Great Lakes Amber Ale★★★**; the drier, more aromatic, hoppier, golden **Bell's Beer★★**; the remarkably warming **Third Coast Old Ale★★★**, starting malty and finishing dry; the malty-chocolatey **Expedition Stout★★★**; and some outstanding specials.

Lakefront

Tiny micro established by enthusiasts in Milwaukee. Products include creamy, hop-accented, golden **Klisch Lager★★→★★★** (named after one of the founders), billed as a Pilsener but more of Dortmunder; **River West Stein Beer★★→★★★**, a strong firm-bodied, perfumy, malty, Vienna-style lager that in Germany might be regarded as a Festbier; and **East Side Dark★★★**, strong enough to be rated as a true Bock, firm and malty, with a hint of chocolate in the long finish. Seasonal fruit brews include a subtle beer made with Wisconsin's Door County cherries. In mid- to late March, a "Blessing of the Bock" is conducted by a Roman Catholic priest.

Leinenkugel

An old-established small (but expanding) brewery, still operating in Chippewa Falls, Wisconsin, though for some years owned by Miller. The flowery, dry, clean beer known simply as **Leinenkugel★★** (or "Leiny") has something of a cult following. **Limited★→★★** is slightly fuller-bodied, spritzy, with some tartness. **Red Lager★★**, more of an amber colour, has a touch of malt and a light finish. **Bock★→★★** is tawny and pleasantly sweet.

Melbourne's

Vaguely "Australian theme" brewpub at Strongsville, S of Cleveland, Ohio. Products include the dry, malt-accented lager **Bondi Beach Blonde★**; **Wombat Wheat★★**, smooth and peachy; and the chocolatey, grainy, **Down Under Ale★→★★**.

Miller

Earlier essays into speciality brewing never got out of the test market, but Miller seems more resolute with its **Amber Ale★★→★★★**: lightly malty in its aroma and sweetish, soft start; developing to a delicate but definite ale fruitiness; with a hoppy, appetizing finish. Since launching this product, Miller has added a relatively light-bodied, but creamy, chocolatey and fruity, **Velvet Stout★★**. These brews are in contrast to Miller's extremely light, almost water-tasting, mainstream products.

Mill Rose

Country store, restaurant and brewpub in the outer suburbs of Chicago, at South Barrington (45 S Barrington Rd). Products have included a clean, malty **Pilsner★★**; a perfumy **Oktoberfest★★**, the malty **Panther Ale★→★★**; the smooth, hoppy **General's Ale★★→★★★**; and a hazy, very spicy (lots of coriander) and aromatic, soft, sweetish **Saison★★★**, a style rarely found in America.

Millstream

By a mill stream in the main village of the Amana Church colonies of Iowa. These villages are better known for fruit wines, but this micro adds beer to their offerings. **Millstream Lager★→★★** is sweetish, soft and light; **Schildbrau★★** is a malty, amber lager in broadly the Vienna style.

Mishawaka

Brewpub in the Indiana town whose name it bears. The pub, in a former fitness centre (3703 N Main St), is less than four miles from the University of Notre Dame. Products include the smooth, dry, complex **Founders' Stout★★→★★★**.

Pabst

Pabst Blue Ribbon★ was once the blue-collar beer of America, but that slightly chewy brew has lost sales over the years. The Milwaukee brewer now produces another item of American nostalgia, **Ballantine Ale★→★★**, with its characteristic hint of geranial hop character. Likewise the hoppier **Ballantine IPA★★**. **Old Tankard★★** is similar, perhaps slightly sweeter.

Page

In the old brewery quarter of Minneapolis, a new-generation micro, named after its proprietor. **James Page Private Stock★★→★★★** is a hearty, American-accented, Vienna-style lager, with plenty of malt and hop. Page pioneered the use in beer of wild rice, which is native to the Minnesota lake country. He has two products in this style, both taking their name from a natural park on the borders of Minnesota and Canada. **Boundary Waters Wild Rice Beer★★** is light, clean and dry, but with plenty of flavour. **Boundary Waters Bock★★** is amber, with a clean, sweetish, palate.

Pavichevich

There is truly a Czech accent to the Pilsener with the odd name **Baderbräu★★★** produced by this micro in the suburbs of Chicago. When fresh, it has a delightfully flowery bouquet of hops, and some malty sweetness, and both characteristics are sustained through the palate to a gentle, elegant finish. A **Bock** (not tasted) has proven popular.

Point

This company has remained independent while other old-established Wisconsin breweries have been bought and sold, and is rightly held in affectionate regard for that. **Point Special★→★★** has a sweetish palate, drying towards the finish. The "super-premium" **Special Edition★★** is notably fuller in flavour. **Genuine Bock★★** is malty and smooth, with a dryish finish. Products brewed under contract include **Chief Oshkosh Red Lager★★**, in the Vienna style and somewhat syrupy; and a similar beer, perhaps more aromatic, for a company in the town of Woodstock, Illinois.

Schell

Not only the prettiest location of any brewery in the USA, but also some interesting beers. August Schell, founded in 1860, in New Ulm, Minnesota, has a deer park and gardens open to the public. Products include a hoppy **Pils★★★**; a lightly malty **Export★★**; a tawny, rummy, **Bock★★**; a **Weizen★★→★★★** with an apple-pie fruitiness; and the malty-chocolatey **Schmaltz's Alt★★**. The New Ulm brewery also makes many beers under contract.

Sharky's

Brewpub, grill, aquarium and live music, in Omaha, Nebraska (777 Cass St). Products include the rich, sweetish, complex, dark **Hammerhead Ale★★→★★★**.

Sherlock's Home

Outstanding cask-conditioned ales at a brewpub in a suburb of Minneapolis (11000 Red Circle Drive, Minnetonka). **Bishop's Bitter★★★**, soft but well hopped with Fuggles and Kent Goldings, and with a touch of acidity in the finish, is perhaps America's most English-tasting example of the style.

Piper's Pride★★★ is a malty but beautifully balanced Scottish ale, with a dash of oats and of quassia, a bittering made from tree bark. From Thanksgiving to the first week of January, there is a malty, wonderfully oily, **Winter Warmer★★★** in a "pin" (small wooden cask) on the bar. This last is dry-hopped, and sometimes tips the odd blossom into the glass. **Palace Porter★★** is more on the lines of a strong Mild; and **Stag's Head Stout★★★** dry and faintly medicinal. Owner Bill Burdick is distantly related to the late Peter Maxwell Stuart, of the Traquair House brewery in Scotland. The pub also keeps a good selection of single malt Scotches.

Sprecher

Hearty beers, evoking the traditions that Milwaukee almost forgot. Randy Sprecher worked at Pabst before launching his micro-brewery, across the railroad tracks, down by the riverside, in a an old packing plant. Products have included **Special Amber★★**, a malty but dryish brew broadly in the Vienna style; **Black Bavarian★★★** (15; 1060; 4.8; 6.0), smooth and intense, with hints of treacle-toffee, and a huge finish; **Irish Stout★★→★★★** (15; 1060; 4.8; 6.0), hoppy, roasty, fruity and enwrapping; **Milwaukee Weiss★★→★★★**, a lovely pale amber colour, with both sweetness and acidity; and **Hefe-Weiss★★★**, an unfiltered version that is full of flavour. The beer can be bought at the brewery (730 W Oregon).

Stroh

National brewer headquartered in Detroit (though no longer making beer there). Stroh uses direct flame to heat its kettles. This "fire-brewing" creates hot spots on the kettle which give a caramel tinge to the beer. This is evident in the principal product, called simply **Stroh's★**; the lightly malty, "super-premium" **Signature★**, and the hoppier **Augsburger Golden★★**. Under the Augsburger name, the company is also developing speciality brews. The first example was **Augsburger Weiss★★**, a fruity but very light interpretation of the style.

Summit

Well-established micro in St Paul, twin city to Minneapolis. A summertime **Sparkling Ale★→★★** is light, dry and faintly yeasty. **Extra Pale Ale★★** has a malty middle, a good development of perfumy fruitiness and a dry finish. **Great Northern Porter★★★** is smooth, with herbal and bitter-chocolate notes. Excellent seasonal specials.

Weinkeller

Intended to be a German *weinstube*, and it has a good winelist, but somehow Weinkeller went on the beer. Its many ethnically Bohemian neighbours in the Chicago suburb of Berwyn (6417 W Roosevelt) probably helped. Products have included a lightly hoppy **Pilsner★★**; the oddly named **Aberdeen Amber★★→★★★**, which might better be called Düsseldorfer Alt; the dry, fruity

Dublin Stout★★→★★★, at a hefty 1082, made with yeast from Cooper's of Adelaide; a malty, faintly phenolic Düsseldorfer Doppelbock; a plummy, sweetish **Bavarian Weisse**★★; and a nicely tart but well-balanced **Berliner Weisse**★★★, which the brewery says it makes with a lactic culture. There is a branch at 651 Westmont Drive, near Ogden.

COLORADO AND THE SOUTHWEST

Few Americans would nominate Colorado as the nation's biggest brewing state but, in volume terms, it is. More importantly, it now has one of the liveliest populations of brewpubs and micros.

In large part its best-known brewery, Coors, in Golden, accounts for Colorado's high output of beer. Without Coors, Golden would be a Wild West town, and some consumers still think of Coors as a folksy brewery in the hills, yet its capacity is 15–20 million barrels. There is no bigger single brewery plant in the world. Not far away, in Fort Collins, Coors' rival Anheuser-Busch now has a large brewery. It is curious that, with a further three micros and a brewpub, the 87,758 people of Fort Collins have five local beer-makers. Fort Collins is the home of the tabloid *Rocky Mountain Brew News*, which appears sporadically. Austin, Texas, puts out *Southwest Brewing News*.

From Fort Collins in north Colorado to Park City in Utah, to Virginia City in the far west of Nevada, and from Tucson, Arizona, to Shiner, Texas – the most unlikely towns have breweries. In its broadest sweep, this might be regarded as the Southwest. California, of course, is another country.

Where to drink

Denver has in recent years been the location of the Great American Beer Festival. With about 1,000 beers from more than 200 breweries, all of them American, this event offers a larger selection than any in the world. It is usually held in mid-October (details from the Association of Brewers, Box 287, Boulder, Colorado 80306–0287, ☎303–4470816). Colorado is also lucky to have the Old Chicago chain of pizza restaurants which always have a good beer selection (headquarters: 1102 Pearl St Mall, Boulder, ☎303–443–5031).

Apart from the brewpubs discussed below, there are few well-established and reliable speciality beer-bars in the Southwest. The pickings are especially slim in Nevada and Utah. In Arizona, The Shanty (4th Ave and 9th St, Tucson) looks like a concrete bunker, apart from its copper canopy and door, and serves its beer in frosted glasses – but it does have a loyal following.

At the other end of the region, Texas has several worthwhile spots. Austin is a good beer town, with the Celis micro and at least four new brewpubs, all opened in 1994: Armadillo (419 E 6th); Bitter End (4th and Colorado), Copper Tank (5th and Trinity) and Waterloo (4th and Guadalupe). More are planned. Austin has many bars along 6th St, and the pubby Dog and Duck at 406 W 17th is strongly recommended. Houston also has a new brewpub, The Village (2415 Dunstan).

Dallas has the Yegua Creek brewpub (2920 Henderson). There is a good selection of beers in a cosy bar called Mimi's (5111 Greenville). At the lower end of Greenville (No. 1520), Flip's has a good selection of draughts, art exhibits, and a high-tech interior. There is a branch of The Gingerman (2718 Boll St), though the original, one of America's best beer bars, is in Houston (5607 Morningside).

Assets
Brewpub, bakery and grille in Albuquerque, New Mexico (6910 Montgomery NE). Products include the malty **Duke City Amber Ale★→★★**.

Bandersnatch
Near the Phoenix Cardinals football stadium and Arizona State University, Bandersnatch (125 E 5th Ave, in the suburb of Tempe) is a brewpub with a good, English-style bitter called **Premium★★→★★★**; a pleasant **Milk Stout★★**; and seasonal specials.

H. C. Berger
A collector of John Dillinger memorabilia, and keen home-brewer, Sandy Jones established this micro in Fort Collins in 1992. Beers include the clean, light, sweetish, **Whistlepin Wheat★★**; the maltier, more complex, **Indego Pale Ale★★**; and a dry-hopped **IPA★★→★★★**, aged on oak chips.

Black Mountain
In the fake Wild West town of Cave Creek, near Phoenix. A micro, with the beers featured next door at The Satisfied Frog (6245 E Cave Creek Rd). **Black Mountain Gold★→★★** is a lager with a touch of malt and hop. The very hot **Cave Creek Chili Beer★→★★**, containing a whole pod, is produced under contract at the Evansville brewery (formerly owned by Heileman), in Indiana.

Boulder
See Rockies.

Breckenridge
The Continental Divide provides a magnificent backdrop for this ski-resort (9,600ft/3,200m) brewpub, at the old gold-mining town of Breckenridge, Colorado (600 S Main). Products have included **Avalanche Ale★→★★**, fruity, tart and refreshing; the fuller-coloured **End of Trail Ale★★**, which is drier; a notably creamy **Oatmeal Stout★★★**; and a soft, fruity, unfiltered, **Mountain Wheat★★**. There is a similar range at a newer Breckenridge brewpub in Denver (2220 Blake St).

Carver
Bakery and brewery in Durango, Colorado (1022 Main). Products include the firm, nutty, toffeeish, malty, **James Brown Ale★★→★★★**.

Celis

Pierre Celis revived "white" wheat beers in his native Belgium by establishing the Hoegaarden brewery there. After being bought out by national giant Interbrew (Stella Artois), he left for America. He now works his magic at his own brewery in Austin, Texas. His **Celis White**★★★★ is perhaps lighter, certainly softer and fuller in flavour, than today's Hoegaarden. Other products include the creamy, perfumy, flowery **Golden**★★→★★★; the fruity, dry, almost woody-tasting **Bock**★★ (misnamed; it is a bronze ale, of 4.0; 5.0); and the very aromatic, spicy, golden, **Grand Cru**★★→★★★, a less strong (4.0; 5.0) counterpart to Hoegaarden Grand Cru. Strengths of beer are especially heavily regulated in Texas.

Champion

Sports bar and brewpub in Denver (1442 Larimer Sq). Products have included the golden, light, sweetish **Sports Ale**★→★★ (with a touch of wheat) and the grainy, nutty (peanut brittle?) **Home Run Ale**★★.

CooperSmith's

Smart, successful, brewpub in former bakery in Fort Collins (5 Old Town Sq). Wide range of beers has included **Mountain Avenue Wheat**★★→★★★, sherbety and clovey; a malty **Dunkel Weizen**★★→★★★, with an attractive copper-brown colour; a **Peach Wheat**★★→★★★ light flavoured with the fruit; an assertive but well-balanced **Green Chili Beer**★★→★★★; the light, hoppy, golden **Poudre Pale Ale**★→★★★; the bronze, hoppier, very long **Punjabi Pale Ale**★★; the soft, light, dry **Albert Damm Bitter**★★→★★★; the smooth, nutty **Not Brown Ale**★★→★★★ (with a tawny colour); the smoky, peaty, whiskyish **McScooter's Scottish Ale**★★★; the faintly medicinal **Horsetooth Stout**★★; and the creamy, fruity **Firestarter 500 Barley Wine**★★★.

Coors

The cleanest-tasting mainstream American brew is the one simply called **Coors**★★. The brewery's other products include the faintly fruitier **Gold**★; a seasonal, **Winterfest**★★★, in broadly the Vienna style, with a rounded and sustained maltiness; and **George Killian's**★★, an amber lager inspired by the Franco-"Irish" ale of the same name and brewed under licence. More seasonal specialities are promised.

Coyote Springs

Phoenix brewpub (4883 N 20th), whose wide range includes **Koyote Kölsch**★★★, light, perfumy and perhaps America's most credible example of the style. At the opposite extreme is the slightly treacly, nutty, **Bison Brown**★★.

Crested Butte

Brewpub in the Colorado town of the same name (226 Elk Ave). Very fruity, dryish products include **Red Lady Ale**★★.

Flying Dog

In the chic mountain resort of Aspen, Colorado (424 E Cooper). **Doggie Style**★★ is a bronze ale with lots of hop. **Wolfhound**★★ is an Irish Stout, very creamy.

High Country

Boulder micro founded in 1993, and immediately acclaimed for its golden **Miners' Pale Ale**★★★ and its **Renegade Red**★★★. To taste the first was like biting on hops, to sample the second like chewing them. It is to be hoped that standards can be maintained after a change of brewer.

Holy Cow!

Casino brewpub in Las Vegas (2423 Las Vegas Bvd S), making better beers than the context suggests. The golden **Pale Ale**★★ is soft and perfumy, while the **Amber Ale**★★ is rich and rounded.

Hops

Café-style brewpub in fashionable Scottsdale, a Phoenix suburb (7000 E Camelback). A wide range of products has included a dryish **Pilsner**★→★★; a malty **Amber Ale**★★; a rather stout-like **Bock**★→★★; and orangey-tasting **Barley Wine**★★; and a clean, delicate, soft **Raspberry Beer**★★→★★★.

Hubcap

In the ski resort of Vail, Colorado. Brewpub (143 E Meadow Drive) producing a wide range of products, with a creamy house character. These include the aromatic, hoppy, soft, beautifully rounded **Solstice Ale**★★★ (which has a reddish colour); the almost whiskyish **Beaver Tail Brown Ale**★★★; and the gentle **Rainbow Trout Stout**★★→★★★.

Irons

Very small micro in Lakewood, Colorado. Products, all unfiltered, include the dry, hoppy, resiny, almost chewy, **Green Mountain Ale**★★→★★★.

Judge Baldwin's

Colorado Springs brewpub (Antlers Doubletree Hotel, 30 S Cascade). Early products have included a pale but well-balanced **Amber Ale**★→★★ and a dryish **Porter**★★.

Lone Star

Chauvinistic Texans swear by **Lone Star**★→★★, a dryish mainstream lager with a slight sharpness in the finish, but not exceptional. The brewery, in San Antonio, is owned by Heileman.

Lonetree

Bottle-conditioned ales from a Denver micro established in 1993. Products include a **Cream Ale**★★→★★★ with a hint of honeydew melon and a perfumy, dry finish; **Sunset Red**★★, light sweet and fruity; and **Iron Horse Dark**★★, syrupy and chocolatey.

New Belgium

An enthusiast for Belgian beers started this micro in an old railroad shed in Fort Collins, in 1992. Early products have included a soft, malty, fruity, Belgian-style, amber ale called **Flat Tire★★→★★★** (the name honours mountain-bikers); a tart, well-rounded, **Old Cherry Ale★★→★★★**, with a tempting orange-pink colour, made from locally grown Montmorency sour pie cherries; an **Abbey★★★**, in the Belgian "Dubbel" style, with lots of malt and fruitiness and a touch of demerara sugar (16.5; 1066; 5.2; 6.5); and a hugely flowery **Trippel★★★** (18.5; 1074; 6.4; 8.0).

Oasis

Brewpub in Boulder (1095 Canyon Bvd). Products notably include the soft, complex, hoppy, **ESB★★→★★★**; and the solid, almost tar-tasting, **Zoser Stout★★→★★★**.

Odell

Decorated with sun signs, in a premises that once sold Mexican tiles, but appropriately brewing under a grain elevator, this micro in Fort Collins has made, among other products: a perfumy, fruity, **Wheat Beer★★→★★★**; a malty-fruity **Golden Ale★★**; and a smooth, nutty, Scottish-style **Ninety Shilling★★★**.

Pearl

The light, sweetish, **Pearl★** and the similar **Jax★** are mainstream lagers made in San Antonio, Texas, at a brewery owned by the Pabst group.

Pike's Peak

Colorado Springs micro, opened in 1993. Early products have included golden, hoppy, **Jack Rabbit Pale Ale★★** and tawny, malty, tongue-enwrapping **Red Granite Amber★★**.

Preston

Tiny brewery, operating sporadically in the warmer months. It adjoins the Embudo Station restaurant, where the "Chili Line" railroad once ran between Santa Fe and Taos, New Mexico (State Highway 68). Early brews included a wonderfully aromatic, peppery, **Green Chili Beer★★★** and a honey-flavoured **Stout★★→★★★** that was nonetheless very dry. The original brewer, Steve Eskeback, is now at Eske's, 106 Des Georges Lane, Taos (beers not tasted).

Rock Bottom

Industrial chic brewpub in Denver (1001 16th St). **Premium Draft★→★★** is a light, golden ale; an occasional **Arapahoe Amber★★** has good, leafy, hop character; **Red Rocks★→★★** is lightly malty; **Falcon★★** Pale Ale fruit-accented but well-balanced; **Molly's Titanic★★** a perfectly sinkable Brown Ale that starts sweet and malty but finishes fruity and tart; **Black Diamond Stout★★** is full-bodied, with an emphatic bitter-chocolate note.

Rockies

The original owners of Boulder Brewing, founded in 1979, moved their operation to the present, purpose-built, site but left before the company changed its name to Rockies. Based on that connection, it can still claim to be America's longest-established operating micro. Products include a very sweet, malty-fruity **Amber Ale★★**; a very malty, attractively tawny **Wrigley Red★★→★★★**, in broadly the style of a Scottish ale; and a roasty **Porter★★** that seems to have lost some of its edge.

San Francisco

Brewpub in Tucson (3922 N Oracle Rd) using extract and some grain. Products include a sweetish **Wildcat Ale★→★★**.

San Juan

Restored rail station brewpub in the resort of Telluride (300 S Townsend). Products include the sweetish **Little Rose Amber Ale★★**; the aromatic, hoppy **Tomboy Bitter★★**; and the winey **Boomerang Brown★→★★**.

Santa Fe Brewing Company

On a horse ranch at Galisteo, in the High Mountain Desert near Santa Fe, New Mexico. This micro began with **Santa Fe Pale Ale★★→★★★**, soft and smooth, malt-accented, with some fruit and a long, gentle, hoppy, finish. Several new beers have been added since (not tasted).

Schirf/Wasatch

In unlikely Utah, a brewpub whose products include **Wasatch Premium★★**, a hoppy but well-balanced ale, and the flavoursome **Wasatch Weizen★★**. The brewery is in Park City, a ski resort 25 miles E of Salt Lake.

Spoetzl

Bohemian and Bavarian settlers founded this brewery, which in the early 1990s restored its original name. It is in the tiny town of Shiner, about 70 miles S of Austin, and slightly further from St Antonio and Houston. It is a lovely mission-style building, but its beers are more mainstream: the light **Shiner Premium★**; a dark counterpart described as a **Bock★→★★**; the slightly drier **Kosmas★★**, named after Mr Spoetzl; and a light **Wheat-★★**.

Squatters

Salt Lake brewpub (147 W Broadway). Products include the lemony, gingery, refreshing **Rocky Mountain Wheat★★**; the grainy **Cole's Special Bitter★→★★**; the perfectly described **Hop Head Red★★→★★★**; and the smooth, malty **Parley's Porter★★**.

The Texas Brewing Company

The original 1890s Dallas Brewing Company was on this site. The present micro was established in 1989, originally as Dallas/

West End Brewing. Products are said to have improved greatly since the brewery switched from malt extract to whole grains.

Union

At the Union Saloon, in Virginia City, formerly a gold and silver-mining town, south of Reno, Nevada. There was a brewery on the site in the 1890s, and the present brewpub was established in 1987. It produces a malty amber-coloured lager called **Union Beer★→★★** in broadly the Vienna style, and a darker Munich type (not tasted).

Walnut

Boulder brewpub (1123 Walnut). Early products have included a lightly tart **Swiss Trail Wheat Ale★★**; the soft, dry, hoppy **Big Horn Bitter★★★**; the smooth, clean, **Old Elk Brown Ale★★→★★★**; and the creamy, roasty **Devil's Thumb Stout★★→★★★**.

Wynkoop

Probably the biggest beer-sales of any brewpub in America, yet quality has been maintained and the ambience is still pubby. The brewpub is on a street named after one of Denver's founders, Edward Wynkoop, whose Dutch surname indicates a wine merchant. The establishment is in the old warehouse district of Denver (Wynkoop and 18th). Products have included **Wilderness Wheat★★→★★★**, light and plummy; **Märzen★★→★★★**, golden, smooth and sweetish; **IPA★★→★★★**, fruity, perfumy and oaky; a hoppy, well-balanced **ESB★★→★★★**; a hoppier **Special Bitter★★★**; a chocolatey **Scottish Ale★★**; a malty-fruity, warming Old Ale called **Churchyard★★★**; and a herbal-tasting **Sagebrush Stout★★**. Wynkoop has a branch in Colorado Springs.

CALIFORNIA

There are more breweries by far in California than in any other state – about 100. This is a new phenomenon. There were just four national giants, plus Anchor Steam, when America's first new-generation micro-brewery, New Albion, fired its kettle in Sonoma, California, in 1977.

New Albion did not survive, but its crew and yeast went on to start the Mendocino County Brewing Company, which thrives in the appropriately named town of Hopland.

While Southern California's hot weather encourages lighter-tasting brews (often served undrinkably cold and, in one instance, over ice), and a less wide (or less readily available) selection, the San Francisco area (including the East Bay), and the north, are full of interesting beers.

That first micro-brewery was in wine country, and the grain has been greatly assisted by the grape. Viticulture is a thirsty business, and wine-makers usually enjoy a quenching beer, but their industry also has a more fundamental contribution. Much of northern California is touched by the viticulture, and this means that people are not embarrassed to discuss the aromas and flavours of drinks and foods. The blossoming of boutique wineries set an example that made it easier for micro-breweries to find funding, equipment and credibility.

Anchor Steam's principal, Fritz Maytag, grows renowned Cabernets (and olives, and has a share of his family's cheese business); the founders of the Santa Cruz Brewing Co. were originally wine-growers; the brewer at Butterfield formerly made wine at Heitz; there are many similar examples. The University of California at Davis, which is oriented towards agriculture and wine-making, also has a department concerned with brewing.

Not only in the wine country of California but also in the grapier corners of the Northwest, this soil has proved fertile for beer, too.

Where to drink

Brewpubs aside, southern California's favourite spot for an offbeat beer may be a sandwich shop. Between downtown Los Angeles and Pasadena, at San Gabriel (413 W Las Tunas Drive; an appropriate-sounding address), The Stuffed Sandwich has about 700 beers, 15 of them on draught, and a caring proprietor. In West Hollywood, Barney's Beanery (8447 Santa Monica Bvd) is one of the older generation of "most beers in town" bars. At the seaside community of Santa Monica itself, Father's Office (1018 Montana) features American micros – and wines.

In the middle of the California coast, the town of San Luis Obispo has a beer-bar called Spike's ((570 Higuera). Check here for details of the town's very comprehensive California Festival of Beers, usually in May, around Memorial Day Weekend.

The largest combined festival of American and imported beers to be held anywhere takes place in San Francisco on a weekend in early to mid-July under the auspices of the local public broadcasting station KQED. In eclectic San Francisco, Belgian beers are featured at Le Petit Café (2164 Larkin) and the New Wave club Toronado (547 Haight). The East Bay has many places, including a Belgian bistro called Mrs Coffee (Nob Hill Shopping Center, Livermore), and Lyon's (7294 San Ramon Rd, Dublin). Notable shops are The Cannery Wine Cellars (2801 Leavenworth, San Francisco) and The Wine Exchange, on the town square in Sonoma. America's first brews-paper, *The Celebrator*, is published in the East Bay, at Hayward.

Anchor

Serious beer-lovers worldwide know Anchor as the inspirational "Small is Beautiful" brewery. It was founded in the 1890s, in San Francisco, and given a new life in the late 1960s by its present owner, Fritz Maytag. Its principal product, **Anchor Steam Beer★★★★**, is made by a process unique to the United States (and, for more than 60 years, to this brewery) Anchor Steam Beer is not only a (protected) brand-name but also a style. Before refrigeration reached the West, pioneering brewers used lager yeasts at natural temperatures, in unusually shallow vessels that resemble coolers as much as fermenters.

Anchor Steam is still made in this type of vessel. The result is a beer that has some of the roundness of a lager but the fruitiness of an ale, with a characteristically high natural carbonation. It is also an all-malt beer, with a very good hoppy dryness (the varietal accent being clearly Northern Brewer). It is made to conventional gravity, of around 12 (1048; 4.0; 5.0). The brewery also makes a rich, creamy, faintly herbal, **Porter★★→★★★** (1068; 17; 5.0; 6.25) that might better be described as a bottom-fermenting medium stout. Anchor's intensely aromatic, hoppy-tasting (Cascade), dry, top-fermenting **Liberty Ale★★★★** (4.8; 6.0) is an American classic, widely copied. Its **Old Foghorn Barley Wine★★★→★★★★** (25; 1100; 7.0; 7.0; 8.75) is beautifully rounded, soothing and warming. Its **Wheat Beer★★**, the first in America since Prohibition, is very light, clean and delicate, with a hint of honey and apple; 70 percent of the grist is wheat. From Thanksgiving through Christmas and New Year, **Our Special Ale** is a spiced brew produced for the holiday season. This brew is different every year.

Anderson Valley

The valley has grown grapes, hops and marijuana, and its "secret language" provides the odd names for the beautifully rounded beers of the Buckhorn brewpub (14081 Highway 128), in Booneville, Mendocino County. They include **Poleeko Gold★★**, soft, lightly citric and dry; **Boont Amber★★★**, starting sweet and fruity, finishing dry and hoppy; **Belk's ESB★★→★★★**, with lots of American hop flavours; **Deep Enders' Dark★★**, a chocolatey but dry Porter; the silky **Barney Flats Oatmeal Stout★★★**; and the very fruity **High Rollers Wheat Beer★★**, among many others.

Angeles

British-accented ales from a micro in suburban Chatsworth. **Angeles Amber Ale★★→★★★** has a full, copper colour, a medium body, a malt accent and a pleasing hop dryness in the finish. A similar, perhaps more assertive, ale called **Rhino Chasers★★→★★★** was created here.

Belmont

Beach brewpub at the beginning of the pier at Belmont Shore, Long Beach. Products have included the tart, dry-hopped **Marathon Ale★★**; the sweeter, fruitier, amber-red, **Top Sail Ale★→★★**; and a Porter called **Long Beach Crude** (not tasted).

Bison

A Honey Basil Ale, tasting robustly of both ingredients; a Nutbrown Ale with carob; and a sharp, dry, IPA with wormwood; were among the early products of this post-modernist brewpub (2598 Telegraph) in the university town of Berkeley. Though they defied rating, all were surprisingly drinkable. A Cardamom Pale Ale and a Lemon Thyme Wheat Beer (not tasted) have come along since.

Boulder Creek

Main street brewpub in Boulder Creek, which is between Santa Cruz and Saratoga. Products have included a very hoppy **Kölsch**★★; a malty-fruity, but slightly tart, **Scottish Ale**★→★★; and a grainy **Oatmeal Stout**★★.

Brewpub on the Green

Golf course brewpub at Fremont (3350 Stevenson Bvd), in the East Bay. It started with a lightly fruity **Lager**★ and a coffeeish **Porter**. Now re-launched as Fremont Brewing Co.

Buffalo Bill

Pioneering brewpub established near San Francisco by the feisty Bill Owens, who also publishes *Beer – The Magazine*. His everyday beers are characteristically rough-and-ready, but he always has surprises. He once made an intensely bitter beer called **Alimony Ale** (100 Units of Bitterness), and pioneered pumpkin beers. (1082 B St, Hayward, in the East Bay.)

Butterfield

Ex-winemaker Kevin Cox created the reddish-amber, soft, slightly chewy, hoppy-fruity **Bridal Veil Ale**★★ (named after a waterfall in Yosemite); a clean, well-balanced, light roasty **Brown Ale**★★; and the dry, malty, textured, **Tower Dark**★★→★★★ (somewhere between a strong dark Bitter and a porter) Butterfield is a brewpub and grill in Fresno (777 East Olive Ave).

Calistoga Inn/Napa Valley Brewing

Italianate chalet-style bed-and-breakfast, restaurant, brewpub and beer-garden at Calistoga (1250 Lincoln Ave), Napa Valley. Products include a dryish, hoppy, golden **Lager**★→★★ and a richly malty, spicy, **Red Ale**★★→★★★ with a suggestion of sassafras root.

Callahan's

Irish-accented brewpub in a suburb of San Diego (82880-A Mira Mesa Bvd). Early products have included the sweetish **Shamrock Gold**★→★★ and the nutty **Callahan Red**★★.

Crown City

The city is the old winter resort of Pasadena, where the foothills of the San Gabriel Mountains meet Greater Los Angeles. Crown City is a brewpub in a renovated china pottery, now a shopping mall (300 S Raymond). Early products have included a sweetish, fruity **Amber**★★ and a **Porter**★→★★ with a hint of black-currant. The range continues to develop.

Dempsey's

An **Irish Ale**★★, smooth, slightly oily, soft, and malty, and a **Stout**★★→★★★ that starts creamily and surges to a powerful espresso finish, are among the products of this brewpub in the Golden Eagle Shopping Center, Petaluma. Dempsey's has an excellent kitchen.

Devil Mountain

Began life as the Devil Mountain pub, Walnut Creek, but is now a micro in Benicia, where Jack London wrote and Gentleman Jim Corbett fought. Early products on this site have included the malty, Scottish-accented, **Railroad Ale★★→★★★** and the smooth, coffeeish, **Devil's Brew Porter★★→★★★**.

Downtown Joes

New name for the former Willett's brewpub, in Napa (902 Main St). New owners have pledged to leave the beers unchanged, and it is to be hoped this promise is kept. Products have included the golden, hoppy, appetizing, **Full Moon Light Ale★★→★★★**; the tawny, fruity, **Victory Ale★★**; the very creamy, chocolatey, dry, **Old Magnolia Stout★★→★★★**; and the smooth, malty, dryish, pale **Maibock★★**. The selection changes constantly. Veteran brewer Brian Hunt now also has the Moonlight micro, in a barn among vineyards at Windsor.

Etna

Revival of an 1870s brewery (closed at Prohibition), on the site of its bottling hall, by Andrew Hurlimann, the stepson of the founding family (who came from Alsace-Lorraine). Etna (population 770) was a gold-mining (and hop-growing) town. It is north of Mount Shasta, near Yreka. Early products, unfiltered, have included the clean, soft, fruity, dry, **Etna Ale★→★★** and the hoppier **Export Lager★★**.

Fremont

See Brewpub on the Green.

Golden Pacific

Between San Francisco and Oakland, at Emeryville. Micro, whose products include the aptly named **Bittersweet Ale★★**, with a malty chewiness and a balancing dryness; **Cable Car Lager★★**, with a good hop aroma and firm, malty texture; **Golden Gate★★**, fuller in colour, body and strength; and variations of the theme.

Gordon Biersch

Serious German-style lagers and excellent food in a stylish brewpub in Palo Alto (640 Emerson), with branches in San Francisco, San Jose and Pasadena. Products include a malty but firm **Export★★★**; a smooth, malty, amber, **Märzen★★★**, slightly dry for the style; and a soft, chocolatey, slightly roasty, **Dunkles★★→★★★**. Partner Dan Gordon graduated as a brewer in Germany (at Weihenstephan).

Heritage

At a beach development and para-sailing resort called Dana Point, about half-way between San Diego and Newport, Orange County. Unpretentious bar-restaurant. Products include the malty, perfumy, **Lantern Bay Blonde★★**; the fruity, smooth **Sail Ale★★**; a tart, hoppy **IPA★★→★★★**; a rich **Nutbrown★★★**; a chewy, chocolatey, **Porter★★**; and the creamy, medium-sweet, **High Seas Oatmeal Stout★★★**.

Hogshead

In the Old Town of Sacramento (114 J St). Cellar brewpub founded by micro pioneer Jim Schlueter, and now under new ownership. Products have included the malty, sweetish, **Hogshead Lager★★** and the dark, chocolatey, **McSchlueter★★**.

Hubsch

See Sudwerks.

Humboldt

On Humboldt Bay, at Arcata (856 10th St). A "Frontier" brewpub, whose founders included Mario Celotto, former linebacker with the Oakland Raiders. Products, all top-fermented, include **Gold Rush★→★★**, soft, fruity and dry; **Red Nectar★★→★★★**, smooth, sweetly malty, with a good complex of hop flavours; **Storm Cellar Porter★★**, with a bitter-chocolate character; and the aromatic, big-tasting, coffeeish, **Oatmeal Stout★★→★★★**.

Lind

In the East Bay town of San Leandro, veteran micro-brewer Roger Lind produces the dry, hoppy, **Drake's Gold★★**; the hoppy but smoother **Drake's Ale★★→★★★**; and the big, chocolatey, spicy, **Sir Francis Stout★★★**.

Los Gatos

Lager brewpub south of San Jose, at Los Gatos (130G N Santa Cruz). Early products have included an attractive, pinkish-amber, **Oktoberfest★★**, malty-fruity, with a refreshing hop tang in the finish.

Lost Coast

Humboldt Bay brewpub, at Eureka (617 4th St). Wide range includes **Downtown Brown Ale★★**, tawny, soft, smooth and lightly malty, with chocolatey sweetness and coffeeish dryness.

Mad River

Just inland of Eureka and Arcata, at Blue Lake. Veteran micro-brewer Bob Smith makes the refreshing, appetizing, dry, citric-tasting **Steelhead Extra Pale Ale★★**, with an emphatic American hop character. His creamy **Extra Stout★★→★★★** is full of flavour, with suggestions of toffee, chocolate, coffee and figs, and a long, oily, clinging, finish.

Marin

A ferry ride from San Francisco, at 1809 Larkspur Landing Circle, in Marin County. Wide range includes **Mount Tam Pale Ale★★→★★★**, with a fruity start and a very hoppy finish; the sweetish **Albion Amber★★**; the malty **St**

Brendan's Irish Red★★→★★★; an aromatic, **Imperial-style Stout★★→★★★**; the herbal-tasting, dry-hopped, **Old Dipsea Barley Wine★★★**; a syrupy, delicious, **Wheat Wine★★★**; and several beers made with fruit extracts.

Mendocino

"Son of New Albion", and one of the country's first brewpubs, is about 90 miles N of San Francisco, on Highway 101, in a 100-year-old saloon at Hopland, in Mendocino County. Amid vineyards, the revivalist brewers planted the town's earlier crop, hops, around their ornamental kiln. Their beers include **Peregrine Pale Ale★→★★**, lightly fruity, and sweetish; **Blue Heron Pale Ale★★**, fuller in colour, body and hop character; the justifiably renowned **Red Tail Ale**, copper coloured and beautifully balanced; seasonal specialities like **Eye of the Hawk★★→★★★**, a strong, malty, ale; and **Black Hawk Stout★★**, medium-dry, fruity and chocolatey.

Murphys Creek

About 100 miles E of San Francisco, at the small town of Murphys, in the Sierra foothills. This micro was established in 1993. Early products included an "ESB" called **Murphys Red★★**, very fruity and dry, with good hop flavours.

Nevada City

Despite its name, Nevada City is in California, albeit on the way to Reno. Located in the Sierras, it has become a retreat for writers and artists, who can also enjoy local microbrewed beers. The brewery makes, unfiltered, the malty-fruity pale lager **Nevada City Gold★→★★★** and a Vienna-style **Dark★★**, with a clean, sweetish, palate. This micro has family links with a brewpub at Pizza Junction (11401 Donner Pass Rd), in Truckee, further up the road to Reno.

North Coast

Rightly well-regarded ales from a brewpub in a former Presbyterian church and chapel of rest at the old port of Fort Bragg (444 N Main) in Mendocino County. **Alt Nouveau★★** is golden-to-bronze, and malty-peachy; **Ruedrich's Red Seal Ale★★→★★★** is fresh, fruity and creamily soft, beautifully balanced, with an appetizingly dry finish; **Old No 38 Stout★★★** is creamy and chocolatey, with lots of flavour development.

Okie Girl

In Grapes of Wrath country. The brewery, originally known as Grapevine, is on the winding mountain road of that name, a stretch of Interstate 5, at Lebec (Frazier Park Exit), between LA and Bakersfield. Early brews have included a malty **Lager★★**; a hoppy, well-balanced, **Ale★★★**; and a chocolatey **Stout★★**.

Old Columbia

A German-born veteran of American brewing, Karl Strauss, helped set up this brewpub in San Diego (1157 Columbia, near the trolley). Products include **Columbia Amber Lager★→★★**, lightly malty, with some hop in the finish; **Downtown After Dark★→★★**, vaguely in the style of a British ale; **Black's Beach★→★★**, dryish and porter-like; and **Red Trolley★★→★★★**, a fruity "ESB". The Karl Strauss Brewery Gardens opened in 1994, in the San Diego Tech Center.

Pacific Coast

Beer-lovers visiting San Francisco should take the BART train to Oakland to sample the ales of this brewpub in a city-centre Victorian building (906 Washington). Products include an excellent, English-style dark **Mariners' Mild★★★**; the hoppy **Gray Whale Ale★★→★★★**; the assertive **Blue Whale Ale★★★**, matured over oak chips; and the dry, herbal-tasting, **Killer Whale Stout★★→★★★**.

Pacific Hop Exchange

Tiny micro in Novato making unfiltered beers. These include the soft, yeasty, dryish, **Gaslight Pale Ale★→★★**.

Pete's Wicked

California-based enthusiast Pete Slosberg created these products, which were originally made at a now-defunct micro in Palo Alto. They are now produced at Minnesota Brewing, in St Paul. **Pete's Wicked Lager★★** is malt-accented, with a leafy hop character in the finish. **Pete's Wicked Ale★★→★★★** has a chestnut colour, a rich aroma, and a depth of fruitiness.

Riverside

Brewpub in the former Fruit Exchange, in old citrus country, at Riverside (3394 7th St), E of Los Angeles. Early products have included the light but hoppy **Pullman Pale Ale★★**, which has an attractively pinkish colour; and the toffeeish, roasty, **7th Street Stout★★**.

Rubicon

Well-regarded brewpub in Sacramento (2004 Capitol). Products have included a **Summer Wheat★★** with a lot of hop in the finish; an **Amber Ale★★→★★★** that is also well hopped; an intensely hoppy **IPA★★★**; the coffeeish, burnt-tasting, **Ol' Moe's Porter★★→★★★**; and a spectacular **Winter Wheat Wine★★★** which is fruity, smooth and warming.

St Stans

Stanislaus County, abstemiously Baptist, gave birth to this micro in 1984, and it moved to a brewpub site in Modesto (821 L St) in 1990. A German-accented range began with two brews in loosely the Düsseldorf style: the pale **Amber Alt★★**, with a malty accent and some apple-and-fig fruitiness; and **Dark Alt★★**, which is ruby-coloured and chocolatey, with a touch of roastiness.

San Andreas

On the fault line, in the town of Hollister (737 San Benito). This brewpub suffered only minor damage in the 1989 'quake, but close neighbours were less lucky. Some thought the brewery had tempted providence with its **Earthquake Pale Ale★★→★★★**, extremely dry, but hardly vengeful. **Kit Fox Amber★★**, named after an endangered species, is maltier but still dryish. **Survivor Stout★★** is coffeeish and dry. Several fruit beers and a wintergreen-tasting **Woodruff Ale★★→★★★** are among other eccentricities.

San Francisco

Where downtown San Francisco meets the North Beach restaurant quarter (155 Columbus, at Pacific), a 1907 saloon houses the city's oldest brewpub (est. 1986). Products have varied, but are good at their best. The golden **Albatross Lager★→★★** has lots of American hop character, as well as some Saaz; **Emperor Norton★★** is broadly in the Vienna style, nutty, with touches of vanilla and apricot; **Gripman's Porter★★** is chocolatey and medium-dry.

San Rafael

Golden Ale★★, with 25 percent wheat content, starts sweetly and honeyish, and finishes with a refreshing suggestion of ginger. **Amber★★** is malty, sweetish and smooth, with a lightly tart finish. These products have been variable, but are tasty at their best. They are served next door to the brewery, at TJ's Bar and Grill (7110 Redwood Bvd, Novato).

Santa Cruz

This seaside resort on Monterey Bay gives its name to a brewpub at 516 Front St. Products include the lightly hoppy **Lighthouse Lager★→★★**; an **Amber★★** that is well-rounded with a dry finish; sometimes a slightly roasty, medicinal, **Dark Lager★★**; and a dry, assertive, coffeeish, **Porter★★→★★★. also** seasonal specialities have included a smooth, chocolatey, **Pacific Stout★★→★★★**; a rich but hoppy **Beacon Barley Wine★★→★★★**; and an intensely aromatic Christmas beer called **Hoppy Holidays★★★**.

Santa Rosa

This college town in Sonoma now gives its name to its brew-pub, formerly called Kelmer's (458 B St). The beers are now more assertive, and the sports theme has gone, since new owners arrived. Products include a grainy, dry, hoppy, **IPA★★** and a somewhat medicinal **Barley Wine★★**, with a warming finish.

Seabright

Outstanding beers from the second brewpub established in Santa Cruz (519 Seabright Ave). Products include **Pelican Pale★★**, lightly malty with a dry finish; **Seabright Amber★★→★★★**, fruity and hoppy, with a long finish;

Amber Banty Rooster IPA★★★, with a hoppy nose and palate, very dry, especially in the finish; **Pleasure Point Porter★★★**, with a coffeeish, malty, start and a dry finish; and a smooth, winey, **Oatmeal Stout★★→★★★**.

Shields

Between Los Angeles and Santa Barbara, in Ventura (24 E Santa Clara), this family-run brewpub produces the dryish **Gold Coast Beer★→★★**; the creamier, maltier, amber, ale named after the **Channel Islands★★** off this stretch of coast; and the dry **Shields Stout★★**.

Sierra Nevada

One of the earliest new-generation breweries in the US, in 1981, and now established as the Château Latour among American micros. **Sierra Nevada Draught Ale★★★** is very slightly sweeter in palate than its companion bottled **Pale Ale★★★★**. This American classic has an teasing balance between the floral Cascade hops and the fruitiness of the top-fermenting yeast. The **Porter★★★** is among the best brewed anywhere in the world: firmly dry, but with a gentle, coffee-toffee finish. The strong **Stout★★** (4.8; 6.0) is very smooth, with a powerful roastiness in the finish. A **Celebration Ale** is brewed for the winter holiday period, to a different specification each year, sometimes with experimental new varieties of hops. In late winter and early spring, Sierra Nevada has its **Big Foot Barley Wine★★★★**, with a huge hoppiness in its earthy aroma and chewy palate. This is among the strongest beers in the United States, at 8.0–10.0 by weight; 11–12.5 by volume. This beer is bottle-conditioned for four weeks at the brewery, and begins to become winier if it is kept for a further three months. Properly cellared, it should remain in good condition for a year or two. There is also a range of characteristically well-made seasonal lagers.

SLO

The town of San Luis Obispo gives its initials, and a location, to this brewpub (1119 Garden St). Products include a **Pale Ale★**, with a dry maltiness and some fruit; a smooth, fruitier, **Amber Ale★★**; and a fruity, chocolatey, sweetish, **Porter★★**. Specials have stretched to a very distinctive **IPA★★★** matured over oak chips.

Sudwerk/Hubsch

From *Sudhaus*, German for "brewhouse". Hubsch is a family name. A splendidly enthusiastic Bavarian brewer makes robustly German beers at this pub in Davis (2001 2nd St), home town of the University of California's beer and wine departments. Hubsch beers include a soft, malty, **Lager★★→★★★**; a **Pilsner★★★** with a beautiful balance of malt and hop; a deftly malt-accented **Märzen**; and a **Dark Lager★★★** with a good bitter-chocolate character.

Tied House

The name first manifested itself at a brewpub in Mountain View (954 Villa St), a town S of San Francisco. The description, the British term for a pub "tied" to one brewery, implied a planned chain. There are now further Tied Houses in Alameda and San Jose, but they have their own breweries. Principal beers are a lightly fruity **Pale★**; a fruitier, pleasant, **Amber★→★★**; and a fuller-flavoured **Dark★★** in broadly the style of a soft English Bitter.

Triple Rock

Well-established, studenty, brewpub in the college town of Berkeley (1920 Shattuck Ave). Principal products are **Pinnacle Pale Ale★→★★**, dry, lightly hoppy and fruity; **Red Rock Ale★★**, sweeter, still fruity, with more hop in a late finish; and **Black Rock Porter★★**, light to medium in body, but dry and quite complex.

Twenty Tank

San Francisco brewpub (316 11th St, S of Market, near Folsom) established by Triple Rock. Products include the robust, perfumy, full-coloured, **Red Top Ale★★→★★★**.

Willet's

See Downtown Joes.

THE NORTHWEST

No American city can match Portland, Oregon, in its number of breweries. The metro area has at least a dozen, and the state as a whole more than twice that number. The neighbouring state of Washington has more than 20 breweries, almost half of them in the Seattle/Puget Sound area.

Portland specializes in brewpubs, while Seattle has more free-standing "ale houses", but in both cities micro-brewed beers are more widely available in ordinary bars and restaurants than anywhere else in America.

Both states grow barley for malting, and between them have the principal regions for the cultivation of hops in America (the Willamette Valley in Oregon and Yakima in Washington.

The two major cities are small enough to have a local pride in their beers but sufficiently large to offer a worthwhile market to their brewers. With their relatively cool weather, both states favour indoor drinking, in taverns, and draught beer is more widely served here than elsewhere in the USA. This has helped micros begin without the expense of a bottling line. The climate also favours the fuller-flavoured speciality beers, as opposed to light quenchers.

Seattle is known for its interest in food and drink, and Portland quietly shares the same enthusiasm for civilized living. Seattle also has America's most adventurous importer of beer, Merchant Du Vin.

With the economic growth of the Pacific Rim, Seattle – long the gateway to Alaska – has become a commercial capital for a wider region. Its beery influence crosses the border into Idaho, Montana and, at a pinch, Wyoming.

Where to drink

The Oregon Brewers' Festival, a major public tasting, has been a model for similar events elsewhere in the USA. It is usually on the third weekend in July, in Portland. For information, check any of the city's three old-established micros (Bridge-Port, Portland Brewing, both with tap-rooms attached, and Widmer).

Apart from brewpubs, the best-known speciality beer bars in Portland are The Horse Brass (4534 SE Belmont), Produce Row (204 SE Oak) and The Dublin Pub ((6821 Beaverton and Hillside Highway).

The elegant Heathman Hotel (SW Broadway and Salmon) is the place for the well-heeled beer-lover. Its two bars offer differing selections of micro and imported beers, and the hotel also owns the nearby B. Moloch bistro, which has its own associated brewery (see entry for **Widmer**).

In Seattle, the best place for beer gossip is Liberty Malt (1432 Western Ave). This is ostensibly a home-brew store, but also has a remarkable selection of books and guides on beer, and is associated with the nearby Pike Place micro.

Speciality bars include The Pioneer Square Saloon (73 Yesler Way), The Belltown Pub (2322 1st Ave), Murphy's (1928 N 45th), Coopers (8065 Lake City Way NE), the Red Door (3401 Fremont Ave N), the 74th St Alehouse (7401 Green-wood Ave N) and the Latona (on the avenue of that name, at 6423). The Blue Moon, famous as a picaresque and vaguely literary tavern (712 NE 45th), has a better range of beers than might be expected. F. X. McRory (419 Occidental Ave S), a bar-restaurant near the Kingdome, has a large selection of micro-brews on draught. Cutters (2001 Western Ave) is a beer-aware establishment, with sister restaurants in other cities.

Alaskan Brewing

Outstanding, quality-conscious micro in Juneau, the state capital of Alaska. Renowned for its Christmas seasonal **Smoked Porter★★★★**. The malt is smoked over alder twigs, across the street from the brewery, at an establishment that normally gives its attention to Alaskan salmon. The end product has a powerful smokiness and treacle-toffee in the nose, a mellow woodiness, a faint hint of fruit (raisins?), and a oily, roasty, finish. Regular products include a notably soft-bodied, very fruity, hoppy, **Pale Ale★★** and a remarkably smooth and malty Altbier, **Alaskan Amber★★**.

Bay Front

See Rogue.

Bayern

The name is German for Bavaria, and Jurgen Knoller's prod-ucts have an authentic character, judging from his **Pilsener ★★→★★★**: firm-bodied, with a tasty malt character and a delicately hoppy finish. This brewpub is in a former rail-road building in Missoula, Montana (North Higgins and Railroad).

Big Time

Creative classics from a brewpub in Seattle (4133 University Way NE). Brewer Ed Tringali makes hoppy interpretations of a golden **Pale Ale★★**; a fruity **Amber★★★**; a malty, rounded **ESB★★→★★★**; a very creamy **Oatmeal Stout★★→★★★**; a smooth **Porter★★**; a very malty barley wine called **Old Woolly★★→★★★**; and a spicy, chewy, spicy-minty **Hefe-Ryzen★★★→★★★★** (a rye beer). Cask-conditioned ales served on Friday evenings.

Bird Creek

Named for Ike Kelly's birthplace, but his micro is 25 miles away in Anchorage, Alaska. **Old 55★★** commemorates the year of his birth. It is a Pale Ale, well balanced but accented towards perfumy hoppiness and late dryness.

Blitz Weinhard

Best known for **Henry Weinhard's Private Reserve★★→★★★** an aromatic lager that was one of America's most distinctive beers before microbrews became readily available. **Henry Weinhard's Dark★→★★** is light and dry. **Blue Boar Ale★→★★** is gently fruity and popcorn sweet, but its claims of Irish heritage are nonsense. This old-established regional brewery, in Portland, is owned by Heileman.

BridgePort

Founded by wine-makers Dick and Nancy Ponzi in 1984, this is the oldest of Portland's new brewpubs and micros, making malt-accented ales. Its signature **BridgePort Ale★★★** is ruby-coloured, soft and Scottish-accented. The amber-red (despite its name) **Blue Heron Pale Ale★★★** is again malty, but develops a tasty, aromatic, hop character. The stronger **Pintail★★** (just under 4.0, 5.0), a full gold colour, is fruitier and tarter, but still well-balanced. **Ross Island Ale★★** is stronger again (around 5.4, 6.6). sweetish and satisfying. **Double Stout★★** is smooth, toffeeish, fruity and dry, with a good length. **Old Knucklehead★★→★★★** (around 7.4, 9.2) is a rounded, warming barley wine. On its own premises (1313 NW Marshall), BridgePort always has three or four of its ales cask-conditioned.

Coeur d'Alene

A resort in Idaho. The Coeur d'Alene brewery and T. W. Fisher pub (204 2nd St) produce a **Pale Ale★→★★** and a **Festival Dark★→★★** that are both somewhat grainy and acidic. Other beers not tasted.

Deschutes

The town of Bend, Oregon, takes its name from a twist in the Deschutes River. Its Deschutes Brewery and Pub (1044 Bond St NW) has produced an enjoyably dry **Pils★★**; a hop-accented **Kölsch★★**; the soft, sweetish, **Cascade Golden Ale★★**, with an appropriate dash of hops in the finish; the firm, fruity, **Bachelor Bitter★★→★★★**; the aromatic **Mirror Pond Pale Ale★★→★★★**; the smooth, well-balanced, **Anniversary Alt★★★**; a coffeeish **Scotch Ale★★** that was almost a sweet stout; the slightly burnt-tasting **Bond St Brown Ale★→★★**; the dry, oily, chewy, nutty, complex, **Black Butte Porter★★→★★★**; and the fruitier, sweeter, smokier, **Obsidian Stout★★→★★★**, among others.

Eugene City Brewery

Brewpub established in 1993 in Eugene, Oregon (844 Olive St). Early products have included a very aromatic, fruity and dry **IPA★★→★★★**.

Full Sail

Brewpubs in Portland (307 SW Montgomery) and the town of Hood River, Oregon (506 Columbia St), the latter also serving as a micro. The name Full Sail was inspired by the popularity of wind-surfing near the confluence of the rivers Hood and Columbia. Beers have included a Saaz-accented but malty (almost sticky), **Pilsner★★**; a fruity **Golden★→★★**; a flavoursome, malty-fruity **Amber Ale★★★** (inspired by Samuel Smith's Pale); a mahogany **Brown Ale★★→★★★**, with a touch of chocolate; a raisiny **Top Sail Porter★★** (more of an Imperial Stout); the fruity-hoppy **Old Boardhead Barley Wine★★**; and several other styles. It is to be hoped that the quality of the beers can keep up with their popularity.

Grant's

Hop country micro and pioneering brewpub, known for its distinctive products, and making liberal use of the Yakima Valley crop. The beers are created by the equally characterful Scottish-born brewer and hop expert Bert Grant. The fruity **Celtic Ale★★★**, with an Irish-looking label, has the original gravity (1034) and appearance of an English dark Mild but much more hop. The medium-amber **Grant's Ale★★★**, smooth and malty, is billed as being Scottish in style, but again has more hop than that suggests. The **IPA★★★** takes full advantage of that description and permits itself to be very dry indeed, with a powerful, lingering, hop finish. The **Imperial Stout★★★** (5.8, 7.2) is fruity and honeyish, but still dry. The oddly spelled **Weis★★**, made with 30 percent wheat, is light, dry, smooth and tart. Grant's, of Yakima, Washington, originally had a brewery and pub in the town's former opera house. It has now moved to a brewpub across the street, at 32 North Front, in the old railroad station, and a micro-brewery elsewhere in the town.

Hale's

Brewpubs in Seattle (109 Central Way, Kirkland) and the eastern Washington town of Spokane (5634 E Commerce St).

Products have included the pale, dry, **Cascade Mist★→★★**; the thinnish, lightly fruity, **American Pale Ale★★**; the fruitier **Moss Bay Amber★★**; the slightly tart, hoppy, **Moss Bay Extra★★**; a maltier, rounder, softer, but aromatic, **Special Bitter★★→★★★**; a malty-fruity **Irish Ale★★**; a roasty, dryish, **Porter★★→★★★**; a light, apple-ish, **Wheat★★**; a tart-and-sweet **Honey Wheat★★→★★★**; and a powerful **Wheat Bock★★→★★★**.

Harrison Hollow

At 2455 Harrison Hollow Boulevard, Boise, Idaho. This brewpub makes a **Western Ale** (not tasted) and a very refreshing, clean-tasting, **Ginger Wheat★★→★★★**.

Hazel Dell

Brewpub just over the river from Portland in the Washington town of Vancouver (8513 NE Highway 99). The general manager is called Joe Moran. Early products have included **Captain Moran's Irish Stout★★**, deliciously oily, sweet and chocolatey.

Thomas Kemper

A ferry ride from Seattle, to the Kitsap Peninsula and the old Norwegian settlement of Poulsbo (22381 Foss Rd). Thomas Kemper is a brewpub that produces lagers, beautifully made, in classic styles. The pale **Lager★★→★★★** has an excellent malt character; the **Pilsner★★★** is hoppy in both flavour and dryness; a **Maibock★★** falls away a little towards the finish; a very yeasty **Hefe-Weizen★★→★★★** soft and lightly fruity, with a nicely tart finish.

Kessler

Dryish, malty beers from a brewpub in Helena, Montana (1439 Harris St). Examples include a full-bodied ale that is relatively low in alcohol (2.8, 3.5), called **Number Seven★★**, and a rich, malty-spicy **Doppelbock★★→★★★**.

Leavenworth

Located in the mock-alpine tourist town of Leavenworth, Washington (636 Front St). This brewpub has produced has a **Friesian Pilsner★★★**, perfumy, dry and assertive (loosely modelled on Jever, but using St Christoffel yeast); a hoppy-fruity **Wheat Beer★→★★**; a well-balanced, fruit-accented, **Altbier★★→★★★**; a dry, hoppy, **Bitter★★**; a hoppy-fruity **IPA★★**; and a **Stout★★→★★★** with lots of bitter chocolate.

MacMenamin's

Grateful Dead "heads" and remarkably expansive brewers, ten of whose pubs, all in Oregon, make their own beers. Icons of the 1960s are often in evidence. There is now a parent brewery, called Edgefield, offering bed-and-breakfast. It is at the stylish former "poor farm", once a county facility, at

Troutdale (2126 SW Halsey), 20 miles E of Portland. The quality of the beers in the pubs has varied, but Edgefield has made some impressive specialities. These have included a **Pilsner★★→★★★** with very good hop flavours; a soft, rounded, fruity, **Kölsch★★**; a very hoppy bitter called **Hammerhead★★★**; an **IPA★★→★★★** that starts malty and finishes with lots of hop flavours; an especially hoppy ale called **Ananda** (not tasted); a fruity special with the name **Centennial★★→★★★**, made with hops of that variety; a spicy **Scotch Ale**; a chocolatey **Porter★★**; a roasty, coffeeish, **Stout★★→★★★**; and a toffeeish **Doppelbock★★**.

Maritime Pacific
Seattle micro. Products have included a grainy, tart, spritzy lager called **Northwest Common Beer** (too early to rate) and a ruby-coloured, fruity, clean, light, **Flagship Red★★**.

Milestown
Tiny micro in Miles City, in the Yellowstone Valley of Montana. Products include an assertive Munich Helles called **Old Milestown** and the fruity, tart, indeed witty, **Coal Porter**. Too early to rate.

Mount Hood
Brewpub in ski country at the town of Government Camp, Oregon. Products have included the hoppy-spicy **Pinnacle ESB★★**.

Olympia
Light-tasting mainstream beers from a brewery owned by Pabst located in Olympia, state capital of Washington. Olympia contract-brews **Smith and Reilly★★**, a firmer lager with a touch of grassy hoppiness.

Onalaska
Midwife Susan Moorehead and husband Dave run this tiny micro and tavern, in the old sawmill town of Onalaska, Washington (248 Burchett Rd). Their robust, earthy, products include the bronze, nutty, perfumy, **Onalaska Ale★★** (4.0, 5.0) and the maltier, slightly stronger, **Red Dawg★★** (4.25, 5.3).

Oregon Trail
Hop country micro in Corvallis, Oregon. Recent products have included a mild-tasting rendition of a Belgian-style wheat beer, with oats, **Oregon Trail White Ale★★→★★★**. Also a darkish, sweet, malty, abbey style (too early to rate).

Otto Brothers
Charlie and Ernie Otto, and their partner Don Frank, brew in the town of Wilson, in Jackson Hole, Wyoming, and have a tasting room (1295 West St). They make very acceptable beers from extract. **Teton Ale★★**, modelled on an English Bitter, is malty and fruity. **Old Faithful★★**, an American Pale Ale, is drier and more fruit-accented.

Pacific Northwest

Brewpub, in the heart of downtown Seattle (322 Occidental Avenue S). Products, with a hop accent, have included the perfumy **Blonde★★**; a fuller-coloured, hoppier, **Gold★★**; an English-accented **Bitter★★→★★★**; a well-balanced **Amber★★→★★★**; a very fruity, dry, **Stout★★**; and aromatically malty **Winter Warmer★★★**.

Pike Place

Quality beers, full of flavour, from a tiny micro (1432 Western Ave) two doors from Liberty Malt and adjoining Pike Place Market, in Seattle. Principal products are a creamy, nutty, beautifully balanced, **Pale Ale★★★** and the soft, smooth, toasty, dryish, **5X Stout★★★**. Specialities have included an astonishingly refreshing **East India Pale Ale★★★**; **Birra Perfetto★★★**, heavily seasoned with oregano; **Cerveza Rosanna★★→★★★**, a lightly peppery chili ale; a rich, salty, **Oyster Stout★★★** flavoured with the liquid from the shellfish; and **Old Bawdy★★★**, an oak-aged barley wine made with peated malt and finishing with a whiff of smoke.

Pizza Deli/Wild River

Sophisticated beers from a brewpub in the S of Oregon, near the California state line, at Cave Junction (249 N Redwood Highway). Wide range has included an assertive **Kölsch★★→★★★**; a well-balanced **ESB★★→★★★**; a creamy, whiskyish, **Barley Wine★★→★★★**; a lightly fruited **Blackberry Porter★★**; and a chocolatey, roasty, warming **Imperial Stout★★**.

Portland Brewing

Classically Northwestern-style ales from a cosy brewpub (1339 NW Flanders St) and a grander newer micro and tasting room (2730 NW 31st). Products include **Oregon Honey Beer★★→★★★**, primed in the kettle and emerging with just the faintest hint of clover in its smooth palate; the light, dryish, **Portland Ale★→★★**; **Mount Hood★★**, aromatized with that variety of hop, and with a late dryness in the finish; the hoppier, yet sweetish, Scottish-accented, **McTarnahan's★★★**; a smooth, dryish, iron-tinged **Porter★★→★★★**; and a strong **Stout★★→★★★** with a touch of burnt currants. There has been a honey-primed strong brew called **Pollinator** (not tasted).

Pyramid

The allusion is to a peak in the Cascades. The brewery, also know as Hart (perhaps after co-founder Beth Hartwell), is north of Portland, across the state line at Kalama, Washington. Its well-rounded beers have included the oddly named **Wheaten Ale★★→★★★**, firm, crisp and dry; an orangey-tasting **Hefeweizen★★→★★★**; a light but flavoursome **Amber★★→★★★**, on the lines of a low-gravity English bitter; a **Pale Ale★★★** that resembles a British "Best"; a sweetish, fruity, flowery, **Brown Ale★★**; a firm, medium-bodied, very coffeeish, **Sphinx Stout★★**; the beautifully balanced, long, **Snow Cap★★★**, a barley wine; and a top-fermenting **"Bock"★★**, malty and fruity (lemony?).

Rainier

Once dubbed "The Green Death", but **Rainier Ale★★** today seems a shadow of its former sins. Even the regular **Rainier Beer★** seems sweeter and less firm-bodied than it was. Rainier, in Seattle, is owned by Heileman.

Redhook Ale

One of the first micros in the Northwest and now by far the biggest with its own tap room, in a former streetcar barn (The Trolleyman, 3400 Phinney Ave N), and a lager brewery planned. The original **Redhook Ale★★★**, intensely fruity (and whimsically brandishing a banana on its neck label), now makes only occasional appearances. **Red Hook ESB★★** has a paler amber colour, is more conventionally fruity, and has a hoppy finish. **Ballard Bitter★★**, named after the site of the original brewery, is pale, fruity and dry. **Blackhook Porter** is smooth and dryish, with a hint of treacle-toffee. **Wheat Hook★★** crisp, firm and tart. The most interesting beers are the "blue line" specials. They have included a lightly spicy **Redhook Rye★★→★★★** and a smooth, malty, peated, **Scotch Ale★★★**.

Rogue

The old coastal resort of Newport, Oregon, boasts a busy micro, with a separate tasting room (748 SW Bay Bvd) and an affiliated brewpub in the theatre-festival town of Ashland (31B Water St). Products, which tend toward maltiness, have included the very hoppy, Saaz-accented, **Waterfront Lager★★**; a soft, slightly oily, **Golden Ale★★**; the firmer, amber, **Rogue Ale★★→★★★**, with an East Kent bitterness in the finish (the Ashland counterpart is maltier and slightly chocolatey); the rounded, malty but dry **St Rogue Red★★**; the very hoppy, long, **Old Crustacean Barley Wine★★★**; the aromatic, chocolatey, **Mogul Madness★★**, a winter brew; the syrupy, coffeeish, roasty, **Dark Ruby★★**; the creamy, coffeeish, **Shakespeare Oatmeal Stout★★→★★★**; the whiskyish, very smooth, **Imperial Stout★★★**, with lots of oats and some licorice; a moderately peppery jalapeño ale called **Mexicali★★**; and the lightly fruity **Rogue 'n' Berry★★→★★★** (the fruit being marion berries. The brewery takes its name from the Rogue River.

Roslyn

The television series *Northern Exposure*, set in Alaska, was filmed in the Washington town of Roslyn, once a mining community. Thirsts can be quenched at the tap-room of Roslyn Brewing (33 Pennsylvania Ave). The principal product is **Roslyn Beer★★→★★★**, reddish-brown, with chocolatey sweetness and herbal, robust, hoppy dryness.

Saxer
Named after an Oregon brewer of frontier days. Micro at Lake Oswego, near Portland. Early products and policies changeable.

Spanish Peaks
Mountain brewpub in Bozeman, Montana (120 N 19th Ave). Early products include a somewhat medicinal, dry, **Porter** and a sweeter, oilier **Oatmeal Stout**. Too early to rate.

Star
Psychologist Jack Norman and metal-worker Scott Wenzel set up this micro in Portland in 1993. Early products, all ales, have included **Hop Gold★★→★★★**, with wonderfully earthy aromas; a well-balanced **IPA★★**; a firm **Nut Brown★★**, with a touch of roastiness; and a clean, lightly tart, **Raspberry Ale★★**.

Steelhead
Hugely characterful and impeccably well-made beers from a brewpub in Eugene, Oregon (199 E 5th). Products include the russet-coloured, complex, hoppy-tasting, dry-finishing **Emerald Special Bitter (ESB)★★★**, named for the local baseball team; an explosively hoppy IPA, called **Bombay Bomber★★★**; an astonishingly nutty-tasting **Brown Ale★★**; the fruity, sweet-and-dry, smoky **French Pete's Porter★★→★★★** (15; 1060; 5.2; 6.5); and the complex, rounded, creamy **Oatmeal Stout★★★** (17.5, 1070, 5.8, 7.2), with the aroma of the grain itself.

Sun Valley
Ski-country brewpub on Main St, Hailey, in Sun Valley, Idaho. Early products include amber, toast-tasting, **White Cloud Ale★★**.

TableRock
Near the mountains, in Boise, Idaho. This brewpub (705 Fulton) uses orange blossom in its light, very dry, smooth, **Dog Days Pale Ale★★→★★★**.

Umpqua
The name is Native American. This brewpub is Roseburg, Oregon (328 SE Jackson). Early beers have included the hazy, orangey, herbal-tasting, Belgian-style, **Rose Garden White★★★**, featuring oats, curaçao, coriander and Goldings hops; and the sweetish, syrupy, fruity, warming, **Roseburg Red★★**, in the style of an ESB.

West Seattle
Brewpub at the intersection of California and Alaska Streets, whose names it also uses. Has made a wild-fermented raspberry and cranberry beer, on the lines of a Belgian *lambic*, and a fruity, tart **Old Stock Ale**. Too early to rate.

Widmer
German-style beers from a family-run pioneering micro in Portland. In recent years, Widmer has enjoyed great success

in the Northwest with its (intentionally) densely sedimented **Hefe-Weizen★★★**, which tastes somewhere between a beer and a fresh, sweetish, grapefruit juice, but deserves points for that curious distinction. Its filtered counterpart, called simply **Weizen★★**, starts softly and finishes crisply, with a late, wheat-beer, tartness. The brewery's outstanding product is its hard-to-find **Altbier★★★** – firm bodied, with excellent malt and hop characters, in perfect balance. Other products have included a full-coloured, malty, **Märzen★★→★★★**; a slightly paler, malty-fruity, **Oktoberfest★★**; and a bronze, malty, **Bock★→★★**. Widmer has a smaller brewery at the bakery-based restaurant B. Moloch (901 SW Salmon).

THE CARIBBEAN

Emigrants from the Caribbean have helped spread the popularity of several beers from the region. The best-known internationally is **Red Stripe★★★**, light-tasting, soft-bodied lager from Jamaica. Other examples include the maltier and fruiter **Banks Lager★★★** from Barbados; and the malty, but drier **Carib Lager★★** from Trinidad. Gravities are typically in the classical Pilsener range of 11.5-12 Plato (1046-48); units of bitterness low (15-19); and lagering times short (two weeks is common). In Caribbean ethnic markets in Britain, Red Stripe has an extra-strong lager called **Crucial Brew★**. Several Caribbean breweries also have sweet or medium-dry stouts, often bottom-fermented, and usually at "tropical" gravities; in the range of 15-20 Plato (1060–1080), with alcohol contents of between 4.5 and 6 percent by weight; 5.75–7.75 by volume. Some of these are produced in unlikely places, Haiti, for example, has the dry, fruity, **Prestige Stout★★**.

For some years, St Thomas on the US Virgin Islands offered the curiosity brew **Spinnaker Lager**. Sad to say, this venture has now ceased.

LATIN AMERICA

All the countries of Latin America have brewing industries, some very large. All produce beers distantly derived from the Germanic tradition, including the occasional dark speciality. A good example is Brazil's tasty **Xingu★★→★★★**, marketed in the USA with a tenuous story linking it to the Indians of the Amazon.

Outside Latin America, the sub-continent's best-known beers are those from Mexico, many of which are exported to the USA. The success in the USA of a product called Corona (see entry, under Modelo) has done a disservice to Mexican beer. Corona is a cheaply made, watery-tasting , sweetish, beer, originally intended simply as a thirst-quencher for manual workers in Mexico. Each of the brewers in Mexico has such a product, usually bottled in plain glass, with an enamelled name instead of a label. By a freak of fashion, and initially with very little promotion, Corona became a cult beer among sub-Yuppies in the southwest of the USA. This has encouraged Mexican brewers to concentrate on such products, at the expense of their several more interesting beers. It has also encouraged Americans to believe that all Mexican beer is light and bland. The way things are going, that will soon be true.

Cuauhtémoc

Second-largest of the Mexican brewing companies. Also owns Cruz Blanca. (It is itself owned by the same holding company as Moctezuma.) The Cuauhtémoc products are lightened by a high proportion of corn, and tend to have a dry, slightly tannic, finish. The company has a typically Mexican range. The "clear-glass" brand is **Chihuahua★**. The dry, crisp, quencher **Tecate★** began as a regional brand. **Carta Blanca★** and (in the US market) the smooth **Carta Blanca Dark★→★★** are mainstream brands. **Bohemia★★** is a pleasantly hoppy Pilsener with a high gravity for the style (13; 1052; 4.2; 5.4). **Indio Oscura★→★★** is a reddish lager, broadly of the Vienna type but a little thin and dry for the style. **Commemorativa★★→★★★** (14.3; 1057; 4.3; 5.6) is a medium-dark Christmas beer.

Moctezuma

Biggest exporter, but smallest in the Mexican market. Uses a lower proportion of adjuncts and makes a point that they include rice. Its beers tend to be relatively smooth, with a spritzy finish: *kräusening* is another point of policy. **Sol★** is another sub-Yuppie quencher; **Superior★→★★** is a lightly fragrant, spritzy, Pilsener-type (11.5; 1046; 3.6; 4.5). Then comes the rather confusing Equis range. **Tres Equis★→★★** is a marginally fuller Pilsener-type. **Dos Equis Lager Especial★→★★** is fractionally fuller again (12; 1048- 3.7; 4.6). The best-known version, simply called **Dos Equis★★**, is amber-red in colour, and broadly in the Vienna style. It, too, has a gravity of 12 Plato. The dark brown **Noche Buena★★★** Christmas Beer (15; 1060; 4.2; 5.4) is very full-bodied, with both malt and hop in its long finish, but there are doubts about its continued existence. Tres Equis Oscura has been discontinued, because the company has more faith in its less interesting beers.

Modelo

Biggest of the Mexican brewing companies, also owning Yucatan. Its most noteworthy product is the **Negra Modelo★★★**, on the dark side for a Vienna-style beer, creamy in body, with a hint of chocolate (just the thing with chicken molé). The Yucatan brands include a similar beer, the tasty, hoppier, **Negra Leon★★**.

ASIA

Western-style beers were introduced to several Asian countries in the mid- to late 1800s, and have been brewed with the greatest enthusiasm in Japan. A potent blend of traditionalism and inventiveness has been brought to brewing there as it has been to other industries. This may become even more evident with changes in the law to permit micro-breweries.

The established breweries of Japan are among the world's largest, and have by far the most advanced equipment. The biggest, Kirin, honours tradition in its regular range with a treacle-toffeeish, strong (6.4; 8.0) Stout★★★ and a faintly smoky, Kulmbach-style Black Beer★★→★★★, as well as its crisp, dryish, everyday Lager★★. Further essays into traditionalism have included the hoppy Spring Valley ★★→★★★ lager, brewed at its micro in Yokohama, and an Alt★★→★★★, with a touch of roasted malt, produced in Kyoto. Inventive experiments have included the all-malt Heartland★★, intended to be as fresh and crisp "as a washed-cotton shirt"; Kirin Draft Kojo★★, with a touch of sulphur to suggest the bath-house; Ichiba★★ , made from the "first pressing" of the malt; Golden Bitter★★, a lager with "matured" hops for an "earthy" flavour; and Ad Lib★, brewed to 10 percent alcohol by volume and diluted with club soda to taste.

Sapporo has a Black Beer★★★ with a touch of licorice toffee; the nutty, Vienna-style, Baisen Beer★★→★★★; an aromatically malty brew called Yebisu★★→★★★ that is somewhere between a Dortmunder and a Pilsenser; and a fragrant, hoppy, Edel-Pils★★★ in its regular range, as well as its spritzy Original★→★★. Experimental brews have ranged from the lightly smooth Ginjikomi★★, made from de-husked malt, to a lightly fruity Alt★★→★★★.

Asahi is known for its slightly grainy-tasting Super Dry★, and a similar, top-fermenting beer called Z★, but also makes a caramelish Black Beer★★; and an outstandingly traditional strong Stout★★★→★★★★, with notes of sherry and whisky in the nose.

Suntory has been emphasizing a soft brew called Malt's★★, with a gently hoppy finish, but it has also test-marketed beers in almost every classic style, all made to impressive standards. A clovey Weizen★★★ was outstanding. More offbeat essays have included a beer called Dynamic Draft★, made with Canadian yeast.

Japan's brewers launch new beers with every season, but the rest of Asia is less hasty. When Germany enjoyed a colonial "concession" in Shantung, China, a brewery was established in the resort town of Tsingtao. This is now one of China's major exporters, and Tsingtao Beer★→★★, a hoppy Pilsener, is a popular accompaniment to its national cuisine in New York and San Francisco. The very sweet Tsingtao

Porter★ is harder to find in the West. Many Chinese beers have made brief appearances in the USA, sometimes under Anglicized names invented by importers. Meanwhile, China now has a British-style micro-brewery, producing ale, at Changsha, in Hunan Province.

German technical help was used in 1934 to set up the Boon Rawd Brewery, which produces the outstandingly hoppy **Singha Lager★★★** (13.8 Plato; 1055; 4.8; 6; and a hearty 40 units of bitterness) in Thailand. The local rival **Amarit★→★★** is milder.

While the Singha is a mythical creature resembling a lion, Tiger Beer is a legend in its own lunchtime, perhaps because it entered literature through the pen of Anthony Burgess. **Tiger Lager Beer★★★** is a hoppier cousin to Heineken. The same brewery has in its range the creamy, roasty, medium-dry **ABC Extra Stout★★→★★★** (18.2; 1073; 6.5; 8.1). These products are made in Singapore and Malaysia.

India has a large brewing industry. Its beers tend to be on the sweet side. Examples are **Cobra★→★★**, brewed in India for the British market, and **Kingfisher★** lager, brewed under licence in Britain. In Sri Lanka, McCallum makes an all-malt **Three Coins Pilsener★★** and a smooth, chocolatey, bottom-fermenting **Sando Stout★★→★★★** (15; 1060). The rival Ceylon Breweries has the fruitier, top-fermenting (in wood) **Lion Stout★★★**, also all-malt, at a similar gravity, producing 5 percent alcohol by weight; 6.3 by volume. Astonishingly, Ceylon Breweries' lager and stout are available, unpasteurized, from wooden casks, drawn by hand-pump, at The Beer Shop, in the brewery's home town of Nuwara Eliya, and at UKD Silva, in the holy city of Kandy.

Except in fundamentalist Muslim countries, almost every corner of Asia has breweries. In a reversal of colonial roles, Spain's San Miguel breweries have their parent company in The Philippines. In addition to the light, smooth, dry **San Miguel★→★★**, a pale Pilsener, the Filipinos also enjoy **Gold Eagle★→★★**, lower in gravity but fuller in colour, and the stronger (14; 1056; 5.5; 6.8) **Red Horse★→★★**, soft-bodied, with some fruity notes. **San Miguel Dark Beer★★** also has an above-average gravity (13.5; 1054; 4.1; 5.2) and a good toasted-malt character.

AUSTRALASIA

The New Zealand brewing group Lion Nathan has in recent years swallowed, in one fell swoop, Toohey's (of Sydney), Castlemaine (of Brisbane) and Swan (of Perth), and subsequently Hahn (of Sydney) and South Australian (of Adelaide). All still brew in their own territories, but Australian pride has been shaken. Lion Nathan now owns almost half the Australian brewing industry, while Foster's (which also has Tooth's, of Sydney, and Power's, of Brisbane), controls most of the rest.

New Zealand's mainstream beers are all lagers, though those with a fuller colour, often identified as "draught" are often considered locally to be ales. Many of them are very sweet. There is a similar sweetness to many Australian beers, which use sugar cane as an adjunct to barley malt. In Australia, "Bitter" often simply means an allegedly hoppy lager, but "Old" indicates a dark, top-fermenting, ale. There are also some very tasty stouts.

The only old-established independent brewing company left in Australasia is Cooper's, of Adelaide. The micro movement that has spread throughout the brewing nations of the developed world arrived in Australia on the eve of an economic recession far more severe than that experienced in Europe and North America during the early 1990s. The result is that some very promising breweries failed, and the continued operation of others is uncertain.

Australian Pizza Kitchen

Pizza restaurant with a tiny brewery behind the bar, in Canberra. Products have included a smooth, golden, **Lager**★★ and a sweeter, maltier, **Dark**★★→★★★, made from grains roasted in the pizza oven.

Boag's

Old-established brewery in Launceston, Tasmania, tracing its history to 1827. The beer's house character embraces a touch of new-mown hay. **Boag's Bitter**★→★★ has a good dryness in the finish; **Export Lager**★→★★ is slightly honeyish; **XXX Ale**★→★★ is slightly tart.

Cascade

Oldest continuously operated brewery in Australia, having first fired its kettles in 1824. This very attractive brewery, near Hobart, Tasmania, has undergone several changes of ownership. Its beers have some subtleties of hop character. They include the firm, smooth, **Cascade Draught**★→★★; the slightly crisper **Lager**★→★★; the fruitier **Bitter**★; the maltier, fuller-flavoured **Premium**★→★★; a slightly sticky **Pale Ale**★; and an oily, roasty, **Stout**★★. All are bottom-fermented, though there have been some experiments with an ale yeast.

Castlemaine

Major brewery in Brisbane, Queensland. Its beers have a little more malt character than those of other big Australian brewers, and it is unusual in its use of hop blossoms rather than pellets or extract. **Castlemaine XXXX★★** also has a touch of new-mown hay in the nose. Although it is a lager, it is identified as Bitter Ale in Australia. This beer is available dispensed by gravity from the cask at the Breakfast Creek Hotel in the Brisbane. **Castlemaine Malt 75★→★★** is firmer and drier, but less hoppy. The bottom-fermenting **Carbine Stout★★** has a good malt note, and a roasty, dry, finish.

Cooper's

The only independent brewery to have survived in Australia since the early days. Cooper's, founded in 1862 on the edge of Adelaide, is now in the middle of residential suburbia. Its ales, all heavily sedimented and very fruity, are Australian classics. They include **Original★★** (3.6; 4.5), with touches of apple, pear and banana; **Sparkling★★★→★★★★** (4.7; 5.8), with more banana flavours; a fruity-chocolatey **Dark★★**; and a fruity, coffeeish, oily, **Stout★★★→★★★★** (5.5; 6.8). Cooper's owns the Earl of Aberdeen pub in Adelaide, and its beers are very well presented at The Bull and Bear (91 King William St).

Dominion

National brewer in New Zealand. Products include the lightly malty **DB Draught★→★★**; **DB Export Lager★**, with a touch of spiciness; the more assertive **Double Brown★★** (less full in colour than its name suggests); and **Kiwi Lager★★**, wonderfully aromatic when it is sampled really fresh.

Dux de Lux

Located in the old college and arts area of Christchurch, New Zealand (Hereford and Montreal Sts). This brewpub produces a very malty **Lager★★→★★★**; the malty-roasty **Hereford Bitter★★** (closer in style to a strong Mild); a very well-balanced and drinkable strong (5.6; 7.0) Pale Ale called **Nor'Wester★★★**; and a licorice-tasting Old Ale of the same strength, **Sou'Wester★★-★★★**.

Forge

Micro in Christchurch, New Zealand, making mainstream beers.

Foster's

Major brewery in Melbourne, Victoria. Its **Foster's Lager★**, sweetish, with a hint of banana, has lost sales in recent years to the same brewery's fractionally drier **Victoria Bitter★**. There is yet a further fraction of hoppiness to **Melbourne Bitter★**. **Carlton Genuine Draught★** is perhaps lighter, crisper, and less fruity. **Abbot's Double Stout★★**, which is bottom-fermenting, is roasty and coffeeish.

Geebung Polo Club

The name derives from an Australian tale. It is, in fact, a Victorian pub, with its own brewery, in Melbourne. Its products have included a refreshing, tasty, wheat beer,

Yellow Mongrel★★; a fruity, hoppy, English-style Bitter, **Cobungra★★→★★★**; a very fruity **Pale Ale★★**; and the richly creamy, delicious, **Razorback Stout★★★**.

Grand Ridge

In the Strzlecki Hills of the Gippsland region of Victoria. This area grows peaches and berry fruits, and makes blue cheese. Its local micro-brewery, at Mirbo North, has made a sweetish **Pilsener★→★★**; a hoppy **Gold★★**; a well-balanced **Mild★★**; and a fruity, vanilla-tinged barley wine, called **Moonshine★★★**.

Hahn

Ambitious micro, making lager in Sydney. Established in 1988, but subsequently acquired by Lion Nathan. Principal product is all-malt **Hahn Premium Lager★★→★★★** with good hop flavours and bitterness.

Harrington's

A Victorian brewery building in Christchurch, New Zealand, houses this micro, making a sweetish **Wheat Beer★→★★**, a coffeeish **Dark★★** and other more mainstream products.

Kitty O'Grady's

Brewery, bar, wine shop, café and restaurant (originally called Kelly's) at 521 Stanley St, Mater Hill, Brisbane. Products have included an aromatically hoppy lager called **Super★★→★★★** and a sweet, rich and coffeeish **Dark Ale★★**.

Lion Brewing

This independent micro, in a restored 1850s brewery building in Adelaide, has had its ups and downs. recently, it has been producing a flavoursome **Pilsner★★**, a hoppy **Sparkling Bitter★★ ★** and a smoky **Porter★★→★★★**.

Lion Nathan

National brewer in New Zealand. Products include the sweetish **Rheineck Lager★**; **Steinlager★★**, lightly malty, with a flowery, pollen-like, dry finish; the firm-bodied, all-malt, **Red Band Export★→★★**; the caramel-tasting **Lion Red★★**; and the even sweeter **Lion Brown★**. Its regional **Waikato Draught★★** has something of a reputation for hoppiness, but is still quite sweet.

Loaded Hog

Brewpub in Christchurch, New Zealand (39 Dundas St). Its products include a refreshing, lemony, **WeissBier★★**; an English-style brown ale called **Hog's Head Dark★★**, and several other beers in a more mainstream New Zealand style. The Loaded Hog now also has a branch pub on the waterfront in Auckland.

Lord Nelson

Pub, restaurant, hotel and brewery at the corner of Kent and Argyle Streets, in The Rocks area of Sydney. Products have included a dryish, spritzy, wheat beer called **Quayle Ale★★**; the well-balanced **Trafalgar Pale Ale★★**; the soft **Victory Bitter★★**; and the malty-fruity **Old Admiral★★★**.

Mac's

Pioneering micro in New Zealand. Established in 1982 by former All Black rugby player Terry McCashin, near Nelson. Products include **Mac's Gold★→★★**, a sweetish lager; **Ale★★**, amber in colour and tending towards a chocolatey malt character; and malty **Dark★★**.

Matilda Bay

Pioneering micro in Perth. Produces a filtered version of **RedBack★★→★★★** wheat beer, pleasantly fruity (hint of apples?) but less spicy than it once was; and **Dog-bolter★★→★★★**, once an ale but now a malty, chocolatey, **Dark Lager**.

Moonshine

A tiny brewery at the Reflections café-restaurant (☎97–552277), on the Kidepo Valley vineyard, Wildwood Rd, Yallingup, in the Margaret River region of Western Australia. Early brews have been somewhat astringent.

Newbegin

Micro near Auckland, New Zealand, producing the all-malt, **Silver Fern★★** lager, with a touch of lemony hop flavour; and the coffeeish, herbal, hoppy, **Old Thumper★★→★★★** ale.

Old Goulburn

In the old wool-gathering town of Goulburn, between Sydney and Canberra, a maltings and brewery established in the 1830s and closed a century later, still stands. In 1991, a catholic priest, Michael O'Halloran, installed an extract brewhouse, in which he began to produce a **Sparkling Ale** (not tasted) and a thinnish, roasty, somewhat acidic, dry, **Stout★→★★**, served on the premises (☎048–216071). Father O'Halloran, who has become something of an expert on 19th-century brewing, operates the establishment as a rehabilitation project for handicapped people.

Port Dock

Brewpub in Port Adelaide, producing the malty-fruity, golden, **Lighthouse Ale★→★★**; the creamy **Black Diamond Bitter★★**, closer in style to a Northern English brown ale; and the syrupy **Old Preacher★★★** (4.8; 6).

Powers

Established in 1987, near Brisbane, to fight the domination of the giants, but now controlled by Foster's. Beers include **Big Red★→★★**, a relatively robust lager by Australian standards.

The Pumphouse

The 1891 pumphouse once provided water-pressure for hydraulic lifts in Sydney. Now the building, at 17 Little Pier St, in Darling Harbour, is part of a brewery and pub. Products have included the top-fermenting **Bull's Head Bitter★★★**, full of hop flavour and dryness; and **Federation★★★**, in broadly the style of a Northern English brown ale, nutty, with notes of vanilla, and lots of flavour development.

RedBack

Brewpub in Melbourne that is an offshoot of Matilda Bay, in Western Australia. Its products include an aromatic, fruity, **RedBack Hefe-Weizen★★★**; and a soft, malty, delicately hopped, **Pils★★★** that dries towards the finish.

Rifle Brigade

In the old gold-mining town of Bendigo, Victoria. Brewpub that has produced the light **Koala★★** wheat beer; the assertive **Old Fashioned Bitter★★→★★★**; and a more flowery, bronze **Premium★★**, among a varying selection.

Sail and Anchor

Pioneering brewpub in Fremantle, Western Australia. Products have included the top-fermenting **Traditional Bitter★★★**, fruity, slightly sweet, and kept under blanket pressure; and the gently roasty, coffeeish, **Brass Monkey Stout★★★** (4.8; 6), served under nitrogen and CO_2.

Sanctuary Cove

This yacht marina, golf resort and playground of the super-rich also has a micro. Products have included a soft, malty, **Lager★★**, with a nice touch of hop; and a strong lager called **Cane Toad★★→★★★** (5.6; 7), slightly syrupy, but with a dryish finish.

Scharer's

This Zurich family emigrated to Australia four generations ago. Geoff Scharer runs The George IV, a historic bar and hotel, in the coal town of Picton, 50 miles SW of Sydney. Products include a hoppy, resiny, **Lager★★→★★★** and an extremely creamy, malty, clean, **Bock★★★**. Scharer now also owns The Australian Hotel, at 100 Cumberland Street, The Rocks, Sydney.

Shakespeare

Brewpub in Auckland (61 Albert St). Products have included a refreshing, hoppy, **Lager★★→★★★**; a lightly malty **Red Ale★★→★★★**, in broadly the Scottish style; a very hoppy, English-style Bitter, called **Falstaff Ale★★★**; a rummy **Old Ale★★→★★★** and a thinnish, roasty **Stout★★**.

South Australian

Major Adelaide brewery. Its beers tend to be slightly drier than those of other big Australian brewers. They include the all-malt **West End Premium★→★★**; the fruitier **Southwark Premium★**; and a very tasty, chocolatey, **Stout★★★** (6.5; 7.6). This company has also brewed the heavily sedimented **Kent Town Real Ale★★★**. This beer, top-fermented at the nearby Kent Town maltings, is pasteurized, and thus does not qualify as a "real ale" by the British definition. Nonetheless, it is full of flavour, with a very soft fruitiness, reminiscent of gooseberries with sugar.

Stockan
Micro near Auckland, New Zealand, making a sweet, spicy, then winey, **Trad Ale★★** and a chocolatey, pruney, **Trad Dark★★**.

Strongcroft
Micro in Petone, New Zealand. Products include a very malty **Bitter★→★★**.

Sunshine
Micro in Gisborne, New Zealand. Products include a well-balanced lager called **Gisborne Gold★★**; a malty **Bitter★→★★**; and a **Dark★→★★**; and a so-called strong Pilsener, called **Moonshine★**, which is very fruity.

Swan
Major brewery in Perth, Western Australia. Products include the clean, lightly hoppy, **Emu Bitter★★**; the dryish **Emu Export★**; and the light, firm, slightly tart **Swan Draught★**. All are lagers. Emu was originally a rival brewery.

Toohey's
Once the Catholic, "Irish" brewery in Sydney, now owned by Lion Nathan. Pioneer, in the early 1990s, of low-alcohol (2.2; 2.7) beers like **Blue Label★★**, with a touch of flavour and colour from crystal malt; a lager, though it is labelled as a **Light Bitter**. Another lager described as a Bitter, **Toohey's Red★★**, has a dry maltness and a late touch of hop; no additives or preservatives are used in this beer. A wide range also includes the light-bodied but fruity and chocolatey **Toohey's Old Black★★→★★★**.

Tooth's
Once the Protestant, "English" brewery in Sydney. Now owned by Foster's. Products include **Resch's Draught★★**, relatively assertive in both malt and hop for Australia, and with a touch of colour; the sweetish, fruity, earthy, top-fermenting, **Kent Old Brown★★→★★★**; and the tar-like, almost oaky, **Sheaf Stout★★→★★★** (4.6; 5.7).

AFRICA

The continent of Africa might claim to have had some of the first brewers, as the ancient Egyptians produced beer in at least 3000BC.

These beers were brewed from barley that was "malted" by a process germinating the grain and then baking it into a bread-like condition. This was then fermented, and must have produced something like the *kvass* that is still widely consumed in Russia. The unfiltered beer may have resembled the turbid, porridge-like traditional brews that are still made in Africa, from millet, cassava flour, plantains, or whatever is locally available.

However, all except the most fundamentalist Muslim countries of Africa have their own breweries producing modern beers. Most of these beers are of the Pilsener type, though the odd *bock* can occasionally be found – and there are one or two ales (in South Africa) and stouts (in several countries, notably Nigeria). Namibia Breweries' **Maibock★★→★★★** (4.8; 6.0) is tawny, syrupy and slightly iron-ish. The stouts are usually dry, and sometimes of considerable strength (the tropical version of Guinness, at more than 18 Plato and 1070; around 8 percent alcohol by volume is typical).

Household names in most western European nations have established in Africa, or contracted or licensed their products to be made there. Or they have acted as consultants or partners to local breweries, often with participation from national governments. In all, there are about 175 breweries in Africa, in at least 45 countries. By far the most heavily breweried country is Nigeria, with more than 50, most of them built in the last two decades. Zaire and South Africa are also significant brewing nations in terms of volume. However, some very well-made beers are brewed in very small countries, like Gambia, Togo and the Seychelles. Several African breweries have at times exported. A super-premium version of Kenya's **Tusker★★** lager, much more aromatic and hoppy than the usual domestic products, has attracted some attention.

Africa's first micro-brewery went into operation in 1984, in Knysna, Cape Province. The brewery began with an all-malt draught lager, then began to experiment with seasonal ales and stouts, cask-conditioned. Knysna is on the south coast, between Cape Town and Port Elizabeth. A second micro, called simply Our Brewery, has since opened at St George's St, Johannesburg. It produces a filtered but unpasteurized ale. There have also been tentative attempts to start a wheat-beer brewery in South Africa. Such are the ambitions of the beer renaissance.

INDEX